Anarchy
in High
Heels

Anarchy in High Heels

A Memoir

DENISE LARSON

SHE WRITES PRESS

Published 2021
Printed in the United States of America
Print ISBN: 978-1-64742-136-6
E-ISBN: 978-1-64742-137-3
Library of Congress Control Number: 2021900231

For information, address:
She Writes Press
1569 Solano Ave #546
Berkeley, CA 94707

Interior design by Tabitha Lahr

She Writes Press is a division of SparkPoint Studio, LLC.

"Les Nickelettes Bite into 'Peter Pan'" by Sharon R. Skolnick (a.k.a. Sharon Skolnick-Bagnoli) used with permission by *Berkeley Barb* (www.berkeleybarb.net).

Dedicated to Vinny and Nikki,
and Les Nickelettes everywhere

Contents

CHAPTER 1

BEHIND THE GREEN DOOR: VIRGINS!

"What do you want for a nickel?"

I am a feminist by destiny. A few years after the events chronicled in this book took place, I sat facing half a dozen psychic interns, who were "running my energy." One of the students reported, "Your soul chose to be born in this lifetime because there was about to be a great advance in women's liberation, and you wanted to be a part of it."

The truth of this pre-birth spiritual perception sent a shiver down my spine. How did she know? How could a young woman at a Psychic Horizons clairvoyant reading look at my aura and "see" my designated life's mission? Walking down the sidewalk afterward, I mused about what she *didn't* see. My spirit also sought to discover a hidden, offbeat, bawdy female humor at a time when being a funny feminist was deemed an oxymoron.

In 1972, I had little sense of this destiny, even as the winds of change were blowing a second wave of women's liberation across the land. I was twenty-four. My generation grew up in the 1950s. We were raised to be nice girls, groomed to become housewives, secretaries, nurses, or teachers. But coming of age during the cultural revolution in the explosive, ragged 1960s changed everything.

Ms. magazine hit the stands for the first time in 1972. Gloria Steinem and other women activists were leading marches demanding equality. The in-your-face Helen Reddy pop song "I Am Woman" topped the Billboard charts. Saturday morning TV aired *Josie and the Pussycats,* the first all-female animation series. But the blueprint for female equality was still being mapped out. Like other women my age, I was trying on this new suit of feminism to see if it fit.

Boomer girls wiggled out of restrictive bras and girdles. Rejecting current fashion, we opted for thrift-store duds and bell-bottom pants from the Army/Navy Surplus Store. We replaced high heels with low-heeled boots. And hair—instead of teasing and spraying our hair into elaborate dos, we parted it in the middle and let it hang down, long and natural. Shunning norms, we refused to shave our legs and armpits and glorified in the forbidden hair. We experimented with drugs; it was just "part of the scene, man." Birth control gave us sexual permission, and boy, did we take advantage of this new freedom. We "lived in sin" with our sexual partners. Our parents didn't approve, but we didn't care—creating a "generation gap." In 1973, the game-changing Supreme Court case of Roe v. Wade ruled abortion legal, giving us something our mothers and grandmothers had been denied: choices. The door opened to a counterculture shift, and we stepped over the threshold.

In the midst of this atmosphere, the accidental creation of Les Nickelettes happened, a collective unconscious synergy of an eclectic group of women coming together in the right place at the right time. I didn't plan it. It was 1972 in San Francisco, and it took on a life of its own.

It all started as a lark, at midnight on February 8. Breathless, drunk, and stoned, three novice Nickelettes arrived late for the first Nickelettes performance. Janet, Karin, and I stood on a black, sticky floor behind the porno movie screen at the Mitchell Brothers' O'Farrell Theater. In nervous anticipation, we waited to make our debut as cheerleaders, looking like an unlikely cross between high-class hookers and naïve teenage girls out for a night on the town.

Why had I let Vince talk me into this?

"Lead a cheer, sing a song, do a dance, like the Rockettes," he told me.

"But we're experimental theater artists, not chorus line dancers," I explained.

"Not like real Rockettes, more like vaudeville—Nickelodeon cheerleaders—the Nickelettes."

Nine months earlier, Vince had launched the People's Nickelodeon as an after-hours event to present vintage movies, and now he wanted to jazz it up with live vaudeville performances.

I talked Karin and Janet into joining me in this goofy, off-the-wall adventure. It appealed to a fantasy of overcoming my failure to become a popular cheerleader in high school. I bought a thrift-store sweater and sewed on a big block letter "N," and matched it with a cute miniskirt. Janet, likewise, added "I" to her sweater, and Karin claimed the "C." It was a long way from spelling out "Nickelodeon," but it would have to do. To go along with the costumes, the three of us lathered our fresh-scrubbed faces with foundation, rouge, and eyeliner, then teased and hair-sprayed our loose locks into puffy dos. The image in the mirror of faux cheerleaders made us laugh.

Outside the Mitchell Brothers' O'Farrell Theater, the stoned freaks lined up for the midnight event as the horny loners straggled out after the last hard-core loop. Self-consciously slipping into the lobby in our "cheerful" outfits, we awaited our big premiere. Art Mitchell eyed us as he passed through on his way up to his second story office. Uh-oh: Art had a reputation for hitting on every attractive chick who walked into his theater. Not five minutes later, Vince invited us upstairs for a doobie.

This was a big deal, like going backstage at a rock concert. We got buzzed through the locked door that guarded the second level of the theater. Topping the stairs, we entered the projection booth where Vince worked. Art handed us an enormous joint and encouraged us to partake freely. I'd never smoked pot before a performance, but hey, this was just for fun. After the second joint, Art said, "Let's go over to Roberts."

"There's not enough time," I replied. "It's almost time for us to go on."

"Come on," cajoled Art, "just for a few minutes."

Roberts was an opulent restaurant owned by Frenchman Robert Charles a couple of doors down from the O'Farrell Theater. The Victorian building housing the restaurant had once been a site where exotic 1930s burlesque performer Sally Rand did her teasing fan dance. It was also rumored to have been a brothel. Passing through the foyer into a large hall, I took in the baroque walls painted red and gold and looked up at the high ceilings covered in colorful frescoes of men and women engaging in Dionysian excess. A second-floor balcony supported by grand Roman columns displayed small curtained rooms. Aha, the rumor was true; these were perfect salons for a discreet rendezvous.

Via a plush red carpet, Art escorted us to a long table set in the middle of the grand hall. Robert, seated at the head of the table, greeted us and introduced six male French tourists. Art guided each of us strategically to seats between two men. Jeez, this was another one of Art's setups. The smile on my face froze, completing the look of an American cheerleader doll. Janet and Karin glanced at me apprehensively, but then eyed the expensive French wine, cheese, petit fours, and other delectable French edibles. Soon, we were gulping wine and laughing at

French jokes we didn't get. My college French vaguely bobbed to the surface and I blurted out, "*Où est la bibliotèque?*" The men laughed. I followed up with, "*Oui, oui,*" and they laughed more. Suddenly, it was 11:55, and like obedient Cinderella, we rushed back to our duties at the Nickelodeon.

Panting, we arrived at our spot behind the film screen. With our brains whirling from the pot and wine, I looked at Janet, Janet looked at Karin, Karin looked at me, and we giggled. This two-hundred-seat movie theater offered no amplification, no spotlight, and no stage—just twelve feet of sticky bare floor between the flat movie screen and the first row of seats.

"The People's Nickelodeon is proud to present the premiere of the Nickelettes," yelled an anonymous voice.

From behind the screen we pranced out singing a cappella, "Music! Music! Music!" camping it up with Karin's choreographed 1920s-style dance. The song had a bouncy beat, and the lyrics mentioned putting a nickel in a Nickelodeon. My dope-shrouded brain told me to kick right, but I noticed that Janet and Karin kicked left. I remembered the lyrics, despite the wine, but Janet and Karin dissolved into giggles. Recovering our composure, we overcompensated for the lack of a sound system by shouting the words into the faces of the too-close audience, and aimed our chorus-line kicks at the teeth of the front row patrons. Wild.

Wheee! We turned around, flipped up our skirts, mooned the audience, and scampered offstage. The crowd awarded us with boisterous applause. What a rush! We laughed so hard we could barely breathe.

The movie started, and we trooped back upstairs as our giddy high slid into recognition of guilty foolishness. The fun had a debasing aftertaste. Like getting away with something you shouldn't. Like darting away from Frenchmen after drinking their wine and gobbling their goodies. Like prostitutes who got paid and didn't have to fuck anyone.

Art greeted us in the projection booth. "Hey, that was great!" he said, as he draped his arm around Janet's shoulders.

"Do you really think so?" Janet asked, removing his hand hovering near her breast.

"The audience loved it," Vince added. "What are you going to do next week?"

"Uh, we don't know yet," Karin tittered, as she shot me a glance that clearly said, "Let's get out of here."

At one in the morning, three embryonic Nickelettes headed for my car. A severe hangover loomed behind my eyes smeared with mascara.

Karin moaned, "I've never been so embarrassed in my whole life. There's no way I'm ever doing that again."

"I agree, never again. I felt like an idiot," Janet echoed.

With my tail between my legs I vowed never to mention the Nickelettes again, delegating it a one-hit wonder.

The following weekend, Janet, Karin, and I performed *White Blackbird*, our original play based on the diaries of Anaïs Nin. As if the Nickelettes had never happened, we comfortably slipped back into our experimental theater roles. On Saturday, after the final performance, we were in the dressing room changing into our street clothes, when out of the blue Karin asked, "So what are we going to do for the People's Nickelodeon on Tuesday?"

And with that, the Nickelettes (*The* Nickelettes would become *Les* Nickelettes later) took on a momentum that refused to be ignored.

In August 1967, I escaped the stifling hot California Central Valley with acceptance to San Francisco State College (now San Francisco State University) as a drama major. As soon as I arrived in the fog-draped city, it felt like home. To me, it was like going to sleep in black-and-white Kansas and waking up

People's Nickelodeon Poster announcing
the debut of the Nickelettes

in the glittering city of Oz. Although I missed the Summer of Love by a hair, there still remained an ambiance of radical culture shift in the air. In this hippie environment, I became an actress who rejected "straight" theater in favor of alternative experimental plays and embraced street theater's revolutionary avant-garde message.

In the college drama department, I found a kindred spirit in Janet Croll. We were the only two women cast in *Epidermis,* a student-written play. I confided to Janet, "Until I got cast in this play, I felt like an outsider."

"Me too. I don't really want to do *Carousel* or *Romeo and Juliet,*" Janet said with a withering glance around the lobby of the main theater where the drama students hung out.

"I think it's cool that this new play presents the Prometheus myth in present day. But the rehearsals are so intense."

"That's what I like about it; it gets under your skin. Here, read this." Janet handed me *Towards a Poor Theatre* by the Polish theater artist Jerzy Grotowski. I took the book home and devoured it in the span of a couple days. Grotowski's technique led an actor to strip away everything and delve into the deepest part of the psyche to unleash genuine emotions that could be expressed truthfully on stage. I ached to be authentic. To me, Janet embodied the deeply serious actress I wanted to be. From then on, we were inseparable.

Getting to know each other, we exchanged childhood stories. I told Janet about growing up in Southern and Central California residing in working-class suburban tract homes. "My parents struggled to pay the bills paycheck to paycheck. Sometimes there wasn't much food in the house. There were times we only had pancakes for dinner. But I always felt unconditional love, even though both of my parents worked, and me and my siblings were on our own after school."

"Wow, my story couldn't be more different," related Janet. "I grew up on New York City's Upper East Side. My father worked day and night on Wall Street, and my mother disappeared to Arizona for months at a time during a series of nervous breakdowns. But I had a nanny. I loved my nanny and she loved me." Janet showed me a beloved comforter that her nanny had given her, and hugged it as if it were the woman in the flesh. "Then they sent me off to finishing school. But I rebelled, got drunk every day, and they kicked me out." She threw back her head of wild brown hair and laughed like a hyena. "Mommy was livid when I enrolled at San Francisco State College and moved three thousand miles away."

I admired Janet's impulsiveness and the way she walked with willowy limbs all akimbo. And I suspected she admired my ability to stay firmly grounded. We fell in love, not physically, but spiritually. This was the first time I'd experienced such a deep-level connection in a female friendship.

After rehearsals of *Epidermis*, Janet and I talked for hours. I confided to her, "My boyfriend James wants to keep me all to himself. He took out the telephone over the holiday break and insisted we hole up in the apartment and not see anyone."

"You called me."

"I had to sneak out to the pay phone on the corner."

"That sounds pretty controlling."

"I love him, but he only wants me to go to school and then come back to the apartment and be alone with him."

"But you're doing the play."

"He knows I have a passion for acting, and that I won't give it up for anything or anybody. But the only time we socialize is with his friends. People ask me questions, and he answers."

"Don't you see? He's obliterating your personality. He's immature, and this relationship is not healthy for you."

It took many of these talks for me to admit Janet was right. One cold, rainy night I called her from the corner pay phone, suitcase in hand. "I left him," I told her, bursting into tears. "Can I stay with you for a while?" She saved me.

After college, Janet and I rented an apartment together as we scrounged around for acting roles. One night, we went to a party at a sprawling communal flat on Fourth Avenue and were reunited with Tom Usher, another theater major alum from San Francisco State College. We fell into reminiscing about our unsatisfying experiences in the drama department.

Tom regaled us with his intellectual vision of a new kind of theater. "I want to broaden the concept of traditional theater by fusing symbols, music, folk dance, and myth with a Jungian archetype narrative. I'm forming a new theater company and calling it the Blue Lantern Theater."

"That sounds so interesting," I replied.

"You and Janet could join our troupe," he offered. I was thrilled.

At the first meeting of the Blue Lantern Theater, Tom introduced Janet and me to his girlfriend, Karin Segal, a dancer. Karin was short for a dancer but made up for it with a fluid, kinetic energy. Tom wanted her to add modern dance elements to the project.

"I'm taking classes with Margaret Jenkins," she enthusiastically told us. "She studied with Merce Cunningham and John Cage in New York, but now is teaching in San Francisco and creating her own modern dance collaborations with other art forms in the same way that Tom is talking about doing with theater." I liked her passion, and also her easy, infectious laugh.

Under Tom's direction, the Blue Lantern Theater staged *Rites of Passage: An Exercise in Archetypes*, and during that run Janet, Karin, and I discovered a shared obsession. We were all besotted with Anaïs Nin and had read every one of her diaries as soon as they came out. Like millions of other women of the time, we daydreamed of stepping into Anaïs's shoes and drifting through one gauze-covered, erotic, poetic encounter after another.

After *Rites of Passage* ended, we talked Tom into collaborating on a project based on the diaries. The title *White Blackbird* emerged from the writings. Anaïs used a white blackbird (*merle blanc*) as a symbol of something rare, exotic, and improbable.

"I want to play the part of Anaïs," Karin proclaimed. "I would have loved to be in Paris and New York in the '30s and '40s and lived the life she describes."

"I would have loved to hang out with Antonin Artaud like she did," weighed in Janet. "His theater of cruelty was surreal and wild." Janet envisioned portraying Artaud's descent into madness as a woman.

I was drawn to the earthy and sexual character June Miller, wife of Henry Miller. The script was developed during a series of workshops. I created a solo scene depicting June giving birth on stage. I sat on the floor upstage raging about the loneliness of my heavy body. "I'm hot, I'm parched. Now I'm cold, cold as ice. I push and I push and I push." I related these feelings to the audience as I inched my body closer and closer to the lip of stage center while slowly spreading my legs in a birth-giving position. "Why am I alone in this pain?" I cried out at the climax of this metaphoric birth. At the end, I bitterly accused mankind of womankind's predicament: "You lie in my womb only to gain strength, and then you leave."

I experienced a catharsis doing that scene. I had never before allowed myself to shout out such rage. There was a freedom in doing it so publicly. It was the first hint of my destiny bubbling to the surface.

During the process of developing and performing this play, a sisterhood formed between Janet, Karin, and me that often excluded Tom. This newfound connection would become the foundation of the Nickelettes.

The convergence of events that sparked the Nickelettes took place in a house of porn, but that says more about the times than the evolution of the group. The upheaval of the late 1960s sexual revolution, with its attitude of free love, opened the door for the acceptance of hardcore porn. Add to that mix a baby-boom generation consuming mass quantities of recreational drugs and liberated from youthful parenthood by birth control pills, and you have a hip counterculture thumbing its nose at past hang-ups. The Mitchell Brothers brought pornography from hidden back rooms and put it on display in a movie theater under the banner of a bright neon marquee.

I was pursuing my acting career in the Blue Lantern Theater, but needed a day job. I took a position as a nursery school teacher that left me exhausted. One day, I complained to Tom, "This job is wiping me out."

"My roommate is a manager at the Mitchell Brothers' O'Farrell Theater, and they're hiring cashiers," he told me. "It would be easy work."

"I'm not sure I want to spend all day in a porno theater."

Tom shrugged, "Porn is no big deal anymore."

I met Tom Volnick, the manager, and he told me the salary would be fifty cents more an hour than my current job, and I would only have to work thirty hours a week. I accepted. This cushy employment in a relaxed atmosphere fit my needs. In between customers I could memorize lines or do research for theater roles. And Art and Jim Mitchell were friendly, laid-back bosses.

Six months after I was hired, Vince Stanich started the People's Nickelodeon. Vince worked as one of the theater's three projectionists, churning through endless porn loops in twelve-hour shifts. To ease the boredom, he concocted the People's Nickelodeon, a midnight event held every Tuesday and Wednesday after the regular porno movies ended. Everything cost a nickel. A nickel to see a classic film, a nickel for a cup of coffee or a box of popcorn, a nickel for a peanut-butter-and-jelly sandwich. The intent of the People's Nickelodeon was fun, not profits. Vince never had to pay film rental fees—he got vintage reels (Charlie Chaplin, Betty Boop cartoons) from his archivist friends, and cult classics like *The T.A.M.I. Show* from fellow projectionists willing to bootleg. Tom Volnick, the night manager, donated his services, as did other staff. It was a perfect happening for the low-income, underground counterculture of the time.

The Mitchell Brothers allowed their union projectionist to stage this weekly event in their theater because Vince convinced Artie and Jim that the People's Nickelodeon would make them more hip and help them become known as more than just pornographers. Vince, in his early thirties, was older than Jim, Artie, and the rest of us. He used this "wiser" status to his advantage. His magnetic personality also contributed to the success of the venture. He sent out word of the event to his influential friends, and they to their friends, and there was an audience the first night.

The scene at the O'Farrell was unfamiliar to me. I held back and observed. Then, Vince, making it sound as if working for free was doing him a big favor, asked me to cashier for the midnight movies. I was thrilled to be asked to be a part of this cool avant-garde happening. However, it also drew me more into the culture of competitive seduction at the theater.

The day manager smiled seductively as he blocked the exit to the popcorn nook, and I had to learn to maneuver like a snake past him. Jim Mitchell winked and invited me up to his private office for a drink, and I learned to laugh it off as if a prank. Art Mitchell cut to the chase: "Come on, baby, take your clothes off and let's do it." I learned to duck his blatant invitation, but he didn't give up. A few days later he invaded my space by slithering up close, breathing into my ear, "Baby, I could drink your bathwater." I rolled my eyes and pivoted back to my cashier station.

Survival in this game was a rite of passage for all young women. Like other female employees who encountered this workplace behavior and wanted to keep their jobs, we had to pull off a delicate balancing act. Boomer girls invented new strategies in this tricky era of sexual liberation.

Behind the projection booth was a small room known as Vinny's Clubhouse, where the guys hung out and smoked weed. Vince had furnished the clubhouse with comfy second-hand sofas, chairs, tables, and a year-round Christmas tree. Except for the odor of marijuana and the psychedelic posters on the wall, it was reminiscent of a set from the 1950s TV show *Father Knows Best.* On the nights Vince and I worked the same shift, he invited me up to the clubhouse to share some pot during my break.

Once, he asked about my theater activities and sat listening intently to my stories.

"My biggest fear is not being taken seriously," I confessed.

He squinted at me with a Slavic, hooded-eyed stare reminiscent of Humphrey Bogart in *The African Queen.* "My biggest fear is being the lonely projectionist with my nose crushed against the glass porthole viewing the party below."

I didn't know what to say. His genuine honesty took me by surprise—this was not his usual playful bantering. I let my eyes gaze around the clubhouse. "It looks like you're pining for the good old days."

"These *are* the good old days," he shot back. Then he lifted one eyebrow and said, "What are you doing after work tonight?"

It was in the clubhouse that the idea of the Nickelettes was hatched and where Vince's effortless charm reeled me in. We went out after work and had drinks. We became close friends.

Nothing in the first year of the Nickelettes was calculated. After our third outing in front of the movie screen at the People's Nickelodeon, a fellow cashier said, "I want to be a Nickelette."

This unexpected request was from Elaine Schelb (nicknamed "Schelby"), who had no performing experience and the demeanor of a mild-mannered librarian, with looks to match: petite, slender, with waist-long auburn hair and granny glasses. We did need more cheerleaders to spell out "Nickelodeon," so why not? Schelby sewed a "K" on her sweater and became the fourth Nickelettes cheerleader. Schelby was even less adept at singing and dancing than Janet, Karin, and me, but by now we grasped that the audience liked it that way.

Next, Debby Marinoff, who had helped with costumes for the Blue Lantern Theater, also asked to come aboard, saying, "The Nickelettes look like tons of fun." Debby was a painter and sculptor who had recently graduated from the San Francisco Art Institute. In her studio she transformed vintage formals, bras, and cocktail dresses into art by applying paint, glitter, and decorative materials, then covering it all in a plastic resin. The most distinctive feature of these sculptures was that the breasts and nipples were on the outside of the garments. "I always secretly wanted to be in the theater," said Debby. "I wanted to get involved because for me it was like a forbidden thing."

The week Debby joined, the featured movie at the Nickelodeon was *The Seventh Voyage of Sinbad*. "We can lead cheers for Sinbad," I suggested.

Debby had a different idea, "Think about it, a 'Voyage *of* Sin-bad.'"

We scampered out chanting: "Sin-bad is a sea-man, a sea-man, sea-man, se-men, se-men . . ." The audience caught on to the pun and joined in. Then we launched into our song:

By the sea, by the C
By the C-U-N-T
You and me, you and me
Oh how happy we'll be . . .

The audience stomped their feet, hooted, and whooped. We ran backstage laughing until we peed our pants. Maybe this was tame by today's perspective, but in the early 1970s, nice girls didn't say such things in public.

With our inner bawdiness unleashed, the cheerleading was left in the dust. The next week we entered as cowgirls running down the aisles shooting cap guns and singing our version of "Home on the Range," ending with the line: "And my pants are real cloudy all day."

After that we skewered the lyrics to "Raindrops Keep Falling on My Head":

> *Sperm drops keep falling on my thigh . . .*
> *Those sperm drops keep sticking,*
> *They keep sticking to my thighs. . . .*

It was silly stuff, but for us it was liberating, like reclaiming our sexuality. We broke the rules and received showers of approval. "I had stage fright, but the adrenaline rush once you were on stage, it was such a trip," Debby said. "I loved it."

With the cheerleader costumes in the trash, we dressed up any way we fancied. Debby favored bright, satin Chinese pajamas. I preferred fluffy formals from the 1950s with silver high heels. Janet tended toward slinky silk dresses from the '40s, with rhinestone jewelry and feather boas. Schelby chose flashy miniskirts. Karin wore a belly dancing outfit. Lucky for us, secondhand shops in the early '70s were full of these inexpensive treasures. Forbidden fantasies hid beneath each costume, so in between group numbers, each "individual" took center stage to do her own thing.

As we were hanging out in the lobby after a show, an unknown woman rushed up to us. "Your show is wonderful," she gushed. "I'd love to be a part of it." Taken by surprise, we ran away giggling like shy schoolgirls. Up to this point, the group had expanded only with friends. But this woman was a stranger.

Later, Vince took me aside. "A girl I know is a fan of the Nickelettes and wants to join the group."

"But we don't know her," I replied.

"Her name is Bonnie Solliman. She's been in some of Art and Jim's movies."

"A porn star? Are you kidding?"

"The People's Nickelodeon is for everyone, and the Nickelettes should be, too."

I made the case for Bonnie to the others, who reacted the same way I did. "The whole point of the People's Nickelodeon is that it's not exclusive, but instead accessible for everyone," I said, repeating Vince's admonishment. We arranged a meeting with Bonnie.

She burst in, and hugged each one of us. "You're all so terrific," she said. "Do you know how special you are? How special your shows are? I would love to be a Nickelette."

Won over by Bonnie's enthusiasm and genuineness, I said, "Sure, you're in."

"I'm only working as a porn actress to pay for nursing school," she told us. Bonnie added a new feature to the group, with her individual tap-dance routines and Broadway musical parodies.

After that, membership in the Nickelettes snowballed. Bonnie brought in her best friend Bermuda Schwartz, who declared, "Bonnie told me, 'Anybody who had the balls to do it, could do it.'" Debby brought in a friend from the Art Institute. Women came in via friends of friends. There were no entrance requirements, little structure, and no rules: performance anarchy. Debby described it as a fluid chaotic sculpture. We purposely kept rehearsing to a minimum and adopted the motto, "What do you want for a nickel?"

Vince recruited other acts for an expanded vaudeville lineup, and the popularity of the People's Nickelodeon exploded. It was

Karin, Janet, Diane, me, Myra, Schelby, and
Bonnie at the People's Nickelodeon in 1972

the only stage in town where new acts and fringe types could perform and receive unfiltered acceptance.

Al Rand, fifty-seven, a retired vaudevillian, emceed the show on roller skates and followed up with a soft shoe routine. Freaky Ralph plucked a guitar, attired in a long rainbow-colored wig and an American Revolutionary outfit. During his number he turned around, revealing a Colonel Sanders mask secured to the back of his head. He flipped his guitar over his shoulders and proceeded to sing a strange tribute to the colonel up in chicken heaven.

A few flyers stapled to telephone poles announced the shows, but it was word of mouth that filled the theater. The five-cent admission was so hot that Vince instituted advance sales and put up a "sold out" sign in the afternoon. A rejected, stoned freak at midnight with a nickel in his hand was not a pretty sight. Despite the lack of public outreach, a reporter from the *San Francisco Chronicle* showed up to write an article

DENISE LARSON ★ 19

about the scene. On Sunday, April 9, 1972, "When Sex Ends at Midnight, the Freaks Roll In" appeared in the newspaper's pink Datebook section. David Kleinberg described the Nickelettes as, "The freaks' answer to the Mickey Mouse Club."

We wanted him to *get it.* And I believe he did as he described our main number:

> *"I'm Viva Zapata and I'm here to say, I want Viva Zapata every day," they sang. . . .*
>
> *"When I'm nice and yellow and I'm golden brown, you can zip me open and go to town. Da, da, da, da do." They whirled and displayed a rear view of full panties. There were screams of delight.*

The article featured a photo of the Nickelettes, and a photo of me captioned, "Denise Larson, Head of the Nickelettes." I was famous!

Reveling in validation, the group radiated with an expectant glow. We strutted our stuff as we walked through the lobby, and people pointed us out to their friends. "It was like being stars," said Debby.

"I got recognized on the bus by some woman," Bermuda told us. "'Aren't you a Nickelette?' she asked." It was so cool to share this sense of identity with a group of female friends.

As newly minted underground celebrities, we started getting mentioned in the alternative press. The *Berkeley Barb* described us as "having one-fifth the no-talent of the Cockettes."

"Ha, ha, ha!" we laughed. The Cockettes were notorious gender-bending performance artists who did outrageous cabaret shows at the Palace Theater in San Francisco's North Beach. In 1971, after seeing one of their shows, Gore Vidal observed, "No talent is not enough." The blurb in the *Berkeley Barb* was a funny joke, but I feared people would think we were

Me at the People's Nickelodeon in 1972

drag queens. Many did. The Cockettes were men *and* women in drag. But we were something else; we personified little girls playing dress-up, using a wacky show-and-tell performance art approach to let out our real feelings.

Speaking of drag queens, one night the female impersonator Divine came to a Nickelodeon show. Divine had worked with the Cockettes and was featured in the John Waters film *Pink Flamingos*. This evening, however, he wasn't in drag. Without his sequin dress, wig, makeup, and false eyelashes, he was an overweight, balding man in overalls. As he walked through the lobby, Tom Volnick pointed him out to Schelby, who was basking in all her Nickelettes glory of having found just the right secondhand outfit for the evening: "Shelby, it's Divine!"

"Thank you," she said, pleased he had noticed her dress.

Debby took a day job at the O'Farrell Theater selling popcorn and candy. Like me, she had to pay the bills until her artistic career took off. We often worked the same shift, and in the downtime between customers, we strategized about the Nickelettes.

Debby envisioned the group as a live version of her sculptures—the resin sprayed dresses with the tits on the outside. "You know what the critics say about my art?" Debby asked. "They say I'm rehashing the first art from the cave paintings about fertility symbols. My art is a revolt against art. The Nickelettes are a revolt against theater. It's a symbol of all women, for all women. It's female art. That's totally the statement."

"The Nicks are like a primordial awakening," I added. "I've always felt like I had to hide my humorous side, like it wasn't allowed."

"We need to jazz things up," Debby said. "Take the art concept up a notch."

"The Nickelettes are like virgins," I replied, "like babes in the woods."

"That's it—virgins! We'll tell everybody we reclaim our virginity. Nobody tells us what to do, and nobody owns us. Never, never compromise."

"And never sell out. Virgins are incorruptible and pure as driven snow. Once a virgin, always a virgin."

"Once a Nickelette, always a Nickelette!"

Debby and I spread the word about this new concept. "The Nickelettes are virgins. Get it?"

Imagine claiming to be virgins in a porn theater at the height of the sexual revolution. The guys snickered, "We know you're not virgins, we know you've had sex."

I replied, "You don't get it. We're saying and doing whatever we want for the first time in our lives. That makes us untouched and virginal."

We had grown up believing that whenever two or more women got together, the natural result was a catfight. But we had fun together; we didn't compete for men or scratch each other's eyes out for the title of Queen Kitty. And we shared a sense of anarchistic humor with gusto and glee.

One night, as we tossed around ideas for an appropriate— or better yet, inappropriate—ending to the show, someone suggested, "Why don't we throw up our panties?" A synchronous "Yes!" rang out.

That night the Nickelodeon emcee announced: "And now the Nickelettes will throw up their panties." Whistles and hoots from the crowd. Turning our back to the audience, we stuffed panties into our mouths, which was difficult because we were laughing so hard, then turned around as a group, and *blaaaaatt*, barfed our panties all over the stage. The crowd went ballistic. This stunt epitomized our campy, off-the-wall, feminist statement.

In late spring of 1972, the Mitchell Brothers released their infamous hardcore movie *Behind the Green Door*. They threw a lavish premiere party (à la Hollywood) and invited the Nickelettes and other acts from the Nickelodeon to perform. Recently, the Miss America pageant had come under attack from liberated women who labeled it a meat market. The feminists pointed out that the parade of young women strutting their stuff in bathing suits and high heels was solely for the crass entertainment of leering men. A Nickelettes spoof was a no-brainer; we called it "The Ms. Hysterical Contest."

Art Mitchell insisted that Marilyn Chambers, the star of *Behind the Green Door*, become a Nickelette for the gala. We had no entrance requirements, so how could we say no?

We chose satirical contestant names: Bonnie claimed Ms. Understood; Karin, Ms. Judged; I was Ms. Stake; Janet, Ms. Guided, and Debby, Ms. Bizarro. Marilyn chose Ms. Pussy. We wore thrift-shop formals. Marilyn chose an itty-bitty bikini. One by one, the Nickelettes parodied hysterical talents: absurd baton twirling, mimed accordion playing, and bad cabaret singing. I placed a champagne bottle between my legs, yanked out the cork, lifted the bottle to my lips and took a hearty swig of the bubbly contents—virginal talent takes many forms.

Marilyn sashayed up to the mic with practically nothing on and did an act that Art Mitchell had written for her: "How would you like to kiss Ms. Pussy, boys? I'd really like to get connected with you," she cooed. "I've got everything you need. Herpes. Crabs. Syphilis. Clap. Come on, I'd like to get to know you better."

The audience self-consciously tittered. Nice-girl Nickelettes played at being naughty. Marilyn played at being smutty. When I explained to her our virgin concept, she replied, "What's that supposed to mean?" If you have to ask, honey, that means you don't get it.

A recruited audience member drew the name of the winner out of a hat. "Ms. Hysterical is . . . Ms. Pussy." A half-baked beauty queen smile stayed plastered on my face as I watched her be crowned.

This event opened a can of worms. Should anyone who walked in the door be allowed into the group? "We should only let in women with the Nickelettes spirit," Debby demanded.

"But how can we tell if someone has a virgin spirit?" I asked. We contemplated this question as the People's Nickelodeon closed down for the summer.

Karin, Janet, and I reassumed our theater careers with a two-month run of *White Blackbird* and relegated the Nickelettes to the back burner. But sometimes they would crop up in conversations. "What if this audience saw us perform as Nickelettes? What would they think?" asked Karin.

"*White Blackbird* is our true theatrical calling, and the Nickelettes are just a goof, right?" asked Janet.

"Yeah, right," I said.

But the run for *White Blackbird* was cut short when we received a cease-and-desist letter from Anaïs Nin's representatives. One of the author's friends attended a performance and reported back to Anaïs on how we interpreted her material. She didn't like what she heard. It never even occurred to us to get permission to adapt the material. We worshipped her diaries, and this rejection was so mundane. We altered the title and changed the character names, but it was never the same.

Debby and I continued our strategic talks as we counted down the days until the fall reopening of the People's Nickelodeon. "I'm itching to get out there again and be even more outrageous," I said.

"I get it," said Debby. "I'm hot to trot, too, like an eager beaver."

"Yeah," I laughed. "Virgin eager beavers."

Debby created two rubber stamps. One said, "The Nickelettes are Virgins," and the other, "The Nickelettes are Eager Beavers." Winking, she told me, "That'll confuse them."

Vince and I also spent more and more time together after work, collaborating on the future of the Nickelodeon. This, mixed with Vince's unwavering support for the Nickelettes and his patient seduction, was a combination I could no longer resist. Our shared passion became a convenient excuse for a love affair.

In October, the People's Nickelodeon reopened, having lost none of its momentum. A month later, on Tuesday, November 7, 1972, in a landslide victory over George McGovern, Richard M. Nixon was reelected president of the United States. It would take a couple of years for the public to learn about the tactics the Nixon reelection team used to win the largest popular vote in the history of the United States, but the counterculture had no illusions about his character. At midnight, after voting results were affirmed, the People's Nickelodeon presented the Tricky Dick Tribute Show. The biggest laugh of the night came when the Nickelettes said, "The country decided, it's unwise to switch Dicks in the middle of a screw."

Vinny's clubhouse hosted celebrities from San Francisco's counterculture: Ron Turner, owner of Last Gasp Comix (the first to publish underground cartoon artists R. Crumb and Bill Griffith); Dan O'Neil, creator of the hip Odd Bodkins comic strip; Karl Cohen, film archivist (the source of Charlie Chapin films and Betty Boop cartoons shown at the Nickelodeon); and Clay Geerdes, underground journalist and photographer. Clay published articles and photos of the Nickelettes. In "San Francisco Report" for the *Los Angeles Free Press*, he wrote:

The notorious Nickelettes are doing their thing. Just what that is has yet to be determined. These chicks are

*a paradox and a parody. . . . [They] are keeping alive
the high points of woman's existence.*

Clay Geerdes attempted to put into words the fact that
the Nickelettes were singular in what we were doing: liberated
women following an inner zeitgeist that at this point defied
categorization.

❧

Art and Jim Mitchell made a ton of money from their surprise
hit *Behind the Green Door*. Now internationally famous, they
crowed and preened like peacocks following their return from
the Cannes Film Festival. And Marilyn Chambers was the most
famous porn star in the world.

The Mitchell Brothers planned to continue this success
with a follow-up film for their new star. They came up with
a coming-of-age story, *The Resurrection of Eve*, and began
shooting soon after the People's Nickelodeon reopened. There
was a scene in the script where Marilyn and her boyfriend
attended a party as sort of foreplay before the climatic sex
scene. Art came up with the idea of filming this party at the
People's Nickelodeon. He enticed the Nickelettes to be in the
film by convincing us that appearing in this new movie could
lead to national attention and our big break. Plus, we would
get paid.

The shoot was scheduled to start at midnight, in sync with
the actual Nickelodeon. But delays in setting up the camera
pushed the start time to one in the morning. Then they turned
on the huge movie floodlights. This illumination revealed an
audience under a cloud of illicit weed.

The crowd got rowdy as the shoot dragged on and on.
This was not fun. Art directed the Nickelettes to alter our act
to fit his script. We balked. "Then he told us to go into the
audience and sit on people's laps," Bermuda later remembered.

I vacillated between my duty to comply with the director's request and my instinct not to. I didn't say anything, but I didn't sit on anyone's lap. Afterwards, I staggered out of the theater in the wee hours of the morning with a bad taste in my mouth.

The next day, Jim Mitchell called Vince into his office and lowered the boom. "No more midnight shows." The reason: Jim and Art didn't want freaks and junkies running amok in their theater. Art recounted witnessing a guy shooting up in the men's restroom. Jim stated that the stoned weirdo culture of the audience was bad for business. Now that the Mitchell Brothers were Big Rich Fucking Stars, the People's Nickelodeon was history.

I didn't want the Nickelodeon shut down. The Nickelettes were just getting revved up. I regretted appearing in that stupid movie *Resurrection of Eve*, an eventual dud. But there was something deeper. The Mitchell Brothers faced a counterculture patriarchal dilemma: How do you promote gender sexual equality and freedom, but still retain power over women? "The Nicks were *for* women, the Mitchell Brothers *used* women," Debby later declared. "We could not be bought and sold, which was the antithesis of what the Mitchell Brothers were about."

Later, when we were alone in my apartment, Vince told me, "I'll let things simmer overnight and talk them out of it tomorrow." The next morning he walked into Art and Jim's office with a persuasive last-ditch plan to save his beloved project. After the meeting, I ducked into the clubhouse, and his crestfallen face told me everything. His usual stoic demeanor failed to hide the disappointment that his dream of creating a 1970s version of vaudeville had bit the dust.

I vented, "How dare the Mitchell Brothers brush the Nickelettes off as if we're pesky gnats?"

"It's not about the Nickelettes," Vince said as his shoulders sagged in melancholy resignation.

"The brothers can close down the People's Nickelodeon but they can't close *us* down," I stubbornly declared. "But where else can we go?"

"Don't worry, I'll help you find a place for the Nicks," Vince assured me. His commitment to the group brought us even closer together.

I could have dropped the whole thing and gone back to being an experimental theater artist. But the Nickelettes had opened a new door. The boost I got from being an eager beaver taking back my virginity was powerful. It was a different kind of second-wave women's liberation, an atypical approach to marching in the streets. A pornographic movie house might be the last place you'd expect to plant the seed of a feminist group, but that's what happened.

CHAPTER 2

URBAN GUERRILLA
SORORITY PLEDGES

"The Nickelettes are Mutants."

Let's have a slumber party," suggested Janet.

"Cool," said Karin, "like high school."

"Okay," I agreed, "but let's use this get-together to plot strategy for the future of the group."

My practical plan of action had as much chance of happening as a pigeon passing up a breadcrumb.

Seven Nickelettes assembled at the apartment Janet and I shared for the faux slumber party. First, we unleashed our inner teenage spirit by dropping a smidgen of LSD. Rocking out to 1960s music in our baby-doll pajamas, we gorged on chips and guzzled Cokes spiked with rum. Our big fat hair curlers jiggled to the beat of rock 'n' roll and the uninhibited abandon of our laughter. Singing along to songs at the top of our lungs triggered the performing bug.

"This is fun, but we need an audience," Debby said. "Where can we go?"

"If the O'Farrell is the bottom of the barrel," I said, "the only place to go is up."

"Right," concurred Debby. "Flaunting it at the top—Top of the Mark."

"Let's go!"

The Top of the Mark is a ritzy cocktail lounge on the top floor of the Mark Hopkins Hotel in San Francisco's upscale Nob Hill. With a 360-degree view of the city and a hundred types of martinis, it has an international reputation as a "must see" destination. So seven high-as-a-kite Nickelettes jumped into a couple of beat-up cars and headed to the swanky side of town.

Scampering through the lobby of the hotel in our pajamas, we giggled at the absurd goofiness of this adolescent stunt. As we popped into the elevator, we faced a no-nonsense matron adorned in a severe black dress and white gloves operating the lift.

"The Top of the Mark," requested Debby. The creaky ride up nineteen floors took forever. Our nervous energy burst out in titters and a fidgety stationary dance.

"Ladies, you're at the Mark," admonished the sober operator.

Karin and I exchanged a glance acknowledging that such silliness was not allowed in these highbrow places.

Stepping out of the elevator into the cocktail lounge, Debby snapped us back on track. "What is this shit? She's not our mother."

The maître d' ushered us to an obscure table next to the kitchen. A waitress came to take drink orders. Uh-oh, no one brought money.

Janet smiled. "Give us a few minutes."

"They're going to kick us out," I whispered in panic.

"Just be cool," said Debby. "Look at this place—it's dead—they need us. Janet and I will go ask the bandleader to play our theme song."

"Do you think they'll do it?"

"Sure, all we have to do is use our charms, a little wink, a little smile . . ."

Off they went. Debby was right—musicians are pushovers for beguiling young women in nighties. Within two minutes, we were onstage at the Top of the Mark singing and dancing "Music! Music! Music!" and mooning the audience with our pajama-clad bottoms. The polite applause from the audience was unlike the catcalls and whistles we were used to at The People's Nickelodeon, but who cares? The house band at the Top of the Mark just backed us full blast, baby! In flushed triumph we returned to our table, the cocktail waitress hot on our heels. Karin waved her off: "Oh, sorry, we gotta go."

"We got another gig to do," added Debby.

As we headed for the elevator, a well-heeled lady patron approached Debby and asked, "What sorority are you pledging, dear?" We laughed ourselves silly all the way home over that one.

"It's all right to *be* crazy, it's not all right to *act* crazy," chortled Debby.

But the society lady's observation was on to something. Our newfound sisterhood *was* like a sorority—not a college sorority, but a performance-art urban guerilla sorority. We stayed up until dawn talking about the possibilities of this new identity: street-wise sorority pledges doing stunts. If we couldn't find a new home for our act, we could just show up at events and ham it up.

Some members drifted away after the demise of the People's Nickelodeon, but others came in to take their place. There were a dozen women in the group now, with usually eight to ten showing up for any specific group event. Doing every show wasn't mandatory.

Vince got us a couple of gigs at the Roxie Theater in the Mission. The theater had recently transformed from a porn palace into an alternative/cult/third-run movie house. Vince hit up his fellow projectionist at the Roxie to let us do a skit before the films.

Bonnie and Bermuda invited their friend, Roberta Coleman, to be in the skit. "Roberta was a Nickelette," explained Bermuda. Roberta, a San Francisco native from a solid middle-class family, had long raven-black hair and smooth flawless skin. She fit right in with us nice girls and also shared our love of bad puns.

"I always wanted to perform," Roberta said. "As kids, my sister, cousin, and me sang songs like 'Sugar in the Morning' and 'Oh, You Beautiful Doll.'" She was different from the rest of us in one aspect: she was a single mom with a four-year-old son. Nonetheless, Roberta pledged the sorority, later saying, "It was a place I could let out a lot of pent-up hostility, emotions, and energy."

The funky Roxie Theater had no backstage, and the only way up to the tiny stage in front of the movie screen was to walk down the aisle in full view of the audience and ascend a mid-stage ladder-like stairway. Try that in a tight dress and high heels. Our skit satirized the Society Against Drugs and Sex, so we changed the lyrics of our theme song, "Music! Music! Music!"

Put another nickel in
In the nickel bag of sin
All I want is smoking dope
And grass and hash and cocaine
I'll do anything for dope
I would even blow the Pope . . .

Our naughty-girl act went over well, but the Roxie didn't fit as a permanent home for us.

In January 1973, as the country watched the Richard Nixon inaugural ball, a friend of Vince's put together a West Coast counter-wingding at the San Francisco Art Institute dubbed the In-Nauseating Ball. The Nickelettes were invited to perform. Our skit scoffed at the president's mandate by marching to the "Grand Old Dick":

Every heart beats true for the red, white, and blue
And there's never a spy or a trick
Should your old acquaintance be forgot
Keep your hand on that Tricky Dick

In the midst of the after-show party, Karin summoned me to the basement restroom. Janet had locked herself in a bathroom stall and refused to come out. From the retching sounds I heard behind the door, I guessed she had consumed too much beer and psilocybin.

"Come on, Janet, open the door," I coaxed.

"Everyone's laughing at me," she sobbed uncontrollably. "I can't take it."

"No one's laughing *at* you, just *with* you," I said through the slit in the stall door. "It's all in fun. Come out."

"No. No. I can't face anyone."

"Well, you can't stay in there all night," I reasoned. She wouldn't budge. Ruining my sequin outfit on the cement floor encrusted with the filthy evidence of several generations of college art students, I wiggled under the door. I led her, pale and shaking, out of the restroom. "Come on, honey, let's go home. I'll drive your car."

Heading across town to our shared apartment, I mustered all my coping skills to navigate the streets of San Francisco. I sobered up by imagining a police officer pulling me over and shining a flashlight into my glitter-rimmed eyes, only to discover dilated pupils sparkling from the ingestion of illegal drugs. Plus, I had to keep an eye on my scantily clad backseat passenger. Twice I swerved to the curb and, in the glare of the streetlight, watched Janet throw up in the gutter. I saw my mission as a symbolic supermom rescuing her wayward daughter. Mama Nickelette made it home without incident and tucked her woozy ward into bed.

Vacillating between the satisfaction of helping a friend and resentment at missing the party, I sat up wide-awake for hours, and memories from high school floated up. I understood Janet's fear of being laughed at. In the summer of 1961, my family moved from the sprawling Los Angeles middle-class suburb of Torrance to Manteca, a small town in Central California. In the early 1960s, the Southern California coast was ground zero for the latest rage in hot-rod, surfing, and Beach Boy culture. In comparison, Manteca was a rural hick town eighty miles from the ocean. My first impression of the place was the smell. Driving south on Highway 99, my father merged into the turnoff for Manteca, and the sickening-sweet stench from the Spreckels Sugar Company assaulted my nostrils. The lone industry located on the southern outskirts of town processed sugar beets and gave Manteca an unpleasant odorous reputation. Not to mention that *manteca de cerdo* means lard in Spanish.

Being the new kid in this backwoods town for my first year of high school was tough. At thirteen, I was the youngest ninth grader, and my physical appearance left little doubt that I was a late bloomer—enough fodder for any number of juvenile jokes. Having no friends to clue me in on the local teenage culture didn't make it any easier.

My first week of a full semester freshman orientation class, I was assigned to write an essay: "What do you want to be when you grow up?" It also required an oral presentation in front of the orientation class. I listened as the other girls presented their responses to the essay question: teacher, nurse, secretary. My name was called. I stood up and began to lose my nerve.

Will these sons of farmers laugh at me? Will these daughters of ranchers snicker when I revealed my deepest heart's desire? Maybe I should play it safe, switch my story to wanting to be a teacher. Shaking, I closed my eyes, gripped the paper, and thought, *Please don't laugh at me.*

Opening my eyes, I stared into the gaze of my classmates, blinked hard, and read the words I'd written: "When I grow up, I want to be an actress. Not a movie actress, but a serious theater stage actress. I want to travel around the world and perform on all the famous stages. I want to play roles like Blanche Dubois in *A Streetcar Named Desire*, or Shakespeare's Lady Macbeth."

My words "Blanche Dubois" and "Lady Macbeth" hung in the air like a couple of expletives. The kids looked out the window, down at their desk, anywhere but at me. Even the teacher examined a speck on the floor. Slinking back to my seat I thought maybe they heard the word "hooker" instead of "actress." But they *didn't* laugh at me, at least not to my face.

Now, as an adult, I understand that most of us feared ridicule from our high school classmates, but we all experienced it in different ways. I don't think I've ever met anyone who told me they were a secure, confident teenager. Revealing our deepest instinctual destiny at that tender age delves into the things we care about the most and pricks the things that can hurt us the most.

I was always out of place in Manteca (although my younger brother took to it like a fish to water). But now, I mused, I'm turning my teenage angst upside-down, telling risqué jokes in off-the-wall spoofs, and inviting people to laugh with me. Janet, I feared, took it too seriously.

The next day, Janet and I talked about the conflict between her upbringing and the bawdy feminine humor of the Nickelettes. She was unable to breach the chasm between the anything-goes, throw-out-the-rules attitude of the Nickelettes and the deeply entrenched morals of her childhood. Janet took a break from the group, and a rift grew between us as I fully embraced the campy, suggestive material we were doing. She accused me of abandoning the theater ideals that we once both shared. I refused to engage in this argument. A short time later, she returned to New York City.

Debby had no problem with the lascivious creed of the Nick-elettes. "We need a gimmick for the Nickelettes to get some PR," she told me. "We've got to do something outrageous." Debby's art degree led to a promotion from lobby popcorn seller to upstairs newspaper ad layout designer for the Mitchell Brothers. Coming in weekly contact with the *San Francisco Chronicle* staff gave her insight into how the media worked. "You have to get to the right people," she told me. Her plan was to zero in on John Wasserman, the liberal-leaning theatre arts critic. "If we can entice him to come to our next gig, he might mention us in his column, 'On The Town,'" Debby continued. "Boring press releases don't work; they get tossed in the trash."

"How can we get the man to come?" I joked.

"Sexy underwear always works," winked Debby. "Wasserman's got a sense of humor."

Among the next batch of press releases John received was a note with the place and time of our next gig tucked into the elastic waistband of a pair of purple satin and lace panties with "Please Come" handwritten across the crotch.

But John was nowhere to be found at our appearance in *The Wild West Show*, galloping down the aisles as cowgirls riding stick ponies and singing "Deep in My Solar Plexus." Oh well, we figured he would at least remember our name (and he did). There were many hilarious guesses about what happened to those panties.

Debby didn't give up. "We need to do some stunt like the Top of the Mark, but this time tell the press in advance."

"Like walking down the street topless," I said, "but we can't do that, we're virgins."

"Yeah, besides who can compete with Carol Doda," Debby moaned. "She walks around Broadway topless every night."

"But hers aren't real," I scoffed. "North Beach—the home of silicone breasts."

Debby jumped up, "That's it! On my last trip to LA, I bought a bunch of plastic tits from Fredericks of Hollywood. We can cruise the Condor wearing plastic tits."

"And Girl Scout uniforms, so they know we're virgins," I added.

"Just bring 'em up, and then . . . let 'em down," Debby laughed.

The night of the Condor stunt, we donned thrift-store Girl Scout uniforms, plastic tits ("On the outside of the uniforms," Deb said. "It has to be on the *outside.*"), and sprinkled glitter from head to tit. To bolster our courage, we dazzled our brains with a little dusting of psilocybin.

"You don't think we're going to do this straight, do you?" I laughed.

"Carol Doda. Condor. Tit-land, here we come," Debby shouted as ten brazen women headed out the door to march down Columbus to Broadway.

Debby talked the manager of the Condor into letting us go onstage for one song, but we got stuck cooling our heels outside the front door because Carol Doda insisted that we couldn't enter until her act was over. Hanging out on the corner of the busy Broadway intersection with our glitter-adorned plastic breasts shining in the blinking neon lights, we attracted a cluster of leering guys snickering in the shadows.

I looked up the street, searching for our friends invited to witness the stunt. Being in a group was better than being a lone woman on a street corner, but I also sought the layer of security that our male friends would provide. I turned back to the group and a guy came out from the shadows and grabbed at my fake tits saying, "Are they real? Are they real?"

"Watch it, bubba," I yelled, and without thinking smacked him in the face. Just then my hunky friend Mike walked up and asked, "Are you having a problem?"

"No," I replied, looking the interloper straight in the eye. He backed away.

The club manager opened the door and motioned us in. We dashed onstage and sang:

> Ain't we sweet?
> See us tripping over our feet
> Now I ask you very confidentially
> Ain't we sweet?
> Just throw a pie
> In our direction
> Oh me, oh my
> Ain't that erection? Da da, da da
> Now, I repeat
> Don't you think we're quite a treat?
> [Whispering] Well, I ask you very confidentially
> [Loudly] Can I take a peek at your meat?

Our planted allies hooted and hollered, but the regular patrons squirmed in their seats and looked around furtively. We called out to Carol Doda, "Join us, Carol, we're your sisters. You're a true Nickelette." But Carol never showed her face or her spectacular silicone tits.

We invited underground journalists Clay Geerdes and John Bryan to come and document the stunt. In the next edition of the *San Francisco Phoenix*, a photo of us appeared on the front page with a second one inside. Media coverage: mission accomplished.

Diane, Roberta, Bermuda, Katy, Bonnie, Debby, Joanne,
Mimi, Karin, and me onstage at the Condor Club

"We had this idea and just went out and did it," said Debby.
"That's what makes it real art." For my part, the spontaneity
of taking our feminist urban guerrilla performance message to
the streets harked back to the revolutionary street theater that
I cut my teeth on in college.

After this bold stunt, we celebrated with a pizza party. Reveling in bawdiness, we took off the plastic boobs and placed
them on different parts of our bodies, finally positioning them
on our heads, which made us look like a perverse version of
the Mickey Mouse Club.

"Remember when that guy from the *Chronicle* called us,
'The freaks answer to the Mickey Mouse Club?'" I said.

"I always wanted to be a Mouseketeer," reminisced Debby.
"Hi, I'm Debby," she said, imitating Annette Funicello, the
Mouseketeer heroine of our childhood who sprouted breasts
on TV right before our admiring prepubescent eyes. "I always
had a problem with being flat-chested," Debby confessed. "It
was always in my art. So to wear these false tits was a personal
triumph, it was so literal."

Women have all kinds of issues with their breasts. We're told they're too small, too big, too flabby, too saggy. It felt good to turn the tables on the narrative and present a women's-lib perspective. Our display of plastic breasts exposed a societal artificial construct about women's anatomy.

～～～

We still didn't have a permanent home, but Vince, our unofficial manager, continued to pitch the Nickelettes to anyone who would listen.

"Vince asked me if I would take on the Nickelettes," Karl Cohen later recalled, "and continue the spirit of the People's Nickelodeon." Karl ran a vintage film series featuring Charlie Chaplin and Laurel and Hardy films on Sunday nights at the Intersection Theater. But Karl hesitated.

"Come on, Karl," prodded Vince, "you had the best time of your life at the Nickelodeon—just see what happens."

Karl agreed to a test run.

For our tryout we presented "The Doll Show," a satirical fantasy set in a toy store full of beautiful Nickelettes dolls. The shopkeeper left for the night, and the dolls came to life. Each doll revealed to the audience that underneath her superficial façade was a complex, interesting, and funny woman. As the dawn broke the dolls screamed out, "Help, I'm a doll! Help, I'm a doll!" before their mouths were once more frozen into molded plastic smiles.

We passed the audition and secured a regular bi-monthly slot on Karl's Sunday night program. Karl introduced the Nickelettes as "Virgins in Residence at the Intersection."

"It was exciting," he noted.

The Intersection Theater in North Beach was a deactivated Methodist Church turned center for the arts—an intersection of art and religion. Reverend John Williams ran the place as a (nearly) free haven for artists, where people who didn't have an outlet elsewhere could test their material, to either sink or swim. "At the Intersection," Karl later explained, "there was a coffee gallery, poetry readings, stand-up comics—Robin Williams got his start there—my film series, the Pitschel Players, and then the Nickelettes."

On April 1, 1973, the 100 percent pure Virgins in Residence inaugurated our new home with a show called "The Nickelettes Get Married." We each parodied the picture-perfect wedding that had been touted as our deepest desire since birth. The point was to launder our psyches of old paradigms. Roberta wore a black dress with a scarlet "A" to her ceremony. Debby dressed in the quintessential 1950s white lace-wedding ensemble. I chose a frothy pink strapless formal and topped it off with my preadolescent version of a veil: a white crinoline petticoat. Schelby wore a slinky green lace dress sans underwear, and at the end of her individual wedding rite, mooned the audience with her bare bum.

We sang that our perfect mate would be "acne free . . . and never having a premature ejaculation." But instead of "I do," at the end of the ceremony we yelled, "April Fool! We don't want to get married, we want to go to Hollywood," and bunny-hopped offstage.

Two weeks later, in the follow-up show "Hollywood," we mocked and rejected star-studded show business as well. "When we got together it was like a chain reaction—all this stuff started pouring out," explained Debby. "If you were by yourself, you couldn't say it, but when you were in the group, you couldn't contain it." It was not easy to find one person with whom you could share your innermost thoughts and feelings, so to find a dozen was a revelation.

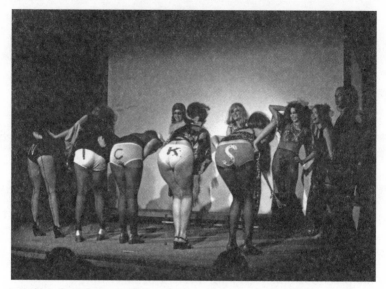

N–I–C–K–S show off their bottoms on the Intersection stage
Photo © Clay Geerdes

Membership in the group still fluctuated. "I brought Kathy in," Debby said. "I dug her so much I wanted her to be in the group."

Kathy Opitz was the product of a rigid military home life and a Catholic school education. When she was fifteen, her father was stationed in Vietnam, and her mother slipped into episodes of manic depression and schizophrenia. She was forced to assume the adult role in the family. As the oldest child, she ran the household, drove the car, and paid the bills. But she also rebelled by sneaking out and smoking pot. Shortly after she left home, she met Debby and saw in the Nickelettes a shared philosophy as well as an opportunity to fulfill her dream of performing. "It was an expression of something taboo, done in a way that was absolutely ridiculous and no one took seriously," Kathy said later. Not being taken seriously had an upside: we got away with it.

Priscilla Alden, an old acquaintance of mine from the San Francisco State drama department, came to a Nickelettes show at the Intersection and fell in love with the group's satirical wit and shameless enthusiasm for bad taste. She was a gifted actress with the ability to grab hold of an audience and not let go. Priscilla hid her bulky body under A-line jumpers designed and sewn personally for her by one of her close friends, but her equally huge personality was never veiled. "The Nicks were a great sorority, based on who knows what peculiar criteria," recalled Priscilla. She pledged and joined the fun.

The group didn't limit performances only to the Intersection. We performed at the very first Comic Book Convention in Berkeley. We found a mutual admiration with the underground comic book scene as we staged a live version of a variety of cartoon characters. Adult comic books were one of the fastest growing happenings in the San Francisco Bay Area in the late 1960s and early '70s. Cartoonists Robert Crumb, Bill Griffith, Spain Rodriquez, and S. Clay Wilson started in San Francisco. Ron Turner founded Last Gasp Comics publishing in 1970. In 1972, he hung out at the People's Nickelodeon. "There are few instances in life where you can tell somebody what's really going on in your brain," said Ron. "Both a cartoonist and a performance artist can transmit a commonality of thought to an audience. I could see the like minds."

On Mother's Day at the Intersection, the Nickelettes presented "A Tribute to Mothers." Allowing the sincerity of our intentions to be the satire, we costumed ourselves in the way we felt our mothers envisioned us. I wore a plaid 100 percent polyester vest and pants ensemble that my mother had given me for Christmas. It would be the first and only time I lovingly wore it.

Individually we paid tribute to our moms. And then summed up our heartfelt sentiments with rewritten lyrics of the "M-O-T-H-E-R" song:

Top: Diane, Bonnie, Priscilla, Karin, Bermuda, Kathy. Bottom: Me, Schelby, Debby, Roberta, Katy, and Mimi. Honoring our mothers
Photo © Richard Alan Smith

M—Is for the many things you gave me.
O—Is for the other things you gave me.
T—Is for the thousands of things you gave me.
H—Is for the hundreds of things you gave me.
E—Is for everything you gave me.
R—Is for the real lot of things you gave me.
Put them all together they spell MOTHER
A word that means the world to me.

Some of us were brave enough to invite our moms. "My parents and family were so outraged and disgusted, they thought I was totally out of line," Debby said. "The mother tribute was sincere and really cleaned up from what we usually did, but my mother took it as a slap in the face."

"I invited my parents," Roberta recalled. "And then at the last minute I chickened out and told them not to come."

My mom drove from Manteca to San Francisco for the event. I pinned a corsage on her shoulder. She smiled at me

after the show, and said, "It was good." But she always unconditionally supported her children's endeavors. I wasn't afraid she
wouldn't get the humor, only that our Hallmark card parody
tribute would be too sappy for her. At the time I failed to grasp
that I had inherited my mom's brazen, somewhat off-color sense
of humor, and that she was, in a way, my Nickelettes role model.

Karin dropped out of the group. She wanted to devote
more time to her dance career. Plus, Tom had enlisted her to
choreograph and perform in his latest Blue Lantern Theater
venture: *Dracula: The Erotic Neurotic.* I was also cast in the
production, and during the summer and fall of 1973, I was
wildly busy, juggling the performances of *Dracula*, Nickelettes
gigs, and my day job.

After the play closed, Karin and Tom went through a difficult breakup, and the theater company disbanded. Like Janet,
Karin moved back to the East Coast. My original collaborators
were now both gone. The Nickelettes wouldn't have existed
without the cohesiveness that the three of us shared at the
moment of the group's conception. But what evolved was a
synchronistic kinship with a new group of women.

Casting about for new show ideas, I recalled a treasured
memory from my childhood. In 1958, I was eleven years old.
On Christmas Day, my mom drove me and a neighborhood
friend to Hollywood for a special taping of the popular TV
show *Queen for a Day.* This classic 1950s show combined two
staples of daytime TV: the game show and the soap opera. The
show was one of my favorites, and this special version, "Princess for a Day," was exclusively for preteen girls. I couldn't
believe I got to have lunch at the luxurious theater/restau-
rant Moulin Rouge, and watch the host, Jack Bailey, bellow,
"Would you like to be princess for a day?" My friend Linda
and I joined the audience in screaming, "Yes!"

The contest challenged four contestants chosen from the studio audience to tell the best (or worst) hard-luck story to millions of viewers, in hopes of being crowned Princess for a Day and winning fabulous Hollywood consumer products. "King" Jack Bailey was a master at capturing the essence of a contestant's sob story, no matter how trivial.

My mom concocted a story for me: I desperately needed an airline ticket to the East Coast to visit my grandparents whom I had only visited *once* in my entire life. "Then try to cry," she coached. Linda had an even juicier story: her father had been canned from his job two weeks before Christmas. She lamented the prospect of a bleak holiday for herself and her five siblings. She failed to mention that her dad was an incurable drunk and this was his third job loss in less than three years. But, alas, neither Linda nor I made it to the top four.

The crowd clapped for their favorite bad luck story as an electronic applause meter measured the decibel level from one to ten, and the highest recorded number determined the winner. The glum losers watched the winner shed cascades of happy tears as Jack placed a princess crown of glittering jewels on her head, draped her shoulders with a sable-trimmed cape, handed her a bouquet of long-stemmed roses, and sat her on a gold-and-red velvet throne. The music ramped up, the curtain opened, and Jack revealed that not only would her wish come true, but she'd also receive a variety of prizes from the show's sponsors.

"Now, little darling," said Jack, the music hitting a crescendo, "your life is complete."

The newly crowned princess sobbed, "Oh, thank you, Jack, thank you so much."

Even at age eleven, I could see that the game was rigged; a brand new Naugahyde living room set or deluxe refrigerator filled with a month's worth of frozen dinners wasn't going to magically turn my life into a fairytale. Jack Bailey's

My mom, my friend Linda, and me at Princess for a Day

demeanor was cheerful, but I detected an underlying layer of condescension.

Queen for a Day was a gold mine for satire. A Nickelettes version would be a snap. Having witnessed the dodgy show up close, I knew the key to the parody was to nail the character of Jack Bailey. I volunteered to dress in drag and take on the part. I purchased a secondhand men's suit, one size too small, unzipped the fly and let my unironed shirttail hang out. On my head, I wore a top hat over a messy wig, and I covered my face with a Groucho Marx mustache, nose, and eyebrows. To complete this effeminate Charlie Chaplin look, I painted my fingernails flaming red. I based my Jack persona on every insincere guy who'd ever crossed my path: "So, sweetie, I understand your husband just died and you have four children under the age of five at home. Sounds to me like you need a washing machine, hee, hee, hee."

The other Nickelettes lined up as contestants vying for the best sob story. Roberta related that her French poodle needed a sex-change operation. Bermuda and Bonnie appeared as one contestant: a two-torso woman with each of them in one leg of an enormous pair of pants. They told Jack (me), "If I fit on your screen, you must make me queen."

Debby, dressed as Shirley Temple in a curly wig and frilly little girl dress, claimed she was candy deprived, and asked for a cruise on the *Good Ship Lollipop*.

"Very cute, Ms. Temple," replied Jack. "Sounds like you need a vacuum cleaner." Jack dragged out a flimsy cardboard cutout Applause-O-Meter. "And now, ladies and gentlemen, the highly sensitive Applause-O-Meter will measure your applause and determine who will wear the crown."

Jack manipulated the arrow of the low-tech device from the back and let Roberta win. The other contestants went berserk and chased Jack Bailey through the audience and out the front door of the theater. This had not been rehearsed.

We hadn't given up on the idea of pop-up street theater. I told the group, "We need to crash some big glitzy event that the press wouldn't miss."

"The San Francisco opera opening!" Debby exclaimed.

"It's the biggest show in town this time of year," Kathy said.

"And every newspaper and TV station will cover it," I added.

"We'll get all dolled up, make an appearance, and then leave," schemed Debby. "Being seen is the point, not seeing the opera."

"But I love the opera," protested Priscilla. "I go regularly."

"So this time you strut your stuff with the high society crowd," I said, "without paying for an overpriced ticket."

"It's silly," chuckled Priscilla. "But I'm up for a display of bad taste."

"It's a power move for attention," noted Kathy. "Let's do it."

Susan Berman reported on the opulent opera opening in the *San Francisco Sunday Examiner and Chronicle*:

Opera's First Night Was
Best Free Show in Town

The entrances had it, and no one could outdo the Nick-elettes, rare coins who called themselves "interpretive performers." They arrived in a funky rainbow-colored VW van, sequins on their eyelids and red mops on their heads, dressed in vintage rags. "We're just here to make an entrance and an exit: we just didn't want to miss it," exulted one woman in the troupe.

David Johnston reported in the *Berkeley Barb*:

Smash Opera Opening

There had been rumors that the Nickelettes were coming. . . . They leaped from the truck smiling. . . . Heads craned and the crowd pressed in with furious elbow and knee attacks. The Nickelettes were being devoured. A horde of reporters crushed in and the Nickelettes hardly had a chance to perform.

Vince volunteered to play chauffeur for this stunt, driving us in his rainbow van. He outfitted himself in dark sunglasses with a cabbie cap pulled down low over his forehead. Picture a security officer watching a rainbow-colored van amid the long line of black Rolls Royces wrapped around the ultra-chic San Francisco Opera House on opening night. As we crouched nervously in the back, Vince inched closer to the entrance. The officer approached asking to see our tickets. Vince kept the window rolled up, playing dumb, pretending not to hear. But push came to shove, and we were forced to make a premature entrance. Jumping out of the van posing as starlets, we smiled, spun, and danced as friends, masquerading as reporters, rushed over and started taking photos with the duped hordes of journalists and paparazzi following suit. Having fulfilled our mission, we leapt back into the van and sped away.

Frances Moffat reported in the *San Francisco Magazine:*

Evening at the Opera House

Stealing the show outside the Carriage entrance of the Opera House were bizarrely dressed non-ticket holders who hopped out of a van . . . young members of the counterculture . . . vying for attention with the chauffeur-and-limousine traffic.

I delighted in the description, "non-ticket holders." Stealing the spotlight from the privileged elite without paying to be in their club was the message. The stunt exceeded our expectations. Not only did the story with our photos appear in mainstream publications, but we also made it onto the eleven o'clock TV news broadcasts.

Me, Joanne, Debby, Priscilla, and Kathy
crash the San Francisco Opera Opening
Photo © Janet Fries

Encouraged by the success of the opera opening, we trolled around for another big event to crash. The opening night of the San Francisco Film Festival was next on the city's social calendar. Debby discovered that Frances Moffat, author of the *San Francisco Magazine* blurb, was the entertainment coordinator for the event. Debby called her and offered our services as a preshow warm up act. She politely declined. Debby persisted; still no dice.

Okay, we'll just buy tickets—an affordable option that wasn't available for the opera opening. This time we would be ticket holders at the preshow reception stealing the limelight with urban guerilla antics. Our performance consisted solely of attention-grabbing costumes. Kathy painted her face, neck, and hands entirely in gold makeup, and posed like an Egyptian statue. Priscilla, as a Spanish *condesa* with a decorative eye mask, snapped open a brightly colored fan and coyly hid her bright red lips. I dressed in an elegant gown from the 1940s, accessorizing with a ratty Janis Joplin feather boa in my hair and a child's party blowout that I blew open into people's faces. Debby, costumed in a pink sequin gown with matching mask and tiara, played with a glittery yo-yo. "You don't need talent," she said, explaining the concept as a live female sculpture. "Let your clothes, props, and accessories do the work."

We searched the premises for celebrities, but they were nowhere to be found. Joanne Woodward, star of the featured movie *Summer Wishes, Winter Dreams*, slipped in through a back door. The nonchalant partygoers barely gave us a second glance. It turned out to be so boring we didn't even stick around to watch the film. However, later, in a roundabout way, we did get a mention in Herb Caen's *San Francisco Chronicle* column:

Wednesday night's opening [of the San Francisco Film Festival] . . . was devoid of glamor or glitter, not that it was headliner Joanne Woodward's fault: she's "normal," intelligent, and a fine actress. Glamorous she isn't, and that brings up a point we'll discuss some other time: do only kooks have glamor?

Kooks? Could he be referring to the Nickelettes? The event was so mediocre you'd think they'd welcome "kooks" with open arms.

Under the headline, "The Nickelettes Are Mutants," Clay Geerdes in the *Los Angeles Weekly News* called us "San Francisco's one and only viable underground feminist theatre troupe." He went on to say about the stunt, "Just say the Nickelettes found out hobnobbing isn't all it's cut out to be." Mutants or kooks, one thing was certain: nobody else was doing what the Nickelettes were doing.

～✦～

Our interest in urban guerrilla sorority stunts waned. We shifted our focus full-time to the Virgin Residency at the Intersection Theater. We moved an old steamer trunk into the dressing room, painted it white, splattered it with glitter, and adorned one side with bold, shiny letters: NICKELETTES. The trunk stored glitter, makeup, wigs, rhinestone jewelry, feather boas, accessories, and other odds and ends that were needed to throw together a last-minute outfit. Settling into this funky, nonjudgmental place was like sinking into a favorite easy chair. Our new home gave us an opportunity to experiment, play, and grow.

Writing, rehearsing, and performing an original show every two weeks meant we had to work fast. But getting everyone together to collectively brainstorm ideas became a challenge. So the group evolved a more cohesive approach, where each performer took a turn writing a script, and then the whole

Me and Debby in front of the Intersection Theater

Photo © Clay Geerdes

group rehearsed and performed it. This allowed every woman in the group the opportunity to write material that inspired her. But we didn't abandon anarchy; the scripts were written with deliberate holes designed for improvisation. The author-of-the-week would direct, "In this part just say whatever comes into your head the night of the show."

"Nor did we stop getting completely stoned before each show," Bermuda commented later.

I concurred. "A performer's high wasn't enough for us, so we downed a couple of beers, smoked some pot, and perhaps had a snort of coke or psilocybin."

"And then we discovered whippets," continued Bermuda. "What do you call it?"

"Nitrous oxide."

Adjacent to our dressing room, the Intersection's café store-room was open and unlocked. One night, rooting around for goodies to eat, we discovered whipped cream canisters along with boxes of nitrous oxide cartridges. We inserted the cartridges into the canister's chamber without the cream, inhaled the gas from the spigot, and got a giddy high. It became the cherry on top of our altered state to take a hit of nitrous oxide as we ascended the stairs to go onstage.

Karl Cohen was left answering to the supervisors of the café. "The whipped cream gas canisters kept disappearing," he said. "It started with just one or two canisters from a box, then every time the Nickelettes did a show, I had to go out and buy a couple of boxes."

Debby's ongoing PR campaign included an oversized, shiny gold 1974 calendar/poster featuring Nickelettes photos and career highlights. The plan was to distribute it to our fans and media as a holiday gift. The calendar sparked an exciting event. Lily Tomlin, one of our comedy idols, was in San Francisco headlining at the Boarding House (a hip nightclub featuring comedy and music acts). Bonnie and Bermuda sent Lily the Nickelettes 1974 calendar, a bottle of champagne, and a gushy fan letter that included an invitation to our show. Lily accepted the champagne, the praise, and the invitation.

"Lily Tomlin is coming to see our show!" Bermuda exclaimed.

"We need to put our best high-heeled feet forward," I said. We even sacrificed whippets for the big night.

Bermuda wrote the skit, "The Maltese Weenie" a whodunit spoof for the occasion, and Roberta played the Maltese Weenie. "I pinned a real hot dog to my shorts, and said, 'You may be a private dick but I'm the Maltese Weenie.'"

After the show we waited for Lily to catapult us out of our funky coffeehouse/theater existence into the big time. That didn't happen, but Bermuda and Bonnie received a note from her a week later:

Dear Bermuda & Bonnie,
I thought the Nickelettes were wonderful and playful and it's so great to see women doing theater together and just generally being inventive and irreverent and crazy and gutsy and assertive. And thank you for the champagne and all your love and support.
Love, Lily

Please let everyone in the Nickelettes know how much I appreciated them.
Lily

If Lily loved us, could real stardom be far behind? The elevator button was pressed *up*. We imagined a call from the Boarding House. It won't happen if you don't dream it, we thought, and there's no sense in dreaming small.

Still, nothing stays the same. Soon after this, Bonnie and Bermuda dropped out of the Nickelettes to form their own group. The majority of the Nickelettes favored irreverent satires of fairy tales and TV shows, while Bonnie and Bermuda leaned toward skewering well-known musicals with off-the-wall song parodies. "We decided we really wanted to do music and learn to sing harmonies," Bermuda said. They formed a vocal musical comedy group called the Pointless Sisters.

Like the People's Nickelodeon, Karl expanded his Sunday night film program to include novice performers looking for a place to test their material. The Pointless Sisters became regulars, as did Freaky Ralph, who often opened for us. Ralph traveled in his own alternative universe. In 1973, Ralph was ahead of his time doing a raw, eccentric act with lyrics and music that tapped into an unconventional male persona.

"And we were giving it all away for a buck," reflected Karl. "It was a fabulous period of wild, liberated, anarchistic theater. And in those days you could even find a parking place in North Beach."

❧

The Nickelettes had a new permanent home, but I avoided planning too far ahead. I honored my audacious youthful confidence to just go with the flow. There was no plan to conform, only the desire to be more outrageous. It was wildly fun to present our rough and raw material out in the open. Having that cutting edge, wearing outlandish makeup and costumes, mixing the metaphors of virgins and eager beavers, and even offending some people thrilled the rebel in me. Nice girls don't make history. Could it backfire? Sure. But eluding female pigeonholes was so much fun it was worth the risk.

CHAPTER 3

SO FAR UNDERGROUND, WE GET WET

"I'm going to do big things!"

The Nickelettes unlocked within me a deep buried sense of humor. The more I allowed my comedic whimsy to escape out in the open, the more authentic I felt. Why had I let my humorous impulses go underground? As an adolescent, I learned that if I wanted teenage boys to like me (and I did), I had to avoid saying out loud the wisecracks that floated through my head. I heeded the unwritten rule for girls of my generation: crack up at boys' inane jokes and stifle your own silliness.

One day, at age sixteen, I caught on to the cultural axiom of the time that boys could say and do whatever they wanted. I was alone at home with nothing to do and a dollar in my pocket. Indulging in a covert pleasure, I walked over to the supermarket to buy a candy bar and a *MAD* magazine. I loved the lowbrow, hilarious, "Humor, Satire, Stupidity and Stupidity" of *MAD*.

I paid for the purchases at the cash register, and the bagger, a male high school classmate of mine, said, "You're not still reading that dumb kids' stuff, are you?"

I looked down and smiled sheepishly.

He smirked. "Do you really think that junk is funny?"

Not replying, I grabbed my bag and fled the store. Walking slowly home, I held back tears and chastised myself for being an immature ninny. If the bagger—a star quarterback on the high school football team—thought *MAD* magazine was kids' junk, shouldn't I also? And if I laughed at the stories in *MAD* magazine, didn't that make me dumb? I wasn't able to enjoy the magazine or the candy bar even in the privacy of my family's empty house. It would be years before I dared to pick up a *MAD* magazine again.

The only safe place an adolescent girl could risk letting the joker out of the bottle was in an all-girl environment, like a slumber party. But that changed when boyfriends entered the picture. Female friendships deteriorated into competition, secrecy, and betrayal.

Flash forward ten years. In 1974, no longer needing the validation of a small-town high school football player, I got to be as brazenly stupid, silly, and *MAD* as I wanted with my circle of campy accomplices.

~~~

The audience at the Intersection never knew what to expect from the Nickelettes, and neither did we. Our bimonthly shows at Karl's vintage movie series included risqué parodies of fairy tales ("Mother Goosed," "Snow White and the Seven Dorks"), and satires of pop culture ("Rock Around the Cock"). We also gave voice to personal obsessions. Debby stayed glued to the tube in 1974 following the unfolding account of the Patty Hearst kidnapping. The bizarre story of the Hearst heiress being nabbed by the Symbionese Liberation Army from her apartment in Berkeley played out more like a fiction thriller than the daily news. We all watched in fascination as Patty denounced her upper-class upbringing, declared she was now the urban guerilla revolutionary Tanya, and demanded that her wealthy parents ("the fascist insect Hearst") host a free food giveaway to the poverty-stricken people of San Francisco.

Inspired by these current events, Debby wrote "Wanderlust." The campy story portrayed Tanya as an underground princess army leader from Symbonia demanding twenty million tons of glitter, sequins, and rhinestones be given away free to all ladies of lesser circumstances.

We also didn't pass up on opportunities to weigh in on political issues. Caitlin Knell, a new member in the group, asked us to perform at a political fundraising party her mother was hosting. Caitlin's family lived in Atherton, a wealthy community near Palo Alto that attracted politicians in search of campaign funds. Caitlin bragged to us that she had run away from this conservative suburb, landed in sin city, and found the salacious Nickelettes. To make her point, the first time she stepped on stage as a Nickelette with a perfectly coiffed, feathered-cut hairdo, she wore a T-shirt that boldly said, "Fuck Off."

The Atherton event was organized to raise money for March Fong, a candidate running for the office of California secretary of state. Caitlin delighted in not explaining to her mother the campy nature of the group. "Let it be a surprise," she said.

One of Ms. Fong's campaign promises was to outlaw pay toilets. In 1974 the public was outraged that, in an effort to keep the riffraff out and the toilet paper in, business and government buildings installed locks on restroom stall doors that required a dime for entry. Opponents argued that it was immoral to make you pay to pee. Roberta wrote a song, "Pay Toilets," for the occasion:

> 'Cause if you gotta go, and you need a dime,
> Under the stall you'll surely climb.
> So, March Fong. So, March Fong
> You know pay toilets are wrong . . .

We danced and twirled our sparkly spray-painted toilet seats in the air. At the end we whirled the seats around and planted them on our bottoms, bouncing up and down, to make the point. The fundraising crowd politely applauded as we pranced off. Caitlin's mother was slightly embarrassed, but the Nickelettes had done their patriotic duty to influence critical political issues: March Fong was elected, and pay toilets were outlawed.

⌒⌔〜

The Nickelettes become *Les* Nickelettes in 1974 for reasons that to this day remain obscure. The only thing I remember is that we wanted to go French. Nickelettes is a French word, so *Les* completed the name, and it made us sound like exotic can-can dancers.

"Yeah, like, 'How you gonna keep 'em down on the farm, after they've seen Paree?'" sang Debby. "But I think it was because we wanted to get laid: *Les*, as in Lay Nickelettes."

"People thought the Nickelettes were all lesbians," piped in Priscilla, "so they thought we were being cryptic by calling ourselves *Les* Nickelettes, as in we're all *les*bians."

But one fan took it in another direction. "I walked into the bathroom at the Intersection," said Roberta, "and read the graffiti on the wall: 'I wish there were *Less* Nickelettes.'" We're famous! Nothing signifies celebrity more than a scribbled pun on a toilet stall.

With the new group name came Debby's idea to launch a new cultural paradigm. "We're deeper than underground," Debby said, envisioning a concept that would take the underground counterculture a step further. "We're so avant-garde, we're underwater; we're the Underwater Ultra Culture."

A few days later, I read a newspaper story about the dauntless swim upstream every spring of scores of salmon. I told Debby about the article: "It sounds like Les Nickelettes's struggle up the raging river of show biz."

"Yeah, and once upriver, they go out with a spectacular spawn!" said Debby. "Think about that."

"Spawning is a perfect metaphor for the Underwater Ultra Culture and Les Nickelettes."

The salmon became the mascot for our new "watery way of life." Pumped up about this new notion, we decided to inaugurate the project with an independently produced variety show and party at the Intersection. Never mind that we had zero experience as producers.

In March 1974, solidifying our relationship, Vince and I moved into together. He hung out at the Intersection when Les Nickelettes performed, and had become a trusted behind-the-scenes advisor. When I turned to him for help in producing this stand-alone show, it was like bringing back the People's Nick-elodeon. In that tradition, Vince and I recruited warm-up acts including a mutual friend, Bill Wolf, to be master of ceremonies. Wearing an old-fashioned top hat and an ill-fitting tuxedo on his lanky frame, Bill used a dummy named Freckles to parody a bad ventriloquist act. Through his goofy, slim-lipped grin, he didn't hide the fact that he was the one telling atrocious jokes. We brought back the original vaudevillian Al Rand, and Freaky Ralph, and added the Pointless Sisters (now a trio with new member Maria Scatuccio), and newcomer Leila the Snake, aka Jane Dornacker, who did a sinuous belly dance while telling outlandish jokes. With very little effort, Vince also assembled a volunteer backstage crew, front house staff, and secured the rock 'n' roll band High Wire to play for the after-show party.

We also welcomed a new member to Les Nickelettes. "It was so cool to be part of this hip San Francisco thing," Roberta said, so she invited her younger sister Carol to share the experience.

"Roberta said to me, why don't you join?" Carol said. "At first I was too shy. But it seemed kind of 'off' in an exciting way, like an inside joke." Carol was nothing like her upfront and outgoing big sister. Her unassuming disposition matched her employment as a preschool teacher. But in her first performance with Les Nickelettes, she surprised me. "I took a risk," said Carol, "playing Trixie Treat." Her gritty hooker character gaily celebrated her job by singing, "'When I come to your door, da, da, da, da, I screw till I'm sore. . . .'" Carol proved that even a sweet preschool teacher could harbor a hidden risqué Nickelettes spirit.

Les Nickelettes kicked off the *Underwater Ultra Culture Show* with "The New Spawning Game," a game show parody of *The Dating Game*. But the highlight of the evening was our satire of the Oscars. I got the idea watching the Academy Awards on TV. I imagined myself being a nominee sitting in the glitzy LA audience. I held my breath as the envelope for Best Actress was opened. I gasped as I heard my name ring out followed by a burst of thunderous applause. Bounding up to the podium, I exclaimed, "Oh, what a surprise!" And grasping the well-deserved Oscar in my tight-fisted grip, I gave a gracious, but self-serving thank-you speech.

I thought, wouldn't it be fun to act out this dream?

Our Salmon Awards spoof set out to roast Tinseltown with over-the-top accolades followed by silly acceptance speeches. For the actual awards, we transformed thrift shop bowling trophies into works of art by gluing on sequins, glitter, and feathers. But the more we planned the show, the more the concept of presenting ourselves with awards became too self-indulgent, even for us. Then we hit on the idea of honoring the people who were helping Les Nickelettes swim upstream. Supporters like Vince, Karl, and John Williams of the Intersection, the backstage crew, and our friends from the press. So instead of honoring ourselves, we switched it up and gave awards to the people on our thank-you list.

We kept secret the names of the recipients until the Fantastic First Annual International Salmon Awards of 1974

From top left: Carol, Priscilla, Ann, Diane,
Roberta, me, Debby, and Kathy in 1974

were announced. John Williams received the Irving Thalberg Memorial Award; Clay Geerdes, the William Randolph Hearst Memorial Journalism Award; and Karl Cohen, the Sol Hurok Memorial Producer Award. All were touched and grinned ear-to-ear as they mumbled, "Thank you." The best was saved for last. Vince Stanich received the Howard Hughes Memorial Award. Despite Vince's enthusiasm for show business, he shunned the spotlight unless in disguise, referring to himself as Howard Hughes (the reclusive wealthy businessman who zealously guarded his anonymity). Vince coveted his Salmon Award.

~~~~~~

Part of our plan to introduce the Underwater Ultra Culture to the masses was to do a stunt. Debby noted that September 16, 1974, was the long-awaited official opening of the Bay Area Rapid Transit (BART) tube—a train tunnel built under the bay to connect San Francisco to the East Bay. With poster board and markers, we designed a sign that proclaimed, "BART IS UNDERWATER AND SO ARE LES NICKELETTES." Debby, Kathy, Roberta, and I headed downtown, waving our sign and wearing bathing suits, swim fins, and underwater facemasks.

At the brand-spanking-new Powell Street Station, we were stopped cold. City officials had placed barriers at the top of the escalator, preventing the masses from going down to the heart of the ribbon-cutting ceremony below. Only a slew of politicians, dignitaries, and press were allowed near the action. On the sidelines, shivering in the fog, we heard speech after speech from the assembled politicians congratulating themselves on their marvelous achievement. In an attempt to stay warm and get attention, we flapped our swim fins, waved our sign, and shouted our message.

At the end of the dreary event, we caught the eye of California Assemblyman Willie Brown who came over to inquire about the purpose of our spiel. "We're Les Nickelettes," said Roberta.

"And we're so far underground that we're underwater," gushed Kathy.

"Just like the BART tube," I added.

"We're part of the new Ultra Culture!" Debby exclaimed.

"Oh," replied the great mover and shaker of California politics as he turned dismissively and walked away.

Maybe the world wasn't ready yet to spawn a female-conceived paradigm shift. Maybe a women's group rising from the underwater primordial soup to usurp the counterculture with an Ultra Culture was ahead of its time.

Still, we resolved that producing and managing our own nouveau vaudeville was the way to go. We printed up and distributed business cards proclaiming our cheeky intentions: "Les Nickelettes: from rudimentary to professional engagements (415) 751-6048."

At a party Debby met a newly hired art director for the glossy *San Francisco Magazine* and gave him one of our cards. He laughed. Then he described to Debby an innovative photographic art technique he was planning to use for the upcoming October issue. A colored light beam would be manipulated around the shape of a person during a camera's long exposure setting resulting in the figure and the light shape captured in a combined image. His idea was to spell out O-C-T-O-B-E-R with a red light superimposed around images of people in Halloween costumes. Debby jumped at the chance to volunteer Les Nickelettes to be models for the assignment.

We hammed it up at the photo shoot, winning over the photographer and art director with jokes about taking over the world with our Underwater Ultra Culture. Debby pushed it further, "You need to do an article about the Nicks to go along with the calendar photos." The art director agreed, and sent a reporter to interview us at our next show. But a centerfold calendar spread plus a featured article in *San Francisco Magazine* was not enough for Ms. Deborah Marinoff. "What do you have planned for the cover?" she asked.

"The BART tube opening," replied the director.

"BART, schmart, this is October, it's Halloween. You need to highlight your unique light-photographic art technique with Les Nickelettes front and center." Debby talked this guy into putting Les Nickelettes on the cover. She assured him this would be a coup that would lead to a big promotion.

The October 1974 cover of *San Francisco Magazine* headlined: "Les Nickelettes: A taste for rudimentary entertainment. . . ." and featured a full-page photo of Priscilla in her Spanish condesa costume, me provocatively pulling up the skirt of a vintage slut outfit to reveal a lacy leg, and Debby looking at me in mock horror costumed as Shirley Temple in a frilly little girl dress, blond curly wig, and white gloves. Opening the magazine to the stapled calendar in the middle was O-C-T-O-B-E-R spelled out in red light with a photo of a Nickelette in the middle of each letter. A two-page story followed: "Direct From Barney's Boom Boom Room—A Snapshot History of Les Nickelettes, Our Center Foldouts." We had co-opted the conservative *San Francisco Magazine*— our best stunt ever.

This kind of publicity was out of reach for starving artists like us. So we reveled in it. Walking into a store and seeing my picture prominently displayed on a magazine rack was exhilarating. We celebrated our coup, but were brought down a bit by Debby's report that after putting us on the cover, the art director got canned from the magazine. The Underwater Ultra Culture apparently didn't resonate with higher corporate powers.

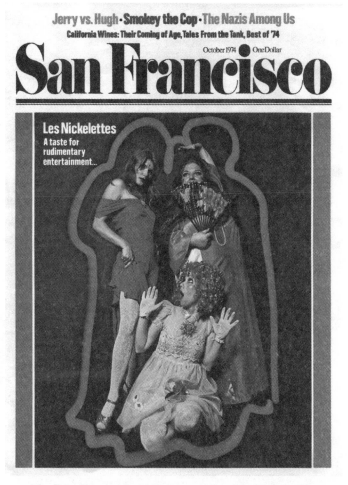

Me, Priscilla, and Debby representing Les Nickelettes
on the cover of *San Francisco Magazine*

Photo © Tim Young Studios

The magazine cover kicked off a flurry of activities for Les Nickelettes in October 1974. We were in high demand. Bill Wolf asked Les Nickelettes to take part in a float he was designing for the Columbus Day parade. Besides acting as emcee for our vaudeville revues, Bill led AAA Productions, a loose group of artists who shared his vision that life was art and participated in his conceptual performance-art projects. Bill's inexhaustible energy and cheerful personality made up for a lack of money. His inventive Columbus Day float was made from used cardboard and recyclables to artfully replicate a royal Italian castle. With the theme, "Queen Isabella Gives Her Jewels to Columbus," he assigned Les Nickelettes to represent the "Jewels" in glittering treasure boxes surrounding Queen Isabella on her throne. Members of the AAA Production Company played the lead roles of Columbus and Queen Isabella.

Riding on a parade float is hard work. The energy from the cheering crowds electrified and drained me. The constant waving wearied my arms, and nonstop smiling made my cheeks

Diane, Kathy, Roberta, and me as "jewels" on
the Columbus Day Float

sore. Debby was feeling awful that day, "I couldn't deal with it, couldn't show my face, so I wore my dog mask. I still showed up, but didn't have to smile." I'm not sure what the crowd made of Queen Isabella's "dog" jewel.

Despite its low budget and no doubt because of Bill's inspired vision, "Queen Isabella Gives Her Jewels to Columbus" won the third place ribbon in the parade competition. After this event, Les Nickelettes and Bill's AAA Productions formed a loose collaboration that came together from time to time to do special projects.

Following in quick succession were Halloween, hookers, and rock 'n' roll. On Halloween we performed "Up Your Vampire" at the Intersection, and then grabbed our makeup bags and hoofed it over to the Longshoreman's Hall to make an appearance at the First Annual Hookers' Masquerade Ball. The event was a fund-raiser for Call Off Your Old Tired Ethics (COYOTE). Ex-hooker Margo St. James, a feisty advocate for sex workers' rights, launched the hookers' union COYOTE to provide dignity, health, and legal protection for prostitutes and to fight to decriminalize prostitution.

The scene at this Halloween shindig, dubbed a "Ball-In," let loose expressions of all sorts of adult erotica. From our repertoire, Les Nickelettes contributed one of our bawdiest numbers:

Would ya like to have whips? Chains? Spikes?
We could have a few shrieks and moans.
Sex offender—I can be offensive to you.

The audience hooted and whistled. Only in San Francisco could you witness feminist naughty virgins fundraising for the hookers' union. Anything goes—no holds barred in this era of sex, drugs, and rock 'n' roll. The notorious Hookers' Halloween Masquerade Ball went on to became an annual not-to-be-missed party in the city for many years.

Next up, Winterland, the biggest rock music venue on the West Coast. The Tubes were the preeminent performance-art rock band in the Bay Area in 1974. Bill Spooner and Prairie Prince, members of the band, had been classmates of Debby at the San Francisco Art Institute performing (as the Beans) at her graduation art show. The Tubes envied Les Nickelettes because we attracted so much publicity. We envied the Tubes because they got paying gigs. The band invited us to sing backup on their finale.

Using my backstage pass, I entered the infamous Winterland, anticipating an even wilder Dionysian scene than the Hookers' Ball. But instead, the grimy backstage rooms in the rock 'n' roll palace matched the somber mood of the band and their entourage. Debby and I took off our coats to reveal our performance-art costumes: lacy little girl dresses. Along with Roberta and Carol and Ann, we went into our act of fawning over the musicians and acting like silly preteen groupies. But the band more or less ignored our shenanigans. "We were just window dressing," noted Roberta. "They barely talked to us backstage."

The lack of stimulating backstage merriment didn't diminish the incredible rush of going onstage. The lead singer, Fee Waybill, as Quay Lewd (a satirical takeoff on quaaludes, a popular prescription barbiturate ingested by hipsters at the time), launched into the finale anthem, "White Punks on Dope," attired in a decadent British glam-glitter outfit with two-foot high platform boots. "We ran out there," Carol said, "and sang, 'White punks on dope, white punks on dope, white punks on dope, white punks on dope, white punks on dope . . .'"

Not able to hear a thing, we still followed the instructions to be as wild as possible while singing the back-up chorus over and over. Fee took the parody up a notch by having his parodied out-of-control rock star, Quay Lewd, trash the entire set. As the music hit the crescendo, he knocked over the huge black-painted faux cardboard speakers. The last note resonated, and with the destruction completed, the lights blacked out. We scrambled offstage.

Grabbing Carol in the dark, I said, "That was unreal; I couldn't even see the audience."

"Me neither, but it was such a rush!"

Despite this big demand for Les Nickelettes's services, our wallets remained empty. Don't give up your day job, girls. Maybe fame *and* fortune don't go hand in hand.

~~~

Perhaps if we were in charge of the shows, we could make some money. With that goal in mind, we visited the Victoria Theater in the heart of the Mission District. This was a bigger theater than the Intersection, with the potential for more ticket sales, thus more income.

During the day, the Victoria housed a strip show called the New Follies Burlesque. The piano player in the house band for the burlesque show knew Debby and told her the place was available for rent in the evenings. Debby finagled a visit to see the strip show and the theater. Kathy, Roberta, Debby, and I were met at the entrance by the manager and quickly whisked upstairs to a vacant balcony. From this clandestine vantage point, we could visually survey the stage and seating below.

The Victoria had been built in the early part of the twentieth century as a vaudeville theater. Now this architectural remnant of past glory was run-down and shabby. But beneath the dust and grime, we glimpsed a potential beauty. Peering over the railing, we watched the auditorium seats fill with a motley assortment of men. The sleazy vibe drifting up from the audience made us glad we were out of sight. The music started, and the strippers came out one at a time.

The young, attractive women each had a different gimmick to appeal to a wide variety of male fantasies. One did a classic tease covering her private parts with feathers and fans; one, accompanied by country music, stripped off her leather boots and cowgirl fringe; another danced to "Let Me Entertain You" as an elegant showgirl stripping off long gloves and nylons held up by a garter belt; and the last one held a huge lollipop that she licked while peeling off her little pink dress.

We enjoyed their art of stripping and teasing, but got a jolt when they danced completely naked, bending over open legs, and lying center stage on a round bed doing spread eagle gyrations that revealed everything. The bawdy Nickelettes were shocked. We were quite willing to tease and stun with our ideas and words, but too modest to flash our pussies for the salacious satisfaction of strange men.

After the show, the strippers trooped up to the balcony, introducing themselves to us as dancers not strippers. The cowgirl said, "We're so thrilled you came to see our show. Our dances are art and can be enjoyed by anyone."

"Do you ever get tired of performing for horny men?" I asked.

"Hell, yeah!"

"You should adopt our philosophy," said Debby. "We're virgins on one side and eager beavers on the other. We do whatever we want and don't have to answer to anyone. We're so far underground we're underwater. Get it? We're taking it back to the womb."

The dancers said nothing.

Breaking the awkward silence I said, "I really like your feathers and rhinestones."

"Do you really get to do whatever you want?" the showgirl asked. "I can't even change the color of my feathers without the manager's permission."

"Yeah, we wear whatever we want," replied Kathy. "How much do they pay you for your act?"

"Usually about $400 a week."

"Wow!" I glanced at Kathy. Most of us made about $400 a

month at our day jobs. But envy at making a lot of money didn't override an aversion to the way they hauled in that dough.

Although we were the same age as the dancers/strippers, we were different as night and day. On the surface, this encounter was similar to girlfriends confiding in each other, exchanging little artistic tricks. But their hard edge clashed with our soft-around-the-edges sensibility. Later, I realized that our uneasiness stemmed from the feeling that someone or something had eroded these women's self-worth.

"Doesn't it bother you when those men in the audience are masturbating?" I asked. The classic stripper said, "I'm so immersed in my dance I just ignore them. It's just a job, a good paying gig, much easier than being a waitress."

"What do you do when you're not stripping?" asked Debby.

"We call it burlesque dancing," the cowgirl shot back.

"Mostly we just hang out at the bar down the street," laughed the stripper with the lollipop.

The manager interrupted the meeting, "Enough of the girly-girly talk. Get your asses in gear for the two o'clock show." The guy made my skin crawl.

As we walked back to the car, Debby said, "I can't believe that's their total life. Every day strip naked, show your cunt to all these bozos, and then spend the rest of your time in a bar getting drunk."

People had been telling us that to hit the big time, Les Nickelettes needed a manager. But if bowing down to some lowlife control freak was the path to stardom, count us out.

We passed on the Victoria Theater and instead put together a holiday vaudeville revue at the Intersection. I relied on Vince to help me navigate this new world of "putting on a show," but Debby and Priscilla wanted the members of the group to be in charge. This was uncharted territory for me. I lacked business acumen, and my only mentor was Vince. I saw no female role models to aspire to. And worse, gender socialization had ingrained in me to be a follower and let men lead. I liked the idea of taking the helm; I just didn't know how to navigate the ship.

Looking at newspaper ads for the winter holiday season, I noted that retailers vying for consumer dollars didn't even pretend that it was a religious celebration; they chopped off "Christ" and just called it "Xmas." Les Nickelettes' irreverent satire, "A Traditionally Plastic Xmas," featured, among other things, a neo-cultural nativity pageant. Kathy jumped at the chance to portray the Virgin Mary, a role she never got picked to play at her Catholic high school. Two "wise gals" (Roberta and Carol) sang a saucy song to the Baby Jesus and offered gifts of rhinestones and glitter.

"I was the Baby Jesus in my white organdy Shirley Temple dress, rhinestone brooch, and blond curly wig," said Debby.

I don't know why, but I really wanted the part of the sheep. What nativity would be complete without sheep? So I outfitted myself in a natural sheepskin jacket and played the part walking around on all fours. Priscilla played the Star of Bethlehem. She held a foil star suspended from a string tied on a stick. "I stood on the piano bench holding the Star of Bethlehem in one hand," recalled Priscilla, "and a box of Ivory Snow in the other."

As the nativity scene played out, the sheep walked under the piano bench, bleating, "Baa, baa, baa." To simulate snow, Priscilla poured soap flakes over the scene.

"I dumped Ivory Snow in the sheep's mouth," said Priscilla with a laugh. The big finale ended with the sheep coughing, the Star of Bethlehem guffawing, and Baby Jesus swaddled in a Shirley Temple costume jumping out of the manger and exclaiming, "I'm going to do *big* things!"

"It was only a fleeting moment, but that nativity pageant

was classic," stated Priscilla. "In its own way it was just as funny as a Gary Larson cartoon,"

Whatever the significance, we specialized in being off-the-wall.

On the night we performed "A Traditionally Plastic Xmas," Karl steered a guy introducing himself as a TV producer to Vince. Dirk Dirksen pitched Vince on featuring Les Nickelettes in a segment of his *Gorilla Video* project for San Francisco's independent public access Channel 6. His pumped up resume claimed he had recently relocated to San Francisco after a successful career as a producer in LA. Vince brought the offer to the group.

"No one watches Channel 6," said Priscilla.

"What's in it for us?" asked Debby.

"Will we get paid?" I wanted to know.

"No," said Vince. "But you will get a professional video."

"It will be something you can show around," added Reese Willis.

"And you can use it to promote your act," argued Larry Reppert.

Reese was Kathy's boyfriend, and Larry was Roberta's boyfriend. They hung out backstage at our shows and became chums with Vince. Also, Kathy, Roberta, and I, along with our boyfriends, had begun to socialize after the shows. The group agreed to meet with Dirk and take it from there.

"Your act is great, just great," Dirk said. "Les Nickelettes have a big, big potential to make it in show business."

We liked the flattery but were wary of the excessive platitudes. Nevertheless, we couldn't refute the fact that a professional video would be an asset.

We trooped down to the TV studio ready to do our Xmas show. Instead, we watched Dirk's protégé (boyfriend?), a cute surfer dude with a blond moustache, frolic around in a gorilla suit. Dirk had picked up this guy hitchhiking from LA to San Francisco and decided to feature him as a new discovery in this video. But he had no performing experience and was awful. The shoot dragged on and on.

As it turned out, the only portion of our Xmas show Dirk wanted was a skit where each Nickelette took a turn sitting on Sugar Daddy Santa's lap asking for X-rated Xmas wishes (Vince, disguised in a traditional red suit and white beard, played Santa). Dirk then directed Debby to duplicate the part in our Nativity tableau where the Baby Jesus in Shirley Temple garb jumped out of the manger and exclaimed, "I'm going to do *big* things!"

"It doesn't make sense out of context," argued Debby.

Dirk countered, "The context doesn't matter; it's funny."

Debby refused, and there was a standoff. Dirk abruptly wrapped the session for the day and told us to come back the next day to complete the taping. But, feigning illness, Debby failed to show up. No way would she let Dirk manipulate her into doing that scene.

Les Nickelettes' appearance in the *Gorilla Video* was cut to only a few minutes, and we never got the promised promotional video.

The next time we all got together, Debby was out of sorts. "I'm stressing out. It feels too Vegas for me. I don't like that these men are getting involved. And the shows are too scripted."

"If we want to take the next step, we have to polish things up," I said.

"We have to get more serious," said Kathy.

"My influence is more sculptural performance art," replied Debby. "I'm intimidated when people expect performing talent from me because I have no talent. The only thing I can really do is fake it."

"You do have talent," disagreed Priscilla.

"I can't sing or dance."

"So? None of us can sing or dance."

"Perhaps your perception of talent is overrated," I interjected.

"No, it's time for me to cut out," replied Debby.

Debby moved to LA. My brain went into a tailspin. Debby and I had been creative partners as we'd plotted and planned the course of Les Nickelettes for the past three years. With Vince's help, I organized and implemented the details of producing, but Debby was the one who initiated the performance-art concepts and publicity stunts. Side-by-side, we had the courage to be virgins and the lustiness to be eager beavers. Whenever my insecurities came to the surface, Debbie whisked them away with a laugh and a wave of her hand. To me she was bold and fearless: calling the media, networking, getting in people's faces. I doubted anyone could fill her red glitter shoes. Debby's brainchild, the Underwater Ultra Culture, was dead in the water. The concept was way too far ahead of its time.

I knew Les Nickelettes had potential to achieve greater success, but without Debby's collaboration, I feared the whole thing could fizzle out. The dream to take charge and produce our own shows waned for me. Of the remaining five sorority members—Priscilla, Roberta, Carol, Kathy, and me—I was the only one who had even a small amount of knowledge about the nuts and bolts of producing. I wasn't confident Les Nickelettes could be Les Nickelettes without Debby.

CHAPTER 4

MABUHAY GARDENS

"It's vicious out there."

As I struggled with what to do next, I didn't want to let self-doubt disable me into inaction. Insecurity had crippled me in the past. My freshman year of college, I dreamt of becoming an actress but was too timid to declare drama as a major. Instead I checked "undeclared" on the application. After I turned in the paperwork, I found out I couldn't take acting classes unless I declared drama as a major. Red in the face, my inner voice yelled, "Stupid, stupid, stupid!" Why did I assume I wasn't good enough? Perhaps not being cast in any high school plays and being ignored by the drama teacher had something to do with it? The admission office informed me that I couldn't change my designated major until the following program year, so I had to wait to enroll in acting classes.

I vowed not to leave the "ticket to stardom" box unchecked. Even though I had qualms about my ability to come up with clever ideas and I missed Debby's inventive spark, my three years in this rare female group had bucked up my courage. It helped that I had Vince's support. One night over dinner, he proposed a plan to support me financially so I could pursue my dream. I quit my day job as receptionist at the O'Farrell Theatre, and Vince, as my boss, signed off on an unemployment claim. Devoting all my time and energy to making Les Nickelettes a serious undertaking and not just a lark was as liberating as it was scary.

The first thing I did was shop around for like-minded virgins/eager beavers to augment the group. Not knowing where to start, I took a chance with a classified ad in the *San Francisco Chronicle* that stated: "Les Nickelettes, an all-women musical comedy group, seeks new members." Jane Huether called, and I invited her to my apartment for an interview. Jane had recently moved to San Francisco from Spokane after graduating from Gonzaga University with a Literary Arts degree and landed a job in the tax department at the Bank of America headquarters. She was originally from the small farming community of Rosalia, Washington, but was now looking for adventure in the big city. "I acted and sang in college," she told me, waving her large, hardy farm girl hands in the air. By way of a Nickelettes introduction I sang her "The Twelve Days of Xmas" from our Xmas show:

> *One Fredrick's of Hollywood bra,*
> *Two Packard limousines,*
> *Three Woolworth's diamonds,*
> *Four chastity belts,*
> *Five—replaceable hy-mens!*

Jane filled the room with guffaws and, on the spot, sang a couple of fitting verses of her own. I was blown away by her pitch-perfect soprano vocal. Jane's zest for life, performing experience, a voice to die for, and bent sense of humor made my invitation to join a no-brainer.

Ellin Stein heard about Les Nickelettes' open call from Bill Wolf after appearing in one of Bill's low-budget film projects.

Ellin had grown up in New York City and attended Wellesley College but transferred in her senior year to the British University of Warwick. After graduation she was lured to the city when she developed a crush on a cute San Francisco resident. The love affair didn't survive. "I knew he was going to break up with me, but by that time I had fallen in love with San Francisco's weather, scenery, and general vibe." Her desire to be involved in theater dovetailed with the pursuit of a journalism career. "I acted in plays all through high school and college," she told me. "I even wrote and directed a satirical musical in the eleventh grade."

She laughed at the send-up lyrics of "The Twelve Days of Xmas," but what stood out to me was her immediate grasp of the cultural significance of Les Nickelettes. "Les Nickelettes are . . . a little different," I fumbled. "We laugh at girl things, and make fun of the things we see going on around us."

"You mean, you challenge the status quo from a unique feminine perspective?"

"Yeah," I replied, "but in an off-the-wall way—some people call us silly."

"It sounds to me like Les Nickelettes are clearly on the cutting edge."

I liked Ellin's ability to verbalize the group's concept in a way I couldn't. I asked her to join.

With five veterans plus Jane and Ellin, we decided to cap the number in the group at eight, so just one more to go. But that decision changed when a musical duo, Janis and Fey, answered my classified ad and would only enlist if I took them both. Fey possessed and played a keyboard, a highly desired addition to the group, so we upped the number to nine. Now, the new group was complete.

But then, my friend Stafford Buckley urged me to meet Betsy Newman. "I took Betsy to see Les Nickelettes' 'Alice in Blunderland' show at the Intersection," reported Stafford, "and she raved about it."

Stafford and I walked up Van Ness Avenue to Geary Boulevard, turned past Original Tommy's Joynt, and came to the Goodman Building, the artists' commune where Betsy lived. We climbed the steps of the run-down Victorian and entered a big common room with dilapidated overstuffed couches and chairs arranged in a big circle. To reach Betsy's tiny room, we had to go up two more stairways and wind our way through a labyrinth of hallways.

Betsy introduced herself by reciting her drama pedigree: a master's degree in theater from the University of North Carolina at Chapel Hill. I was impressed, as well as intimidated. She twirled a strand of medium-length black hair around her finger and told me in a slight Southern drawl (affirming her South Carolina roots): "The first time I saw the Nickelettes, I was bowled over. Y'all connect to a kind of iconoclastic feminism and Dadaism that I'm really into."

"Cool," I said, and then went on to brag, "The Dada mail-artist Anna Banana sent Les Nickelettes a certificate: 'Master of Bananology by the Royal Order of Banana—for having gone bananas beautifully.'"

Betsy laughed. We dove into a discussion about the Dadaism movement of the early twentieth century, sharing our admiration for these anarchistic artists who prized nonsense and sought to subvert the orderly bourgeoisie.

But Dadaism wasn't the only astute observation Betsy made. "In 'Alice in Blunderland,' it looked like y'all might have been on acid."

"Guilty as charged." We both laughed. "Call it method acting," I said. "We took playing those drugged parodied characters in *Alice in Wonderland* literally."

"I loved that part where you were Alice jumping up and down singing 'The Tantrum Stomp.'" She imitated my portrayal of Alice: "'I want my own way / I want my own way / I want my own way!'"

I giggled, "My favorite part was the White Playboy Bunny giving Alice nonsense advice."

"I'm interested in this kind of anti-theater: breaking the rules, being reckless, dangerous, and funny," continued Betsy. "I would love to dress up like the Nickelettes do and wear glitter."

Awkward pause. I knew she was angling for an invitation to join the group, but I couldn't offer it. "Oh gosh, sorry, we already have a full house and aren't looking to take in any new members right now."

"Oh," said Betsy, as her shoulders drooped and her smile vanished.

After we left, Stafford said, "Are you crazy?"

I frowned. I had never rejected anyone who wanted so badly to be in the group. I rationalized that even though I easily connected with Betsy, the group was determined to be less impulsive and more professional.

Nonetheless, I couldn't stop thinking about how my conversation with Betsy resonated. A week later, I got a call from Fey who informed me that she and Janis were dropping out. I immediately called Betsy and told her she was in.

"I was so happy to get that phone call," recalls Betsy. "I was just thrilled to be part of the group."

This sudden turn of events paid off immediately. Betsy offered free rehearsal space in a large storefront on the ground floor of the Goodman Building. Though funky and unheated, this place was a dream come true. No more rehearsals in cramped living rooms.

The eagerness that Jane, Ellin, and Betsy brought to the group created a palpable energy shift. All my dreaded anxieties about the group disbanding were replaced by a shot of positive buoyancy. I worried, though, that with no prospective bookings on the horizon, the newbies' enthusiasm would wane.

One day, Ann Rudder showed up at one of our rehearsals. She had performed in a couple of our nouveau vaudeville shows and was also known as a talented seamstress. In that capacity, Ann was working with the Tubes making costumes and banners for the band. "The Tubes are hoping to get a recording contract with some big shot industry guys coming to their next gig at Winterland," she excitedly explained. "And they want the Nicks to sing backup again on 'White Punks on Dope.'"

"Wow, cool," I said.

"Just one thing," continued Ann, "they only want three girls. Me and two others."

Among the eight of us, how could we fairly choose just two?

Ellin slid to the edge of her chair and said, "I really want to do it."

"Me, too," Betsy echoed in a high giddy voice.

Jane shrugged, "Not my musical taste." Priscilla and Kathy also expressed little interest. Carol, Roberta, and I had done it the first time and wanted to do it again. We had paid our dues and deserved to reap the rewards.

"But, on the other hand, you already got to do it, so let us have a turn," Ellin countered.

Squirming, as if on the verge of wetting her pants, Betsy said, "I agree."

My Mama Nickelette intuition kicked in. I lobbied for Ellin, Betsy, and Ann to do the gig. Not that I didn't want to do it, but I figured once Ellin and Betsy experienced being on a rock 'n' roll stage with the Tubes, they'd be hooked.

"We came out for about five minutes, and there were thousands of people out there screaming," said Ellin later. "It was one of the most exciting moments of my life and the closest I've ever come to knowing what it's like to be a rock star. No wonder they turn into egomaniacs!"

"It was tremendously exciting," continued Betsy. "I wore a bright scarlet wig. I loved that wig; it was all stuck together with some kind of grease because a porno star in *Behind the Green Door* had worn it. I was in heaven."

~⌒~

The newly formed group leafed through previous Nick scripts searching for a vehicle to get the ball rolling. "The Ms. Hysterical Contest" stuck out as a still relevant satirical theme. In the process of reviewing the skit, the newbies weighed in.

"Why is there no Bert Parks character?" Jane asked.

Ellin added, "Without a smarmy host we're missing an opportunity to skewer the demeaning concept of beauty contests."

"It would make the parody sharper," Betsy pointed out.

My mama heart swelled with pride hearing this valuable input.

And Ellin had another suggestion: "We should add a reigning Ms. Hysterical who has to relinquish her title after the new winner is chosen."

"But she refuses," laughed Jane.

"And steals the crown," added Betsy.

"My character, Ms. Laid could do that," said Priscilla. "Just before the coronation, I'll run offstage with the crown, screaming '*Never!*'"

We created the clueless host, Bert Farts, who hawks pussy wipes during a fake commercial break. Kathy volunteered to play the part. Jane, Betsy, Carol, Ellin, Roberta, and I vied as beauty contestants to win the coveted title of Ms. Hysterical in a musical chairs competition. "And let's not script who wins," I added. "It's every girl for herself."

We debuted the revised "The Ms. Hysterical Contest" at a benefit Betsy organized for the Goodman Building. The newly formed group nailed it. This was a turning point. Les Nickelettes pivoted from being an urban guerrilla sorority to being a theater collective with a humorous female message. Now we needed to find a more upscale performing venue.

I had no idea how to find a performance space that would elevate us above the funky Intersection, so I turned to Vince for help. Vince enlisted the assistance of Dirk Dirksen, the director of the *Gorilla Video*. Dirk brought to mind a mischievous elf, with his short stature, prominent hooknose, and ever-present red-and-white-striped wool scarf with matching hat. I was put off by his obnoxious manner, but Vince saw humor in his deliberate surly demeanor. As the three of us traveled around town searching for a space to present Les Nickelettes, Dirk recounted his life story. In 1948, as a young child, he had emigrated from Germany to LA. As a teenager he'd started working in television and produced *Rocket to Stardom,* a twelve-hour live weekly variety show broadcast from a car dealership. The venture was hailed as a feat ahead of its time. Vince convinced me that Dirk's oddball entrepreneurship could be a valuable resource in our elusive hunt for a new home.

One night, dodging barkers along the Broadway strip loudly insisting we take a peek at the topless ladies, Dirk steered us to a quiet nightclub in the middle of the block. Next to the entrance was a bright sign in the window welcoming patrons to the Mabuhay Gardens. A neon palm tree blinked on and off as if swaying in the breeze. We entered the Filipino supper club and traversed the length of a long bar to an open area in the back with scattered tables facing a slender stage set in front of a brick wall. The faux paper palm trees and tropical decor gave the cheesy illusion of a lush island setting. We grabbed a side table as I noticed that the place was less than half full. Over drinks we watched the featured act, Cookie Wong, perform a karaoke set of popular songs.

"This is the perfect place for Les Nickelettes," said Dirk.

"Yeah," agreed Vince.

"Are you out of your mind?" I said. "I can't picture it. People come here to see the Filipino Elvis Presley." I pointed to the poster on the wall of Eddie Mesa posing as Elvis.

Vince smiled, "That's why it's great. It's kitschy enough to appeal to your audience." Dirk told us he had befriended the owner, Ness Aquino, who confided in him that the club was in financial trouble, and he was open to trying something new. "Why not?" Vince asked me.

With nothing else on the horizon, I figured we had nothing to lose. Dirk got a standard deal from Ness: the club got drink profits, and we got ticket sales. The offer was for an open-ended run on Monday and Tuesday nights. The slowest nights of the week weren't what Les Nickelettes had envisioned.

"The place is in a prime location," argued Vince, "and after you broaden your audience, you can negotiate for something better."

No one signed a formal contract, but now we had producers: Vince was the head honcho, and Dirk was the nightclub liaison. Vince subsequently brought in two other guys. Roberta's boyfriend Larry Reppert was recruited to do publicity. Larry worked in sales and dressed like a model for men's cologne. His long lanky legs were clothed in slick gabardine pants, topped with a polyester shirt and a plaid sports coat. It was no big surprise that Larry was Roberta's biggest fan; he rallied for her and even crafted jokes for her characters.

Next, needing money to get the production off the ground, Vince turned to Kathy's boyfriend, Reese Willis. He owned the antique store, Attic Salt—a front for his more lucrative business of selling drugs. With an overflow of cash needing laundering, he was open to investing in the project. Due to the nature of his illicit business, he was guarded and secretive, but his cuddly-bear looks, curly locks, and ever-present Hawaiian shirts offset his aloofness.

I trusted Vince but expressed unease with the other three

of this four-man producing team. "Let the producers take care of business," Vince assured me, "and Les Nickelettes are free to concentrate on writing and performing shows."

Before we could set up shop at the Mabuhay Gardens, we needed to come up with a companion piece to the forty-minute "Ms. Hysterical Contest." Delving into the Nickelettes archives, we searched for something edgier than our pageant show. The nitty-gritty "It's Vicious Out There," a slice of life on the streets, stood out as the vehicle we were looking for. As progressive feminists, we were indignant that women brave enough to report being raped were told, "You asked for it," by dressing provocatively. Men were rarely held accountable for these crimes. Society's message was, "Just get used to it."

The script of "It's Vicious Out There" turned the tables by telling the story of a raped man. A ditzy female police sergeant wielded a glitter-spattered rubber dildo like a nightstick as she questioned the alleged victim. "Your past sex life makes your accusation suspicious. I see no bruises, no signs of battering. Besides, we all know men have a secret desire to be raped." The show ended with the song, "Give My Regards to the Rapists." The goal was to challenge the audience to question how the legal system handles rape cases. It was a risky theme for musical comedy. But what's the point if we shy away from controversial subjects? Our only question was, can we make it relevant *and* funny? If nothing else, by going out on a limb, we hoped to raise a few eyebrows.

Most of our rehearsals now shifted to the nightclub. Sometimes boyfriends dropped by, but Dirk hung out all the time. "You could use a director," he said, breaking into our session. And before we knew what hit us, he'd taken on the task.

He made suggestions to soften the play's radical feminine message. "Here we were this wild and crazy group of gals," said Betsy, "and suddenly, a dork like Dirk was telling us what to do." Having a director was not a bad idea, but having Dirk direct Les Nickelettes was like Napoleon trying to tame the Furies. At first we gently fended off his corny advice, but we finally wound up kicking him out of rehearsals altogether.

But Dirk did introduce a couple of valuable resources to the group: Buddy Smith, a choreographer, and Rick Burnley, a musical director. Buddy Smith worked with us to improve our dance steps and spiced up the finale group number in "Ms. Hysterical" by using chairs to add provocative poses in our parody of *Cabaret*:

And if of late, you masturbate
Well, it's all right to fantasize
But that's no way to socialize

Rick Burnley, the quintessential laid-back musician, wrote and arranged a score. Replacing our practice of singing a cappella, he raised the bar with his three-piece band playing live music every show. His rendition of our narrative song "There's a Rape Going On" gave the show a recurring musical theme and added a down and dirty rhythm that set the tone:

I woke up this morning, my brain in a scare
I looked out the window. There's a rapist out there!

No one had any problem working with Buddy and Rick. They collaborated with us and didn't try to change our material.

But Dirk wasn't the only problem. A wedge formed between the Nicks who had producer boyfriends and the Nicks who didn't. One day, a publicity photo shoot with a professional photographer was set up. This group photo was a vital piece of a planned promotional package. Kathy didn't show up.

"How can she not show up?" demanded Ellin.

"This is important," echoed Betsy.

"She is being very unprofessional," said Priscilla.

I finally got ahold of Kathy, and she excused her absence with, "I had to do an errand for Reese." The photographer had to leave for another job, and we were forced to reschedule.

"So that's how it is," said Jane. "If your boyfriend is paying for the photo shoot, you can do whatever you want."

"Never mind that we have to rearrange our schedules," fumed Ellin.

I was also annoyed with Kathy. But Roberta and I were caught in the middle. We understood the strain of home life brought on by being a girlfriend of a producer. Roberta confided in me: "Having Larry involved in every aspect of my life—Les Nickelettes, my son, my home—it's just awful."

I'd come home from rehearsals, and Vince would confront me with a list of Dirk's suggested script alterations along with reasons why the changes would make Les Nickelettes successful. I disagreed with Vince, but kept the peace by deflecting the argument with, "The other Nicks won't go along with it."

Dirk's revisions made the show more palatable to a mainstream audience, but to us it was a sellout. Kathy and Roberta told me that Larry and Reese also urged them to tone down the message.

"There was tremendous pressure," said Kathy.

"I loathed Dirk and all those men," said Betsy, "but I had conflicting feelings because I liked Vince."

"Larry *thought* he knew what he was doing," said Ellin, "and Reese was clearly just there as a piggybank. At least Vince was in it for love, and he was the most helpful."

That was part of the problem, too. Everyone liked charming Vince, even when he sided with Dirk, Larry, and Reese.

But living with Mr. Nice Guy wasn't easy. The night after the preview, Vince and I got in a huge fight over the artistic direction of the show, and he threatened to quit.

Despite this strong male influence to sway the group's creative direction, the collective held firm. However, we allowed the guys to stay in the driver's seat. Women producers scaling the upper echelons of show biz had scant precedent at the time.

⌒◡◡

It's Cool in San Francisco starring Les Nickelettes in "The Ms. Hysterical Contest" and "It's Vicious Out There" premiered on May 27, 1975, at the Mabuhay Gardens. "More stars than there are in heaven," the poster announced.

Outside the club, hung on the jutting awnings, were Ann Rudder's eye-catching cloth signs. The side banners spelled out in silver shiny script, "LES NICKELETTES — TONIGHT." The front banner, facing the street, displayed a red-glitter-lipstick smile. Inside, the tropical Mabuhay Gardens had been transformed into a Nickelettes version of paradise. Covering the front of the stage hung a deep burgundy velvet stage curtain. Vince had rescued this beautiful but frayed drapery from the demolished Art Deco Fox Theater where it had languished in a box collecting dust for twelve years. Ann expertly trimmed and hemmed it, then sewed on gold lamé stars and glittery letters that spelled out "LES NICKELETTES" when the two panels of the curtain came together. The upstage brick wall was covered with a Bill Wolf spray-painted backdrop of the nighttime San Francisco skyline with an ascending stairway leading to the stars. Added to the entrance window with the swaying palm tree blinked a royal blue neon sign emblazoned with "LES NICKELETTES."

Having the show up and running melted the behind-the-scenes discord with the producers. The positive feedback from the audience buffered the two camps. Everyone was having fun again. Bill Wolf served as our opening act and bridged the gap

The poster for Mabuhay Gardens

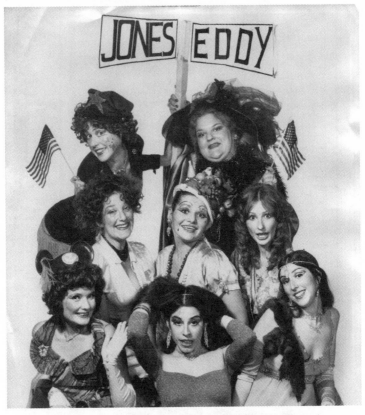

Betsy, Priscilla, Ellin, Jane, Kathy, Me, Roberta, and
Carol in the publicity photo for Mabuhay Gardens

between the two Les Nickelettes sketches. Outfitted in a white
tux and matching top hat, Bill performed his deliberately awful
ventriloquist act featuring the bucktoothed dummy Freckles.
Shortly after we opened, Dirk wrote a musical number for
Bill devised to kick off the show. He proposed Les Nickelettes
provide backup. With our spirits up, and defenses down, we
suddenly found ourselves onstage singing "Hello People":

Hello people, here we are on the strip.
Hello people, we're taking you on a trip.
Throw down your bra—kick off your shoes . . .

Me, glammed up in glitter, rhinestones,
and feathers, for "The Ms. Hysterical Contest"

How had we allowed Dirk to slip this one over on us? "We had to sing that weird song, 'Hello People,'" Betsy complained. "I felt like a jerk."

Everybody hated it. We played along for a short while, but eventually rebelled and refused to do it anymore.

❦

The dressing room at the Mabuhay Gardens was tiny, and the only way to get to it was up a ladder-like stairway. Squeezing in eight performers proved tough, but we soon discovered it had an advantage. It was so small and hard to get to that the producers never ventured in. In this Nickelettes refuge we were free to mingle, have fun, and share a laugh. It eased tensions and strengthened the core component of the group: female bonding. Maybe that's why our shows ended with all the girls banding together.

At the end of "Ms. Hysterical," Ms. Information (Ellin) repudiated the contest: "What are we doing—competing to see who best embodies a value system that only oppresses us?" The contestants then invite the recently revealed transsexual Bert Farts to join them. In "It's Vicious Out There," all the characters agreed at the end that the system was raping everyone and the only way to fight back was to come together in unity.

Our only remuneration was two free drinks before each show, and we took advantage of it. "It was a great time," recalls Roberta. "Putting on our makeup and having a drink." The drinks loosened inhibitions that led to venting about Dirk. Jane had everyone in stitches imitating "Jerk Jerkson" singing "Hello People." One night during a performance of "Ms. Hysterical," Jane's character, Ms. Understood, called Bert Farts "Jerk Jerkson." The other contestants jumped on the bandwagon. Bert introduced Ms. Begotten (Roberta). "I attended Epoxy State and majored in adhesiveness. My ambition is to stick it to everyone. Especially you, Jerk Jerkson," Ms. Begotten cooed.

We expected Dirk to throw a tizzy-fit, but as Ellin observed, "Dirk really liked it."

⁓⚬⁓

Coming off the Broadway strip, guys drifted into the Mabuhay Gardens expecting to see some sort of girly show, not "It's Vicious Out There." At first, they stared bewildered at the spectacle; then came their taunting smartass remarks. One night, Priscilla responded: "You can go home now, your cage is clean."

Emboldened, the heckler shouted, "Yeah, and your ugly dog face can crawl in, too."

"It was a trap," said Priscilla, "because it completely destroyed the timing of the show." Ignoring the heckling proved a valuable lesson for us as actresses as well as feminists.

There were other memorable moments. One performance, Jane, costumed as Carmen Miranda complete with a hat full of plastic fruit, begged not to be arrested as a suspect in the rape case: "They will take away my visa and if they take away my visa I have to go back to Panama City, and that's like being sent to Hayward." She turned her head sharply to the left, and a contact lens popped out. "Oh no," she yelped and fell to the floor searching for it. The performers and musicians stopped the show and joined in the hunt.

Soon, audience members were also crawling around the floor seeking the lost lens. One of the strangers crowed, "I found it!" Jane popped it back into her eye, and the show resumed. Talk about audience participation.

Priscilla played a wino named Ramona Rummage, a washed-up burlesque queen living on the streets as a bag lady. When confronted by the cops as the possible rape suspect of John Dildo, she indignantly proclaimed, "I've never forced myself on any Dildo. I've never had to." From her shopping bag she pulled out a large bottle of Ripple wine, and the stage—concocted of pushed together tables because the built-in stage was too small for our show—shifted. She fell in between two tables and got stuck. Priscilla stayed in character, took an enormous pause, and deadpanned, "That Ripple isn't what it used to be." The house exploded in laughter.

"It was one of the funniest moments of the whole run," recalled Ellin.

Some revelations happened backstage. Looking in the dressing room mirror, one evening, Betsy and I commiserated about getting wrinkles. "We're over the hill," I tittered.

"At the ripe old age of twenty-seven," Betsy deadpanned. I also saw in that mirror reflection a new friendship. Betsy, along with Ellin and Jane, had given new life to Les Nickelettes. This new alliance held the key to the continuance of the group. We all shared the belief that our big break was just around the corner. I took stock of that pint-sized dressing room, laughed, and said, "So this is what's called paying your dues."

Les Nickelettes provoked mixed reactions from the press. The group's new direction confused some reviewers and was misunderstood by others. Carl Raymond in the *Kalendar* summed it up best:

> *Is it the ultimate satire, or poor camp? Was what I saw good, or so bad that it is excellent? . . . At times "LES NICKELETTES" soars, then it falters, only to sneak back up and devastate you.*

Dean Glassbrook of the *Gay Crusader* commented:

> *It is a brilliant job of solidifying contemporary culture and related satire; however, at the same time, the audience often overlooks that there is any purpose to the show because of the untamed looseness in the presentation.*

Margo Skinner in *Bay Area Lifestyle* appreciated the playful antics of our anarchistic presentation style:

The Zany Nickelettes

> *Some of the material's hilarious; some I think is deliberately awful. Apparently there are Nickelettes addicts. Folks at one table were practically rolling on the floor. . . . There's pace aplenty and a lot of laughs with The Nickelettes, a group that could only exist in San Francisco.*

San Francisco Chronicle theater critic Bernard Weiner had a different take:

Amateurish, Allegedly Feminist Satire

Though the all-female group has among its members some of real promise, the overriding impression is that of campy amateurs.

I took exception to Bernie's use of the word "amateurs." It brushed off our intentionally goofy female humor as not on the same level as stupid, silly, male humor. Also, "allegedly feminist satire" stuck in my craw. His message implied that feminist offbeat satire was, at best, "alleged"; ergo, women weren't funny.

∽∾

July 1975 marked the anniversary of the First Annual Salmon Awards. Should we institute it as a yearly celebration? We had to admit our swim upstream had made considerable progress in the past year, and we couldn't have done it without a lot of help from others. I voted to do it. The Second Annual Salmon Awards signaled a truce with the producers. Putting aside past disagreements, we honored them with major awards. Reese received the Sugar Daddy of the Year; Larry the Trigger of the Year (not sure of the origin of this one, except some obscure connection to Roberta's cowgirl character Farfa Knout); Vince was Super Dog of the Year (his favorite character was Snoopy, from the Peanuts comic strip); and Dirk got the David Merrick Award (David Merrick was a stage producer with a prickly reputation).

The spawning celebration served to bring us all together and gave me a sliver of hope that we could jell as a cohesive team.

The future of Les Nickelettes was promising, but I felt I was living inside a pressure cooker. I worked overtime to quell uprisings between the two sides: first, in the dressing room, where Ellin, Betsy, Jane, and Priscilla advocated for more say in how the show was being produced; and next at home, where Vince and I continued to bicker over the group's artistic decisions.

One day, on a routine errand to the bank, my heart started pounding in my chest and my head began to spin. I stopped to catch my breath, only to grow dizzier. To avoid keeling over, I found a bench and collapsed until my blood pressure stabilized. Was I dying? Did I have some rare disease? A visit to the doctor resulted in a diagnosis of "panic attack." The cure: calm down, take deep breaths, and meditate. Easier said than done. How could I relax when everything I ever wanted was on the line? As Mama Nickelette, I strove to keep everybody together, but I couldn't prevent the rapport between the performers and producers from reverting to a disdain that was growing like pus on an untreated wound. At ground zero lurked Dirk's persistence in suggesting alterations to our jokes in the script. "We got so fed up," said Ellin.

One night, Dirk pounded the final nail in his coffin. Kathy arrived at the club with a suitcase filled with $800 in cash. After the show, she was to complete one of Reese's drug deals. She left the case with a friend while she was onstage. With the luggage stashed beneath his table, he briefly left to get a drink, and it disappeared. Livid, Kathy searched every inch of the club for the bag with no luck.

"All of a sudden, Dirk was buying people drinks and acting like a big shot," said Roberta.

"And we wondered where this new-found generosity came from." I added.

"We all suspected him of stealing the cash," said Ellin.

But with no proof, we couldn't accuse him of the theft. This episode brought to my mind some previous instances where objects of value mysteriously vanished. There was no longer any levity to the anti-Dirk sentiment.

The disappearing suitcase incident also highlighted another concern. Kathy's day job interfered with her reliability. Working as a delivery mule for Reese's coke business gave her a never-ending access to the drug. Cocaine was the drug of choice in the underground culture at the time, and we all indulged, but it was taking over Kathy's life. Three months into the run, Kathy began calling herself Ruby Tuesday (from the Rolling Stones song) and taking on the flighty traits of that character. One night, in the midst of our pre-performance routine, it came to a head.

"Well, I see Ruby Tuesday is late again," Betsy said to me.

"She never gets here in time for the preshow fun anymore," I replied.

Thirty minutes later Betsy was in a panic, "Kathy's still not here, and its five minutes until show time!"

"What if she doesn't show up?" asked Priscilla.

Just then Kathy breezed in. "Kathy, you scared us," I admonished.

"What's the problem? I wouldn't miss a show," she replied. After the show I took Betsy aside to address the concern she had about playing opposite Kathy in most of her scenes, "If Kathy forgets about a performance, we'll drop my character, and I'll step into her part."

"That makes me feel better," Betsy replied. "But I wish she would be more reliable." Kathy still talked the talk but sometimes didn't walk the walk.

In the fourth month at the Mabuhay Gardens, boredom and restlessness set in—still stuck performing only on Monday and Tuesday, still being paid nothing, still spinning our wheels. Needing to jump-start our artistic juices, we hatched an ambitious plan to write a full-length play with original music. We informed the producers of this undertaking, knowing full well that a large-scale theatrical production meant the Mabuhay Gardens was out and our nightclub liaison, Dirk, was out. Vince, Larry, and Reese, however, launched plans to produce this new project.

Betsy and Ellin took me aside. "We could do a better job of producing this play than these guys," said Ellin.

"I'm not so sure," I replied. "They have skills and resources we don't have."

"We can do this," Betsy confidently whispered, keeping the conversation out of earshot of Kathy and Roberta. My panic attacks returned. How will this go down? Reese and Larry were one kettle of fish, but how could I tell Vince his services were no longer needed after all he had done for us?

On November 11, after almost six months, *It's Cool in San Francisco* came to a close. The group heaved a sigh of relief when we exited the table stage for the last time. Bye, bye, Mabuhay Gardens. Bye, bye, Dirk Dirksen. Although we suffered through Dirk's apprenticeship as an obnoxious impresario, we couldn't have known that this small liberating step for womankind would have a profound effect on the music scene in San Francisco. Within a year, the Mabuhay Gardens featured a new genre of music, punk rock, and had been rechristened "The Fab Mab." Dirk, "the pope of punk," turned the club into a profitable enterprise by bringing in the Nuns, the Dead Kennedys, Devo, the Ramones, the Mutants, Black Flag, and many others. Dirk and Ness Aquino would go down in San Francisco music history as punk legends.

～～♪～

Les Nickelettes moved on. A couple of weeks after our last show at the Mabuhay Gardens, Betsy put together a Thanksgiving show featuring Les Nickelettes called *Turkey Lips*, a benefit for the Goodman Building. The San Francisco Redevelopment Agency had declared the Goodman Building decrepit and planned to tear it down and replace it with a modern apartment complex. The Victorian hotel, built in 1869, had served as a haven for artists since the 1940s and still provided an affordable living space for creative people to live in San Francisco. As president of the Goodman Group, Betsy led the battle against the redevelopment plan to safeguard this unique enclave. The counterplan devised by the artists in the Goodman Building involved preserving the space as a city landmark, thus preventing it from being torn down. But the process was cumbersome and required bags of loot—hence, never-ending fundraising. "I loved the struggle to save the building," said Betsy, "but it was a heaven and a hell."

Performing "The Ms. Hysterical Contest" without producers overseeing the proceedings for the first time in six months was liberating. It also demonstrated to me that Betsy could lead and organize. At the same time, Ellin told me about her job as assistant to playwright-in-residence Sam Shepard at the Magic Theater. She was soaking up details about the inner workings of a theater company. Add to this mix Jane's skills in accounting from her day job, and I began to feel confident that this new group could become architects of Les Nickelettes' future. But how could I break the news to Vince? Panic attacks intensified.

CHAPTER 5

LIBERATING PETER PAN

"No one is going to make me grow up.
I'm too smart for that."

Turning my attention to the new project, I relegated the simmering clash with boyfriend producers to the back burner. For a full-length play idea, we went back to a skit we had done a couple of years earlier, during our fairytale spoofing period: *Peter Pan*. The skit lampooned Disney's version of the J. M. Barrie classic by recasting Peter as a pompous rock star who refuses to grow up. In 1976, the Peter Pan Syndrome was nowhere more evident than in the boys of rock who wore the never-grow-up motto as a badge of honor.

The casting of *Peter Pan: A New Rock Fairytale* evolved organically as we worked on expanding the script. I took on the role of Peter Pan, and Priscilla revamped Tinkerbell as my exasperated manager. Ellin, in the part of Trendy Wendy, and Betsy, as her younger sister Tammy, became Peter's groupies, as did Kathy in the role of Tiger Lily. Jane morphed the crocodile character into Crock, the impresario of Never Never Land, the biggest rock palace on the West Coast. Roberta transformed Captain Hook into V. D. the Pirate Queen, and

Carol paralleled Hook's right-hand man Smee into V. D.'s manager/lover, Sylvie Snatch. These two lesbian foils vowed to dethrone Peter Pan from his perch as the reigning prince of rock 'n' roll.

Most exciting was the plan to write original music for the play. No longer would we rely on rewritten lyrics to well-known tunes. Each of the characters got a solo song, and the actresses penned the lyrics. We tapped Rick Burnley, the musical director from the Mabuhay, to write the music. I arrived at Rick's apartment to hear him put my words to music. Kathy, Ellin, and Jane also crowded into Rick's tiny living room, jam-packed with a bed, bulky chair, overstuffed couch, and an upright piano. Shivers slid up my spine as I listened to him play the songs. This was a game changer. The songs ranged from spicy to gritty to rhythmic rock, but my favorite was the melodic finale. Tinkerbell dispelled the nasty Battle of the Bands conflict with a wave of her wand: "This reality needs some magic." Transformed, Jane, as Crock, in her beautiful soprano voice, summed it all up:

If this were real life we would have failed
Instead of laughter there would be disaster
But for the time being this is a fairytale
So they all lived happily ever after.

Yep, we held to our tradition of ending with all sides coming together in harmony.

This shift to a traditional theatrical format dictated the need for a director. After the fiasco with Dirk, we searched for a woman with a Nickelettes frame of mind. None of us felt up to the task, plus we all just wanted to perform. But the scarcity of female directors hit home when our search went nowhere.

Betsy recommended a friend of a friend, Martin Worman. A man, yes, but Martin's resume included his stint with the Cockettes (a menagerie of androgynous men and women infamous for performing outrageous shows at the Palace Theatre in San Francisco), and a current membership in the Gay Men's Theatre Collective. He also possessed a degree in theater with playwright and songwriter credits. Those qualifications assured us that Martin was no Dirk Dirksen. His Cockettes background, including coating his face with female makeup undeterred by a sandy red moustache and beard, gave credence to an appreciation of our brand of zany theatrics.

The first thing I learned about Martin was that his wiry physique matched his laser-focused professional intensity. At our first meeting he looked me straight in the eye and said, "Let's drop the bullshit, and cut to the chase." I agreed, and he took the helm at the following rehearsal.

"I was pleased to have Martin Worman on board and being perceived as the second wave of the Cockettes," Ellin later opined, "although it just increased the public perception of us as drag queens instead of actual women." We did dress like drag queens, and sometimes drag kings, but were neither. Being an all-woman group skewered assumptions about us every which way. Some men saw us only as sexy, hot chicks. Hardcore feminists complained that we perpetuated derogatory female stereotypes and disavowed us. Others dismissed us as merely silly. Our humor and collective spontaneous female spirit defied labels. Asked to describe ourselves, we replied, "We're Nickelettes."

I told Martin there was still a big hole in the script. Priscilla had been struggling to come up with a song for Tinkerbell. "It needs to be feisty," said a frustrated Priscilla, "and still show Tinkerbell's mixture of jealousy, anger, and love for Peter Pan."

"Where does this happen in the story?" asked Martin.

"Peter learns that Tinkerbell has betrayed him to his rivals, the Pirate Dykes," I explained, "and he banishes her from his life forever, proclaiming, 'I don't believe in fairies anymore!'" A couple of nights later, Martin showed up with a poignant, show-stopping tune.

"I'm in hot water up to my wing tips," an abandoned Tinkerbell moans. "Every fairy knows when you mess around with mortals you get hurt." The music to "Fairy's Lament" was like a mournful regret:

Although we are immortal
You should know before you start
The only thing a fairy can die of
Is a delicate . . . transparent . . . and gaily broken heart

Martin was shrewd enough to know that the use of the double-entendre "fairy" would not be lost on the audience.

Martin took over rehearsals and watched the group spend precious time goofing off and laughing at our own jokes. At first he said nothing. But after the scene repeated over and over, he challenged, "Are you going to become a serious theatre troupe or just do this for fun on Saturday night?"

His rebuke reminded me of the discipline I had learned in college acting class. "We want to get serious," I replied.

A week later, Martin asked me to stay after rehearsal. "I'm concerned about Kathy," he explained. "She's been late, left early, and even missed one session."

"Maybe you could talk to her, and then she'll shape up," I said.

"I question her commitment," he bluntly asserted. "She's not on the same level as the rest of the cast and should be replaced." This had been building up for some time, but I had let things drift along and allowed my friendship with Kathy cloud my judgment. I gave my blessing for Martin to do the dirty work. But Kathy refused to walk away without a fight. She demanded a group meeting.

Betsy arranged for us to use the common room in the Goodman Building. We settled into the circle of sofas and chairs, filling glasses with wine from a huge jug, and passing around a joint. Martin laid out the basic guidelines: Everyone got a turn to speak. If it wasn't your turn, you respectfully refrained from interrupting.

Soon, pent-up emotions held in for months exploded like a volcano. The first complaints weren't about Kathy, but about boyfriends. Ellin, Betsy, Jane, and Priscilla firmly stated, "No more producers!" Roberta argued in Larry's defense but no one bought it. When it was my turn, I admitted that I didn't like Reese and Larry's involvement, but trying to save my butt at home, I pointed out that Vince had been crucial in creating the group.

"No exceptions," answered Betsy.

"It has to be a clean sweep," said Priscilla.

"We have to have faith in going it alone," concluded Ellin.

I conceded that the jig was up.

Next, the conflict over Kathy's irresponsibility spewed out like hot molten lava. In response, Kathy retorted, "The group should be spontaneous, and rehearsals aren't always necessary."

"We're a theater group now and not a performance art happening," Priscilla pointed out.

"And in theater, the cardinal rule is to show up, on time, period," added Betsy.

"Let me remind you that my boyfriend has invested a sizable amount of money in Les Nickelettes, and you should all be grateful," Kathy spit out.

I noticed that Martin was uncomfortable with where this was headed. Within minutes he excused himself, "Ladies, I'll leave this to you to work out."

He missed the best part. "And if you kick me and Reese out, there will be consequences," threatened Kathy.

Not waiting for details, I said, with more pity than anger, "Kathy you are committed to drugs, not Les Nickelettes. I'm sorry, but the decision is final."

"Well, I quit!" yelled Kathy, as she stormed out.

In the silence that followed, I said, "I just hope she doesn't O.D."

It was past midnight, but this showdown wasn't over. The emotional floodgates had been opened, and it was all going to come out. Next up was Carol. "No one takes me seriously," she said. "You just see me as Roberta's little sister."

I had to admit she was right. I always deferred to assertive Roberta and took quiet Carol for granted.

In her defense Roberta pointed out, "I always speak up for you, Carol."

"I can speak for myself," countered Carol. As I listened to the two sisters confront a sibling rivalry, I reflected on the role Les Nickelettes had in all of this. Carol's newfound boldness could be attributed to the role she played in *Peter Pan*. Carol's character, Sylvie Snatch, dominated the vain and insecure V. D. the Pirate Queen, played by Roberta.

"If the Nicks are a collective, then I should be treated as an equal," protested Carol. In the end, we all agreed to give Carol the respect she deserved. Who knew Les Nickelettes would function as a family therapist? By three thirty in the morning, all the dirty laundry had been aired and cleansed. It was a painful birth into a new era, but I felt purged as I staggered home.

I walked through the door at four and was surprised to find Vince still up. He sat on the couch in his bathrobe, illuminated only by the light of the television, smoking a cigarette. I was so wrung out I could barely speak, but I managed to mumble that the Nicks had had an all-night encounter session.

"Sure," he said sarcastically, staring at the TV screen. Did he think I was lying? Where else would I have been? I stumbled to bed with the vague perception that he might have implied that I had cheated on him. Before I conked out, my last thought was that it would be easier to dissuade him of the notion of an unfaithful encounter than telling him the news that he was no longer Les Nickelettes' producer.

You can't sever an umbilical cord without shedding some blood. The next day Reese called. "Les Nickelettes are horrible and selfish," he ranted in my ear. "Okay, so kick me out, but what you did to Kathy was mean. She's worked hard and deserves to stay."

"Sorry, Reese, the decision is final." More the diplomat, Larry showed up at the rehearsal that night to discuss the situation. We declined. Vince accepted the decision stoically, but added a cynical, "Good luck."

It was time for Les Nickelettes to take off and fly without a net.

In 1976, women were making it big. Barbara Walters became the first female nightly news anchor. *The Bionic Woman* (an action series featuring a woman) and *Laverne and Shirley* (a girl pal comedy) debuted on television. The Episcopal Church approved ordination of women as priests and bishops. Ten thousand Northern Irish women demonstrated for peace. For Les Nickelettes, producing a full-length musical satire play represented a big step up. It was time to shout out that besides being an all-women group of comedy writers and performers, we were also taking charge of the production.

We held auditions to replace Kathy in the role of Tiger Lily and picked Janet Sala. She was an experienced performer who took on the role that same evening. Janet objected to Kathy's lyrics to Tiger Lily's song, "A Love She Couldn't Can":

He was a strong and handsome brave.
And then my heart began to crave
Soon Tiger Lil loved Peter Pan
With a love she couldn't can.

In the play, the song explained why Tiger Lily, a down-to-earth levelheaded Native American activist, would be devoted to Peter Pan. The next night Janet came in with revised lyrics:

I smell wild horses in his sweat
I lose my cool, I lose my pride
I never fell for any man
Till I fell for Peter Pan

Next, we needed a theater space to present the play. Bill Wolf linked me up with his friend Richard Reineccius of the Julian Theater housed in the Potrero Hill Neighborhood House. It was early January 1976, and he told me his only open slot in the next nine months was three weekends in February. I snatched it up, figuring there's nothing like a deadline to get the adrenaline pumping.

With an opening date set, it was all hands on deck, and we called on friends for help. Martin secured set designer John Flowers (from the Cockettes) to construct a cardboard set painted in pastel cartoon colors. Carol's carpenter boyfriend, Doyle Crosby, a shy and unassuming guy, built two essential props. First, Peter's magic sword. This phallic metaphor, a three-foot-long wooden shank covered in silver glitter with a red glittery arrow-shaped head, was used throughout the play to brandish in groupies' faces and ward off lesbian pirates.

The second prop was for the pirates. V. D. the Pirate Queen and Sylvie Snatch schemed to dethrone Peter Pan in the Battle of the Bands: "This little foil will make Peter's sword look like a limp dick," said Sylvie. The script then called for her to whip out a guitar in the shape of a woman's body. Audience reaction matched our initial shock at beholding Doyle's crafted wooden prop. The outrageous, anatomically correct female body in the shape of a guitar featured pink legs splayed spread eagle, and strings stretched over a bright red vagina. In the show, the prop perfectly signaled that Peter had met his metaphorical match.

Ellin lined up Trina Robbins (a cartoonist, and one of the founders of the underground *Wimmen's Comix*) to do a poster. The cartoon design depicted a woman in a saucy Peter Pan style outfit seductively looking at the viewer and clutching a microphone with a cord that looped up to spell out "Peter Pan" then curved down to plug into the pirate ship in the background. I loved it.

Betsy recruited her boyfriend's sister, a modern dancer, to do the choreography. An old friend from the Intersection revue days, Jeff Ross, was brought in to play piano. Another friend, Will Guterman, added percussion. We got by with a lot of help from our friends. This can-do spirit reminded me of the classic Mickey Rooney–Judy Garland movie *Babes in Arms,* where Mickey kicks things off by cheerfully rallying, "Come on, let's put on a show!" With limited resources and against all odds, the teenagers successfully stage a show in a barn.

Even with all these labors of love, we still needed money for materials, theater rent, and publicity costs. Ticket sales would sustain the play, but we needed funds before opening night. I turned to Vince. He had been angry when the producers were ousted, but wasn't the type to hold a grudge. Now that we no longer bickered over Les Nickelettes, we were having fun together again. I had a hunch that easing him into a role of behind-the-scenes advisor suited his Howard Hughes alter ego. I asked him, "How can we come up with some fast cash?"

He suggested we sell ads in the program. "You'll be giving it to every audience member who walks in the door. You can pitch advertisers on that." We picked up the phone and hit the

Poster for Peter Pan: A New Rock Fairytale

Design by Trina Robbins

pavement to hawk our ads to businesses near the theater. In response to our serious hustling, Vince helped out by calling several business associates (who owed him favors) and solicited them to buy ads. Within a week we had raised $300, enough to open the show.

Rushing to opening night, everything was coming together at lightning speed. But jam-packed producing tasks, day jobs, and rehearsing every night left everyone frazzled. With only five days until opening night, Betsy arrived at rehearsal really out of it. Her timing was off, and she had trouble focusing. "I don't feel well," she explained. Martin sent Betsy home to rest and reminded the rest of us that part of our job was to stay healthy.

The next morning, I got a call from Betsy's friend Matthew, "Betsy's in the hospital. She has phlebitis."

"What?" I asked.

"It's a blood clot in her leg. She can't do the show this weekend," Matthew explained.

The thought of canceling the show sent my brain into a tailspin. But how could we replace her on such short notice? I called Ellin in a panic.

"Call Martin, immediately," she advised.

His calm demeanor helped me to breathe. "Canceling the show is not an option," he stated.

Martin recalled that at the recent auditions for Tiger Lily there had been an actress, Linda Dobb, who could fit the role of Tammy, if she agreed to do it. To our great relief she did. A few hours before the rehearsal that night, Ellin, Martin, and I met with Linda and helped her cram for the role. "By golly," Mickey said to Judy, "the show must go on!"

I called Betsy in the hospital to let her know we were going on with the show as planned. She had mixed feelings, happy for the group, sad for herself. She related what happened. "I was wearing my new Frye boots, and it caused a big blister on my heel that got infected. That, combined with tight jeans rolled up tight around my knee, caused a blood clot in my leg." And more bad news: she required hospitalization for two weeks while medication dissolved the clot. She was out for the entire run. "It's awful," she said. "I'm really heartbroken not to be in the show."

On Friday, February 13, I held my breath during final dress rehearsal. The paint was still drying on the sets. The volunteer stage crew was slow on cues. Linda had to carry the script to remember her lines. Janet was tentative in her role as Tiger Lily. And Priscilla, usually a rock solid performer, had an anxiety attack about her show-stopping song. As if that weren't enough, Jeff, the piano player, staged a hissy fit over Will's percussion playing. There's a saying in theater, "Bad dress rehearsal; good show." I went to bed with that theater axiom repeating over and over in my head to the beat of a pulsating headache.

On Saturday, February 14, 1976, *Peter Pan: A New Rock Fairytale* debuted. We did two back-to-back shows and nearly sold out both, a sweet Valentine. Jitters aside, the performers brought it home. Linda and Janet proved to be pros. The musicians and stage crew came through. The audience laughed at all the right places, and Tinkerbell's song stopped the show. As we celebrated our success, Martin rushed backstage to tell us Stanley Eichelbaum, the theatre reviewer for the *San Francisco Examiner,* had been in the audience. The following Wednesday the review came out.

A Women's Troupe Liberates *Peter Pan*

A group of female performers called Les Nickelettes
. . . is dumping all over . . . PeterPan . . . The ladies
(if I may use the term loosely) . . . unleashed a stream

of language that would make a stevedore blush . . .
They are, however, a vivacious bunch, and their spirit
of defiant fun is contagious, despite the ragged, gross
caliber of their work.

Jane, Carol, Priscilla, Ellin, Betsy, Roberta,
and me in the publicity photo for *Peter Pan*

Today, our material would be tame, but in 1976 well-behaved
women didn't talk in ways that would make a stevedore blush.
The review wasn't bad considering that mainstream critic Stanley
Eichelbaum wrote for the conservative *San Francisco Examiner*.

I loved playing Peter Pan. Poking fun at the bad boys of rock by toting an erect "magic" sword and proclaiming, "No one is going to make me grow up. I'm too smart for that," was a gas. Peter acted like a cool dude, but when he didn't get his way, he dissolved into tantrums like a three-year-old, and it was delicious parody. I styled my hair in a unisex mullet and wore a green satin outfit with big padded shoulders. Inside the crotch of my pants was pinned a thick stuffed sock painted pink at the tip. At the end of my Battle of the Bands song, "Don't Grow Up Baby," I unzipped my fly and flipped out the sock.

Ellin played Trendy Wendy, a hippy-dippy groupie giving sage advice to her younger sister, Tammy: "You're not as abnormal as you seem. In the garden of love, your path is that of a late bloomer."

Me in the role of Peter Pan

"My costume was a blond curly wig, camisole, glitter knee socks, silver platform ankle strap shoes, and hot pants," said Ellin. "I don't often get cast as a bimbo so I really enjoyed it." A besotted Wendy defended her devotion to Peter in her solo song, "A Man Who Cares":

And he'll always return to my bed
'Cause he knows I'll always give him good . . . clean sheets.
And that man knows he's in luck
Cause I'm such a good. . . cook.

Casting against type, a hefty 250-pound Pricilla as Tinkerbell provoked a big laugh the first time she appeared on stage in pink overalls and plastic glitter wings. But Priscilla's talent shone in her ability to play the scrappy fairy with shades of sweet femininity. In one scene, after being banished by Peter forever for her betrayal, she downs an over-the-counter overdose of NoDoz and NyQuil and feigns imminent death. The audience totally buys in when Peter discovers the drugged fairy and persuades the crowd to sing a raucous "I believe in fairies, I believe in Tink," until she is revived.

Carol came into her own playing Sylvie Snatch. She created a butch dyke look that included a ragged denim outfit and an Afro wig spray-painted China red. V. D. the Pirate Queen, in contrast, wore a revealing pirate jacket, short-shorts, and a sexy eye patch. "I loved being the star," said Roberta, "it was fun."

One of my favorite scenes was Sylvie telling V. D. (in a song) of her plan to take over the number one spot from Peter Pan:

Picture This. You come out in a barbed wire G-string
. . . Sit on an electric john, with a caca pedal to distort
the sound of your song,
And at the peak of it
You take a shit.

Groupies in Bondage: The Pirate Dykes kidnap Wendy and Tammy
Photo © Ted Milikew

And Sylvie got to deliver the best pun in the show. In a confrontation between Peter and V. D. the Pirate Queen, she gets in the last word: "You're dead, Pan."

"The character empowered me," said Carol. "It was really instrumental to my growth. And things were more balanced with me and Roberta."

The second week of the run, John Wasserman from the *San Francisco Chronicle* reviewed the show:

Nickelettes Are at It Again

Les Nickelettes are an exceedingly plucky group of young ladies . . . spoofing contemporary pseudo-hip society, performing for the sheer fun of it, amateurs in the most exalted, as well as the most pedestrian sense.

. . . But a little talent, ebulliently presented without pretension, is considerably more than nothing. The Nickelettes have their role in God's Great Plan.

The review was witty with several useable quotes for future press releases, but I still bristled at the putdown in the word "amateur." Although used subtly in this review, it still put us in our place. I had hoped to earn more kudos for charting new territory in female satirical writing and producing.

That being said, we took pride in our accomplishment as first-time producers. The fact that the two major newspaper publications in San Francisco reviewed a show mounted with only $300 was huge. And due to healthy box office receipts, we were able to pay the bills. It rankled us, however, that we promised to pay a stipend to piano player Jeff Ross for the length of the run. He constantly hassled us over trivial matters, and if he didn't get his way he threw a conniption fit (it didn't go unnoticed that he was acting just like Peter Pan). I tried to reason with him. Jeff was not a reasonable guy. At one point, he spit on me. Being stuck with this nasty guy for three weeks would be my education on the down side of producing.

Now what? The tiny profit from box office revenue alone couldn't propel us forward. When the dust settled we had less than $200 in the bank. In a discussion on ways to boost our financial bottom line, Ellin proposed that we become a nonprofit corporation.

"What do we know about being corporate?" I asked.

She was one step ahead of me, "I met with Eric Peterson, a lawyer from Bay Area Lawyers for the Arts, and he can help us with the legal process."

"I don't know," I protested. "Sounds too legit for us."

"It's the only way we can become a serious theater company," Ellin countered. "And it will enable us to apply for grants, solicit donations, and get tax-exempt status."

My head began to spin as she described an overwhelming complicated maze of articles of incorporation, bylaws, board of directors, committee meetings, and compliance with state and federal laws. "But Les Nickelettes have always been lawless and noncompliant," I reminded her.

But Ellin was determined. She roped Jane and me into forming an incorporating committee and laid out the details of an organizational structure. "Thrashing out the bylaws with Jane and Denise," said Ellin "was a long haul." The committee, with the help of Eric Peterson, slogged through the paperwork process needed to become a nonprofit organization with the State of California and file for a federal 501(c)(3) tax exemption.

On Wednesday, April 28, 1976, Jane, Ellin and I, dressed in our version of conservative businesslike outfits, traveled to the state capitol in Sacramento to file Articles of Incorporation on behalf of Les Nickelettes, Inc. To us, this giddy monumental moment represented the height of ingenuity. To the clerks in the Office of the Secretary of State, it was another dull day in the office filled with blasé paperwork. Yawn.

After we got the papers stamped and certified, it was lunchtime. In the mood to celebrate, we canvassed the bright, sunny sidewalks of Sacramento looking for an open bar. "We couldn't find a bistro," said Ellin, "so we bought sandwiches and a bottle of wine and went out to a park." Sitting on the grass, with our legs daintily tucked under our respectable ladylike skirts, we ate lunch, passing the wine bottle (still snug in its brown paper bag) among ourselves.

"We're no better than those winos over there," laughed Jane motioning to the sots nearby.

I held up our Articles of Incorporation paperwork, and marveled, "We are now a corporation vested with the official Great Golden Seal of the State of California."

This set off a round of jokes about California's Great Seal, which led to us barking like sea lions. The winos looked over at us, and we muffled manic laughter. I took a couple more swigs from the wine bottle and thought it fitting that this bona fide nonprofit corporation, Les Nickelettes, Inc. still kept intact a little bit of anarchy.

As the incorporating committee, Jane, Ellin, and I were the first members on the board of directors. Bay Area Lawyers for the Arts advised us to recruit other board members who were active in the community and connected to the corporation's stated goals. The first person to come to mind was Bill Wolf, an easy invitation since we already had an alliance with his AAA theatrical production company.

Ron Turner, publisher of Last Gasp Comics, had been a fan and supporter of Les Nickelettes since our early years. A quintessential underground entrepreneur, Ron was the perfect pick for a business representative on our board. "I had been burnt out in the '60s from various political movement boards," said Ron, "and then I got in the comic business, and I ended up on the boards of three corporations with lots of irrational people. It made me have an aversion to meetings. But this was such a neat idea, I loved it." A throwback to the hippie era, Ron dressed in obligatory jeans and T-shirts, and let his hair, moustache, and beard (rumored not have been cut since the '60s) cascade freely down his back and chest.

At an organization information event, Ellin met Jeffrey Tar Genza. As they discussed theater nonprofit status, she discovered that he had worked with her mother in the Development Department of the New York Philharmonic. "I thought, hmm, an art administrator who had worked with nonprofits in New York," said Ellin. "That could look good on grant applications." She invited him to be on our board.

We also nominated Vince. He respectfully declined, comfortable in the role of anonymous advisor. But he suggested Sharon McNight.

Sharon worked with Vince at the Mitchell Brothers O'Farrell Theater. She was originally hired as the Brothers' secretary but graduated to filmmaker when Jim Mitchell asked her to direct *Autobiography of a Flea*, a modern porno adaptation of the ribald nineteenth-century erotic novel. The project was a rare fusion of hard-core sex and narrative storyline. "I was the first woman to direct an adult feature film," bragged Sharon. "The movie made $2 million the first year."

How had Sharon moved so easily from secretary to movie director? For starters, she just so happened to have a master's degree in theater. But the fluke of this story was that I knew Sharon. Back in 1968 we were both drama majors at San Francisco State College, and she had directed me in a one-act play for an acting/directing class. Reconnecting with Sharon in the context of Les Nickelettes inspired me. Here was a mentor with directing experience, a capable female unafraid to take control. I was happy that Vince suggested her for the board.

The board of directors for Les Nickelettes, Inc. valued creativity and fun above business matters, so monthly meetings at Bill's storefront studio in the Mission could be as haphazard and wacky as a Nickelettes script session. Wine, weed, and jokes accompanied old business, new business, and financial reports. Bill was elected president, Jeffrey Tar Genza vice president, Sharon McNight secretary, and Jane treasurer. With this eclectic group in place, we set about the task of fundraising and applying for grants to support and elevate the status of Les Nickelettes. The only one who looked and sounded like an actual arts administrator was nerdy Jeffrey. In wire-rimmed glasses and tweed blazer, he scanned the room in puzzlement. Turning to me, sitting next to him, he intoned in his New York accent, "What have I gotten myself into?"

"I knew exactly where he was coming from," Ellin said with a laugh, "having worked with my mother in the small world of the New York Philharmonic. It was something to watch this anal, buttoned-down Manhattan Club administrator get enmeshed with wild San Francisco artists and slowly become a completely different person." It also didn't hurt that he developed a mad crush on Bill.

On the serious side, the board provided valuable feedback to the performing group from an outside point of view. But the most important function of our board of directors was its focus on fundraising. They had no artistic control (unlike the producers) so they presented no threat to our autonomy.

The success of *Peter Pan: A New Rock Fairytale* called for an encore run. Betsy, back after her bout with phlebitis, proposed we book a six-week run at the newly converted storefront theater in the Goodman Building. The bad news was that the renovation wasn't completed. The good news was that if we volunteered to help with cleaning, repairing, and painting, they would only charge us a nominal rental fee. We pitched in to help convert the storefront into a soon-to-be theater. We also rustled up chairs, lights, and a light board. Bill constructed a large freestanding cardboard backdrop that created a required backstage area.

In the midst of all this activity, Priscilla stunned us with her decision to take a break from the group. She had decided to get back to her dream of becoming a classical theater actress. "I always had this absurd notion that I wanted to play Lady Macbeth," explained Priscilla. Recalling my own early theatrical ambitions, I understood. I wished her luck and left the door open if she wanted to return. But I hated to see her go because the twist of a hefty Tinkerbell worked so well in the Peter Pan satire.

Who could fill those pink sequin fairy sneakers? Betsy, without missing a beat, raised her hand, "I can do the part, and Linda Dobb can remain in the Tammy role." It was a simple solution and eliminated the hassle of auditions. "Who ever thought I would play Tinkerbell?" said Betsy later. "It was so much fun. I could get away with a lot and I did."

And there was no way we were we going to ask Jeff Ross back to play piano. Betsy's friend was dating a guy who had a sister who just happened to be a piano player. Serendipity happens. Twenty-one-year-old Liza Kitchell arrived with a resume as a professional piano accompanist. "I've been accompanying opera workshops in the Oakland adult night school for seniors," she told us. Liza was as authentic as her fresh-scrubbed fair complexion and white blond hair. But this was neither opera nor seniors. "I thought Les Nickelettes' show was pretty wild, and I didn't get a lot of the sexual or drug culture humor," she explained later. "But it was exciting. I was emotionally in a very young place, so it was fun working with women with that kind of spirit." Liza embraced the girl-bonding experience and fit into the group like a hand in a glove.

❧

The Goodman Building run of *Peter Pan: A New Rock Fairytale* proved more successful than the first. In fact, we got such strong word of mouth that it forced us to turn away paying customers.

Part of the allure laid in making it not just a play, but also a happening. That summer Les Nickelettes had become huge fans of the late-night TV cult phenomenon *Mary Hartman, Mary Hartman*. We got even more excited when the credits revealed that this groundbreaking, satirical soap opera had a woman director and female writers. This ahead-of-its-time story chronicled the disintegration of an average American housewife facing the turmoil of modern society dysfunction, while dealing with the suburban distress of yellow waxy buildup on her kitchen floor linoleum. After our Friday night performances, we set up a TV and invited the audience to stay after the show and watch *Mary Hartman, Mary Hartman* with us.

Word got around in counterculture circles that Les Nickelettes' scene was the place to be. Sharon R. Skolnick (a.k.a. Sharon Skolnick-Bagnoli) explained our ahead-of-our-time story in her review for the *Berkeley Barb*:

Les Nickelettes Bite into "Peter Pan"

You can't call Les Nickelettes' transformation of Peter Pan *a feminist statement. But you can't not call it that either. It's ambiguous. Which is both its strength as entertainment and its hallmark as art. . . . Instead of suffragette polemics, Les Nickelettes parade before us a motley assortment of characters, female-style: a funhouse mirror vision of the many ways one can be a woman. . . . Les Nickelettes exploit their "femininity" in the service of satire, and why not? These ladies, tongues ensconced firmly in cheeks, poke fun and worse at everything they can get their hands on. Their dialogue never hides behind anybody's society—pruned ideas of what women aren't supposed to say. It's blunt and bawdy, and unmercifully gets down. Though it could use some smoothing out, the play is a highly creative venture, perhaps possessing earmarks of a pretty big step for Womankind. Peter's sword slices through a whole shitload of stereotypes and "isms" plaguing men and holding women back, piercing the very walls of feminism and letting some light into the mansions of meta-sexual art.*

Wow! This review verified our suspicion that female critics picked up on our message more astutely than their male counterparts. And nowhere was the despised "amateur" word used. Ellin and I were so impressed we invited Sharon Skolnick to be on our board of directors.

What good is sitting at home on your ass?
Playing with yourself all day
Go play with someone else just once
Come to the Salmon Awards.

The metaphor of swimming upstream and spawning against all odds cemented as an ongoing Nickelettes theme at the Third Annual Salmon Awards. New members to the party bought in hook, line, and sinker. Liza received the lovingly decorated Soft Pedal of the Year award.

"I thought, *Me?*" said a surprised Liza. "I was very happy. I kept it on my bed stand with all its glue and glitter and fringe."

Ron Turner was awarded the Hugh Hefner Publisher of the Year.

"I treasured it," said Ron. "It was wonderful. It meant more to me than getting my Outstanding Lineman trophy in high school."

The Tanya Hearst Journalist of the Year award went to Sharon R. Skolnick of the *Berkeley Barb* because she gave us the best review. But we held no grudges. John Wasserman of the *San Francisco Chronicle* got a consolation prize, and he mentioned the honor in his *On The Town* column:

> *I regret to say that I did not get to the Nickelettes'*
> *annual Salmon Awards presentation ceremonies on*
> *Saturday night. . . . I received the coveted Golden*
> *Dildo award. "Where," you ask, "can you go from*
> *there?" Good question.*

In the span of one year, the big picture had changed. Instead of dreaming of a mythical show biz bigwig whisking us off to stardom, we saw our future as a nonprofit theater company sustaining itself through foundation and government grants and private donations. We had a board of directors committed to preserving and supporting the group. Once the bucks started rolling in, we could quit our day jobs and become full-time theater artists. "*Peter Pan* was a real step forward," said Ellin, "in that it was empowering to discover we could write and produce a full-length show."

Finally, I believed, we were on a solid pathway to achieving, as noted by John Wasserman, our "role in God's Great Plan."

CHAPTER 6

NOTHING'S SACRED

"Rhinestones in the Rough."

What do you want? We want it all. When do you want it? We want it now! I made a to-do list:

1. Build on momentum from *Peter Pan*.
2. Secure subsidized government and foundation grants.
3. Receive recognition from the theater community as a bona fide professional company.
4. Create a new show from scratch—not just a parody of a familiar story with a Nickelettes slant.

To accomplish all these ambitious goals, I wore many hats: actress, playwright, producer, art administrator, and Les Nickelettes, Inc. board member.

The possibility of funding the new production in one fell swoop lit a fire under our collective asses. We hustled to "get aboard the government grant gravy train." None of us had grant writing experience, but with help from board member Jeffrey Tar Genza, Ellin, Jane, and I diligently filled out the complex National Endowment for the Arts (NEA) application and managed to send it in by the January deadline.

The process of getting the grant would take time. Meanwhile, we squished a couple of goals into one: keeping our name in the public eye by performing a touring cabaret show (and making some money), while at the same time writing a new play.

A revival of the popular "Ms. Hysterical Contest" offered a quick launch for a traveling show. But that idea slowly dissolved. Linda and Janet had no interest in joining the collective. And Roberta decided to drop out and go solo. Roberta and Larry's relationship was kaput. But Larry and Vince were still good friends, so Larry continued to show up at Nickelettes events. "I don't think I would have dropped out if it hadn't been for Larry," said Roberta. "When I broke up with him, I had to leave the Nicks, because I couldn't get rid of him. It wasn't funny; it was like being stalked. The funny thing was that Larry had introduced me to stand-up comedy, and I left to be a stand-up comedian."

I didn't envy Roberta. She was brave to go off on her own. With the Nicks, it was all for one and one for all, so if we bombed we commiserated together.

The company then dwindled to four after Betsy deserted us for a different sorority. "I had known Terry Baum since college, and she approached me about working with Lilith," said Betsy. Terry, the artistic director of Lilith, launched the theater group "to write, produce, and perform original plays that affirmed the power of women to change the world." Wait a minute, this sounds like competition to me. Was there room in San Francisco for *two* women's theater collectives?

"Lilith was me wanting to do something more serious," said Betsy. "All my life I have had a conflict between the good Girl Scout on one hand, and the bad girl smoking cigarettes out in the back of the school yard on the other."

I went to see Betsy in Lilith's show *Moonlighting* (women work two jobs; one for a paycheck, and one in the home). Their play demonstrated to me that the two groups were as different as night and day, like Betsy's good and bad angel. Lilith's play was a principled, no-nonsense take on feminism, the antithesis of Les Nickelettes' anarchistic satirical approach.

Ellin, Jane, Carol, and I were not enough to stage a "Ms. Hysterical Contest," and barely enough for any sort of cabaret show. Rosalie Schmidt, our volunteer stagehand for *Peter Pan*, came to me and said, "I'd like to perform."

"What kind of experience have you had?" I asked.

"Nothing on the stage, but I've worked for the CIA, the Salvation Army, and the Moonies."

I chuckled at Rosalie's muddled resume.

"I like to try new things," she continued. "I have Jesus in my heart, and I'm bored again."

Always a sucker for a pun, I cracked up. In the spirit of being a breeding ground for women who shared our skewed comedic perspective, the group welcomed Rosalie and stitched together a *Best of Les Nickelettes* sketch show.

There was more good news. Liza Kitchell wanted in on the project to write music and serve as our piano player. Having a female musician eager to compose new music lifted the group up to a whole new level. Liza's first song, "Nothing's Sacred," expressed a desire to resist conformity. In 1977, primitive computers required a user to insert thin cardboard punch cards as protocol for inputting information. Using the cards came with a stern warning: "Do not fold, staple, or mutilate." With that line as a starting point, Liza's robotic "Nothing's Sacred" cautioned not to blindly obey:

Nothing's sacred—all is approved
Do you feel the urge to be rude?
You can live life just as you're told
You don't get wise. You get old.

Inspired by the song's title, I suggested we change the name of the show from *Best of Les Nickelettes* to *Nothing's Sacred*. Looking at it through the lens of a journalist, Ellin objected, "Saddling ourselves with a title like *Nothing's Sacred* will leave us open to reviewers skewering us with our own words," she argued.

"Possibly. But we shouldn't let fear of criticism guide our artistic impulses," I countered. The others agreed with me, and we changed the show's name.

Short skits for *Nothing's Sacred* dovetailed with favorite Nickelettes songs. Two teeny boppers listed the desirable qualities of a mate in "The Boy that I Marry" ("Never have a premature ejaculation"). A delusional bride sang "A Man Who Cares." An audition in Hollywood featured a fairy singing "Fairy's Lament" ("I heard that all fairies make it big in Tinseltown"). In the end, after having their dreams stomped on by a sleazy Hollywood agent (played by Jane in drag), all the characters summed up the rigged game in a reprise of "Nothing's Sacred:"

> *Stardom's road is paved with gold*
> *It can be yours so we've been told*
> *Suckers for another con*
> *And a come on, come on, come on, come on.*

In the midst of performing, writing grants, and squeezing in moments to come up with ideas for a new play, a harsh reality hit home for me. My unemployment benefits ran out. After living on the dole for a year (I thought of it as an artist's sabbatical stipend), I had to get a day job. I didn't want a full-time, full-commitment job; I needed something that provided adequate income but also allowed me time to pursue my Nickelettes aspirations. Scouring the want ads for this kind of dream job left me frustrated. Jobs that fit my criteria didn't want me. Someone suggested I check out Macy's: the pay was good, shifts under forty hours a week were available, and it was easy to get hired.

I costumed myself as a fashionable store clerk, hopped on the downtown bus, and made my way to Macy's Union Square in San Francisco's upscale shopping district. During the trip, I envisioned the interview as an audition for the role of perky salesgirl. The ruse worked. Two days later I was hired. Rather than getting placed in a specific department, the letter of employment assigned me the confusing designation of "flyer." At my orientation I learned that a flyer was a sales associate who filled in at different departments when the regular person was out sick or on vacation. Unsure about this position at first, I soon discovered that I had lucked into the perfect job. I had no set schedule, but instead signed up for available shifts and could work as many or as few hours a week as I wanted. Working as a flyer provided flexibility to pursue my goal of eventually making a living as a theater performer. Nonetheless, the pace of my life speeded up as I added shop girl to all my other activities. I hardly had time to think.

My sales position at Macy's led to a new song in the show. In the 1970s, major department stores had huge sales only twice a year, not practically every weekend like today. Customers waited all year for these sales and then jammed the store to score coveted discounts. Encouraged by management, I signed up to work a full eight-hour shift for my first White Flower Day. Not knowing what I was getting into, I attached the white carnation to my nametag and reported to my assignment in the Domestics Department. I anticipated a leisurely morning selling sheets, pillows, and towels.

The store opened and shoppers descended on the goods like early birds to the worm. After a hectic couple of hours, the pace returned to normal. The seasoned saleslady working alongside me warned, "It won't last—wait till the lunch crowd arrives."

I wasn't an expert on selling bed linens, so I used this slow period to navigate around the floor taking in everything possible about the merchandise so I could answer customer questions. As I tidied up a bin of pillows, a voice behind me said, "Miss, could you please help my daughter?" I turned, and was confronted with the craggy face of William Randolph Hearst, Jr.

Oh yes, I recognized the chairman of the famous Hearst newspaper-publishing dynasty, but more importantly I recognized the father of the notorious Patty Hearst. I blinked hard as movie-like images flashed through my mind of his kidnapped daughter joining the revolutionary Symbionese Liberation Army, changing her name to Tanya, and waving a machine gun around during a bank robbery. I mumbled, "Of course."

Patty walked up behind her father. She was a petite brunette with satin-smooth skin. I was aware of her current status. After being on the run for a couple of years, she had been captured, tried, and sentenced to thirty-five years for the bank heist. She was living with her parents pending an appeal. Her lawyers argued that she had been a victim of brainwashing by her kidnappers. She testified that she'd done what she had to do to survive. A big burly mustached bodyguard appeared and planted himself behind Patty.

Mr. Hearst explained that he had just purchased a new bed for his daughter upstairs in the furniture department and asked me to recommend appropriate sheets. I didn't know sheets from Shinola, but I took a deep breath and willed myself to play the part of a knowledgeable salesperson; in other words, fake it. I figured rich people purchased expensive designer labels, so I led them to the Ralph Lauren section and blathered ignorantly about the merits of these quality sheets.

Patty never made eye contact and was more interested in joking with her big hunky guard than picking out a bedding ensemble. After casually pointing to the bed linens of her choice, she wandered off with the bodyguard. Daddy was left to pay. Poor millionaire.

As I rang up the purchase, Mr. Hearst informed me that he didn't have his Macy's card, only a receipt with his account number written on it from the bed purchase. Now, of course, I knew he was the famous and wealthy Mr. William Randolph Hearst Jr., but Macy's policy required a customer without their card to show a photo I.D. I hesitated, but then thought, why do the rich get away with circumventing rules? I innocently asked him for his California driver's license. He smiled at me with a hint of distain, and indulgently dug out his wallet.

I related this story to the Nicks, and Ellin was inspired to write a new skit and song for *Nothing's Sacred*. Dressed as bank heist Tanya in big sunglasses and black revolutionary beret, she accompanied herself on electric bass guitar as she sang, "I Was Born in Hillsborough" (the wealthy San Francisco suburb where Patty Hearst grew up).

Well I've been bad, now I'm good as gold
I won't make no more trouble, at least till I'm paroled.
. . . Oh Daddy, Daddy, things just ain't the same
Why do you call me Patty, when Tanya is my name?

At the beginning of the year, after receiving our tax-exempt nonprofit status, we discovered one of the perks was reduced bulk-rate mailing. "Let's do a monthly newsletter," I enthused.

"It would keep the fan base informed of upcoming performances," said Ellin.

"And we can spread the Nickelettes philosophy," added Jane. The *Nick News* debuted in February 1977 with the headline, "Why Be a Star When You Can Be a Constellation?" We also used the newsletter to solicit tax-exempt donations:

"Send your check in the name of art to Les Nickelettes, Inc. a nonprofit orgasmization." We hoped puns and jokes would trigger a cascade of greenbacks.

The first big event announced in the *Nick News* was the group's audition for *Nothing's Sacred* at a new club, Chez Jacques, on Hyde Street. In preparation, I asked Sharon McNight to direct the cabaret show. "We haven't been able to find a woman director," I told her. "If you come on board, it will be the first time the Nicks will truly be an all-women group."

"There's not a lot of women directors, let me tell you," said Sharon as she accepted the task.

We had evolved from the early days of no-holds-barred anarchy, but left on our own, we still tended to goof off. Rehearsals began with serious intentions, but then someone cracked a bad joke, which led to an awful pun, and we all dissolved into mirthful chaos.

Sharon admired our spirit, but didn't have time to fool around and thus demanded that we buckle down. "It's my German gene," she explained, "You vill do vhat I say."

I appreciated the needed discipline she brought to the group. I zipped my mouth shut and replied, "Ja, Frau Direktor."

The evening of the tryout, the owners of Chez Jacques allowed us to invite our friends and fans (the cabaret hadn't officially opened yet but we knew the show would go over better with a live audience). Sharon came to cheer us on, "I had to support the troops," she explained. Vince was also in the audience and mentioned to Sharon that the club was looking for singers, and since she was contemplating a singing career, she should audition. "So I did," said Sharon.

A few weeks later, Chez Jacques's big splashy grand opening advertised a show featuring well-known San Francisco cabaret performers Weslia Whitfield, Dana Ballan, and David Raine. "Then Weslia was shot in the spine by a random bullet on the street, and was in the hospital," said Sharon. "They needed a third person right away to do the show, so I got to do it. After that I decided I would go out solo on my own." Good news for Sharon, her career as a cabaret singer was launched. Bad news for Les Nickelettes, we lost our director. But we did book a couple more gigs at Chez Jacques.

And then, more bad news: Liza decided to become a professional chamber accompanist and enrolled at the University of California Santa Cruz to study classical piano. Like Betsy, she was torn between doing something fun and doing something serious, and like Betsy, the serious won out.

Ever the optimist, I refused to be disheartened. I had faith things would work out. And just like that, a spitfire piano player with a mass of curly brown hair and a broad smile entered our circle. Jill Rose wanted to expand her musical skills and saw an opportunity in Les Nickelettes. "I was working at the Jewish Community Center at the time," explained Jill. "But I was looking to be more of a music person, to establish myself as a feminist and musician."

Jill didn't just want to play piano; she wanted to be part of the show. She adapted the position to her own style, adding a solo prelude, and taking on the role of musical narrator. Jill's musical influences were Carole King and Laura Nyro, and so she belted out songs with soul and R&B influenced chords on the bottom and a sweet melody on top.

⁓〰〜

The other big event announced in the February *Nick News* was a two-night gig that Ellin scored at a brand-new club called the New Riverside Back Room in Santa Cruz, seventy miles south of San Francisco. Our first actual out-of-town booking! With visions of lolling in the surf and sand of the sunny beach town in between rollicking performances, we ventured out of the safe and sure Bay Area. But instead of big city confidence, fear gripped us on the first nerve-racking night. There was a good-sized crowd to feed off, but we didn't know them, and they didn't know us. Our mojo was off.

The next evening, the audience was smaller, but we rebounded and got into our groove. After the show, a meeting with the manager of the club squashed my good mood. First, he disparaged our material asking, "Where was the hot babe act I booked?" Then he smiled condescendingly as he handed me a measly $80: "Here's your take of the receipts." The scumbag made me want to puke. Eighty bucks didn't even cover travel expenses.

Ellin's prediction that critics would use the title *Nothing's Sacred* against us in reviews proved unfounded. Instead, Buz Bezore of the *Santa Cruz Sentinel* blasted:

Les Nickelettes Drown in Sea of Ineptitude

Les Nickelettes probably think of themselves as a feminist answer to Saturday Night Live Not Ready for Prime-Time Players, but actually their humor . . . falls somewhere below the broad burlesque of Sha Na Na.

We debated, could that be construed as a put down or a compliment? Comedy is in the ear of the beholder. We bid farewell to Santa Cruz with the grit of sand not only in our shoes but also in our brains.

After tasting crow, there's no food like comfort food. Our March *Nick News* proclaimed that we were "Rhinestones in the Rough" and would perform again at Karl Cohen's Intersection vintage movie series. The home town audience embraced us and revived our spirits.

Next, Ellin snared us a tryout at Shady Grove, a new club in the Haight-Ashbury. But Shady Grove turned out to be not only the name, but also the mood of the place. Stepping into the gloomy interior reeking of stale tobacco and marijuana smoke repelled us. The smell was nothing that we weren't familiar with, but this place had an atmosphere of sleaze. We later learned the owner was a drug dealer who used the club as a front for his real business. During our performance, the furtive patrons were more interested in the wares for sale than the entertainment. This wasn't our crowd.

"I didn't like that show at Shady Grove," said Carol. "It felt weird. Icky. I was trying to decide, at the time, whether I was in or out." Carol dropped out.

Ellin, Jane, Rosalie, Jill, and I carried on. We traveled up the Northern California coast to Point Reyes. The Dance Palace, run by the Palace Players, was housed in an old Emporium on Main Street. The venue served the small rural town as both a cultural and community center.

The Palace Players warmly welcomed us, and we found a collective symbiotic fit. They were in it for the pleasure, not the profit.

Paki Stedwell, reviewing the show for the *Tomales Bay Times*, summed up our reception:

> Nothing's Sacred . . . *is brash, feisty, lusty, and represents satire at some of its feminist best. . . . Simply said, it was hysterical. I applaud Les Nickelettes for their talent, verve, and bursting-at-the-seams energy, even if it appears they worship at the altar of Bawd instead of Bard.*

The newsletter in April announced a gig at the Cabaret Club in Cotati, fifty miles north of San Francisco. The first night was fine, but the following night the club was empty. Zip. Nada. Not one patron. We were beginning to see that touring wasn't all it's cracked up to be. And it was delaying the writing of a new play.

Me, Rosalie, and Betsy throwing up
our panties in *Nothing's Sacred*

We stopped touring but continued to send out the *Nick News*. In the May newsletter, we quoted overheard musings from the dressing room:

"All I want in life is a new dress, a good hairdo, and a decent fuck."

"Are you sure you're not asking for too much?"

"No, I was born with a silver spoon up my nose."

Our mailing roster included fans and media, but I was still shocked a couple of days later when I picked up a *San Francisco Chronicle* and read this blurb in Herb Caen's column:

BODKINS' ODDS: The Nickelettes, those Anza Street terrors, have a friend with a seemingly limitless supply of expensive cocaine. When a Nickelette wondered

*where it all came from, the friend giggled, "I was born
with a silver spoon up my nose!"*

Everyone in San Francisco read Herb Caen, and getting an
item in his daily column was the best free publicity in town.
But his reference to Anza Street hit me where I lived—literally.
The return address on the newsletters was my apartment. I had
visions of the narc squad raiding my home, and hauling me
away for drug possession. Despite my unending devotion to
Les Nickelettes, this disclosure published in *the* major newspaper of Northern California had me shaking in my boots.

The board of directors drafted an official letter to Herb
Caen stating that although we appreciated the mention of
Les Nickelettes in his column, in the future, could he refrain
from revealing our personal residential address? Herb never
responded.

The letter that did land in our mailbox that May was notifi-
cation from the National Endowment for the Arts that our
grant application had been rejected. Disappointed, I still held
out hope that the local funding sources we'd applied to would
come through. But no, the San Francisco Foundation and the
San Francisco Hotel Tax Agency also declined to provide
financial support. We were rookies. We pitched them hilarious
examples of our cutting-edge satirical feminist comedy. The
bureaucrats soberly requested long-range goals, objectives, and
statistics. If we didn't up our corporate game, the gravy train
would pass us by. Discouraged, but still determined to move
ahead with plans to produce a new play, we sought alternative
ways to fund the project.

The board of directors suggested a garage sale. After dig-
ging out unwanted treasures from closets and basements, we
took off early one cold morning to the local flea market. At

the end of the day we made more money selling secondhand goods than performing.

"How pathetic," I said. "To do the thing we love, we have to stoop to peddling used clothing."

"We're slaves to our art," joked Ellin.

It was time to hunker down and write a play. With undaunted moxie, Ellin, Jane, and I set out to change Nickelettes history by becoming playwrights in our own right. Brainstorming through our favorite childhood experiences, we discovered a shared love of Nancy Drew mystery novels and the detective board game Clue. "Let's do a private-eye satire," I suggested.

"A screwball murder mystery," added Jane.

"But instead of our usual raunchy jokes and puns," weighed in Ellin, "we write a genre parody based on funny situations and witty lines."

To my delight, Betsy decided to rejoin the group. "Although the experience of working with Lilith satisfied certain desires to work in a different way," said Betsy, "I missed Les Nickelettes, missed that great anarchistic feeling where you can do anything you want and nobody's going to judge you for it. And, of course, Les Nickelettes were never politically correct, and that's what made them so much fun."

From my perspective, Betsy's input provided a shot in the arm. We needed her. I needed her. And she was jazzed about the idea of a musical comedy/murder mystery. The writing team met at Jane's tiny studio apartment on 19th Street across from Dolores Park. We smoked a joint, opened a bottle of wine, and discussed the elements of plot required to craft a murder mystery.

"We need to understand why a character would kill someone," Ellin began.

"Have any of y'all ever felt like murdering someone?" Betsy asked.

"I wanted to kill my college boyfriend." I replied. "In the winter of 1969, we lived in a cockroach-infested apartment on Divisadero Street. James nailed a sleeping bag over our only window in a quest to shut out the outside world. It was his cave, and I was his captive. He spurned social college events, discouraged friendships, even refused to get a telephone. One time, his sister knocked on the door, and he signaled me to stay quiet, pretending no one was home. She pounded on the door, 'James, I know you're in there!' He didn't relent. I tolerated it because I loved him.

"But I was twenty-one and craved being involved in theater. During our four-week winter break, he decided we would go nowhere and see no one, just hibernate in the apartment. After a couple of weeks, I was bored to death. And then he started talking about a post-college plan that involved retreating to a cabin in the woods and subsisting only on rice and beans. He cited the hippie utopian dream of the time—that living in the wilderness would make us more in tune with nature. But I also picked up on an underlying motive to isolate me so he would have no rivals.

"One night, as he slept next to me, I lay awake daydreaming of escape. I envisioned getting up, going to the kitchen, grabbing the carving knife, coming back to the bed, and . . . the end-deed of this thought jarred me out of inertia and into action. The next day, I packed my suitcase and left. Crying and numb, I couldn't answer his stunned question, 'Why?'"

I finished the story, and everyone was silent. I took a deep breath. "I've never told another single soul about that thought," I confessed. "It was too scary."

"Well, you felt trapped," said Jane. "So you thought about getting rid of the thing that had you cornered."

"But I didn't follow through," I said. "I left. But what if leaving wasn't an option? Would that drive a person to go over the edge? And it not, what would?"

"Rage, jealousy, powerlessness," answered Betsy.

142 ★ ANARCHY IN HIGH HEELS

"Revenge always motivates," added Ellin. "Or the feeling of being disconnected from the world and blaming it on one particular person."

I gave that some thought, "So our murderer could be a disengaged, powerless person pushed over the edge."

"Like the Kafka story about the guy who turned into a bug," said Jane.

Kafka's classic twentieth-century novella *The Metamorphosis* was about an insurance salesman, Gregor Samsa, who feels so alienated from his work, family, and community that he wakes up one morning transformed into a disgusting insect. The story never explains why Gregor turns into a bug, but describes how his family attempts to adjust to his new repulsive body and habits.

"But in the story the bug is not a murderer," I said.

"Well, maybe the murder victim could be dressed up like a bug," said Ellin.

"A singing, dancing female cockroach," said Betsy. We burst into laughter at that vision.

"Squished to death by a critic," cracked Jane.

"But seriously," I said, "instead of the classic male alienated from society, we change it to a woman, the long-suffering housewife stuck in the suburbs, like Mary Hartman, forced to worry about the waxy yellow buildup on her kitchen linoleum. And then, when she decides to break free, she metamorphoses into a giant disgusting cockroach."

"No, not disgusting," said Jane, "a snazzy Nickelettes cockroach dressed in sequins and high heels."

"We could use the cockroach story as a play within a play," suggested Ellin.

"A good plot device for a murder mystery," added Betsy.

We were on a roll, and quickly constructed a rough plot outline. That was the easy part. Coming to consensus about details proved more difficult. The process was agonizing, exhilarating, exciting, and excruciating. Disagreements flared up, especially between Ellin and Jane. In those moments, I was happy to have Betsy as an ally; we both also had strong opinions but were more willing to compromise. Ellin and Jane, on the other hand, dug in their heels and fought like two vicious dogs over the same bone. A running joke became, "I hope we finish this murder mystery script before we kill each other."

"There were writing meetings where we fought," said Ellin. "But also sometimes we laughed so hard, we cried. We would drink and smoke a lot of dope, and somehow the quarrel would just evaporate in the effort of coming up with this stuff."

The next phase proved even tougher: dialogue. Sitting in a circle collectively writing dialogue didn't work. So we pulled out a tape recorder and began ad-libbing. "It was my first real writing experience," said Betsy. "I felt really great about it. We did improvisations and wrote from that. I thought it was a wonderful way to write."

By the end of October, we had the play sketched out, but it was still far from complete. Meanwhile, I was getting nervous about the slow progress. In the past, Les Nickelettes unleashed an idea from our collective unconscious and slammed it on stage as quickly as possible. But getting "serious" and writing an original play from scratch turned out to be harder than we imagined. Nevertheless, we missed the adrenaline of performing, so it was time we got our butt in gear and set a deadline. We arranged a booking at the Intersection Theatre for a May 1978 opening. This gave us six months to complete the script, compose the music, raise the money, rehearse, and ramp up production. "No flies on us," said Betsy.

At the prior year's 1976 Salmon Awards, I had received the first annual Martyr of the Year trophy. It was both a joke and an honor. I did sacrifice my personal life in service to Nickelettes responsibilities.

Competition for this year's 1977 Nickelettes Martyr award had been going on all year. As the celebration neared, the playful contest heated up. Jane, Ellin, and I (who were doing the bulk of the business tasks) pitched our deeds in terms of self-serving toil.

"This week alone, I typed up the script, booked a theater for the new play, *and* put up flyers on Castro Street," I groaned.

"That's nothing," Ellin declared. "I sent out press releases, managed the mailing list, set up radio interviews, *and* put up flyers in North Beach."

"You guys only work part-time," asserted Jane, "I work full-time, while maintaining the books, preparing budgets, *and* putting up flyers on Haight Street."

"Last week, I folded and stapled a thousand newsletters," I countered. "And then took them to the special bulk-rate post office and waited two hours for them to be processed."

Ellin went in for the kill. "Well, I originated, researched, and engineered the idea of us becoming a nonprofit organization, and I refused to back down even when you balked."

Okay, Ellin you win. She had out-martyred me with her relentless effort to turn the group into a legitimate theater company.

During the awards ceremony when her name was announced, Ellin feigned surprise and made a humble speech from the dais: "I would like to thank all the little people that I stepped on as I made my way to the top."

Ellin extended her "Martyr of the Year" status by writing an article published in the *Berkeley Barb*:

Salmon Eggs!

The Salmon Award audience simultaneously pats itself on the back (by taking the award seriously) and trips itself up (by realizing the Awards are a prank).

Me, Ellin, Jane, and Rosalie in the
publicity photo for the Salmon Awards

Photo © Lisa Lloyd

On December 31, 1977, I turned thirty. Milestone birthdays could be written off as no big deal. But turning thirty when you're part of the baby boom generation, who, in our late teens, defiantly proclaimed, "Never trust anyone over thirty," was a bummer. I fretted that my youthful spontaneity would melt away.

Vince, who was several years older than me, scoffed at my apprehension. "It only gets better," he told me.

I brooded for a while, but ultimately chose to embrace my new decade. After all, I'd come a long way. In my early twenties, I thought the only avenue open to me was acting. I never dreamed I would acquire the skills and gumption to write and produce plays. Women weren't supposed to do those things. Cheers to being thirty!

CHAPTER 7

COCKROACH IN
HIGH HEELS

"Kafka Knows Best"

I converted any lingering negative thoughts on turning thirty into positive ones by focusing on building my confidence as a playwright. It helped to be sharing the process with three of my best friends. Vince's support also strengthened belief in myself.

The countdown clock to a May 1978 opening began ticking down in January. The script for the musical murder mystery was almost ready to go, but we didn't yet have a title. The writing group tossed around several options, each of us arguing for the one we preferred:

Murder on a High Note, touted Jane.

Murder Crept In, proposed Betsy.

Ellin favored the grammatical pun *Whomdunnit?*

And my personal favorite was *Bugged to Death.*

The debate centered on whether to choose a tongue-in-cheek name, or to signal a more serious intent with a conventional title. In the end, those early titles were rejected in favor of Ellin's more astute nomination: *Curtains!*

"When the right idea comes up," said Ellin, "everybody knows it."

Maybe so, but I mourned the loss of *Bugged to Death*. We saved the whimsy for the title of the all-American-family show-within-a-show: *Kafka Knows Best*.

Before ramping up production, we had to tackle the question of who would direct the play. Our Achilles heel, for the past three years, had been avoiding filling this key leadership position from within.

"One of us has to direct," I told the group. "As Les Nickelettes, we've become playwrights and producers, now someone needs to become the director." I wasn't prepared to do it, so I pointedly looked at Betsy.

"I did some directing in graduate school and college," Betsy told us as she stepped up to the task. "So it won't be my first directing experience, but certainly it will be the biggest I've ever done." Thus ushered in a new era whereby a core member helmed our productions.

Production duties were broken down among the four of us into tasks that suited our abilities. Jane did the banking and bookkeeping. Ellin covered publicity. I discovered an innate organizing skill that I used to implement the nuts and bolts of the overall production. As director, Betsy, with an easy-going but firm style, demonstrated an ability to work with and, when needed, corral the actresses. I worked closely with Betsy to shape the production and kept everything running smoothly. "We made a great producer/director team," noted Betsy. "We complemented each other in very important ways."

The script called for fourteen characters. With double casting, we planned to have an ensemble of twelve. The core playwright/actress group got cast first.

Ellin was tapped to play Kate Kendall, the director of *Kafka Knows Best*. Ellin immediately wrote lyrics for her solo song conveying Kate's artistic angst, and the Nickelettes worldview that her character embodied: "Slave to My Art."

I work long hours and I work for low pay
But when all's said and done I'll have my say . . .
'Coz I'm a slave, a slave to my art
Nothing else can satisfy this hunger in my heart.

Jane snagged the role of Ethel Featherstonehaugh (pronounced Foon) an entomologist and amateur sleuth who deduced the backstage murder mystery.

Publicity photo for *Curtains!*:
Ethel Featherstonehaugh examining a bug
Photo © Rita Mandelman

I scored the part of Mary Miller, the actress who played Doris, the next-door neighbor in *Kafka Knows Best*. I relished portraying this character. I spent most of the play lying low, and then, in a stunning denouement, Ethel exposed Mary as the murderer. Our plot created more detours and dead-ends than an Iowa corn maze, but I tied up all the loose ends in my gut-wrenching confession. I revealed that the self-involved star of the play-within-a-play was having a ruinous affair with my only son, thus soiling his Gypsy heritage. (Did I mention that Mary was a Gypsy?) I blamed the star for my son's demise in a horrific car crash. "Revenge! Revenge!" I cried as I was dragged offstage, chewing up the scenery as I went.

Betsy offered Rosalie the part of Lawn, a stoned and dim-witted male stage crew member. The running gag was that every time the audience glimpsed Lawn, he was napping. Rosalie also doubled as the actual stage manager for the production.

Now, we needed to recruit seven actresses for the other roles. Betsy set up two consecutive days of open auditions. The first day she cast three roles. A tall, slender Debbie Cavanaugh demonstrating a breezy delivery was cast as Diana Delucca, Ethel Featherstonehaugh's sidekick and intrepid private eye, who did the legwork to untangle the mystery.

A scrappy, wiry Shelly Gordon impressed Betsy with a mannish manner that, along with her short tousled black hair, led Betsy to cast her as Jeff, the father in *Kafka Knows Best*.

The third selection, nineteen year-old Marga Gomez, stood out. "Marga had a kind of light about her," said Betsy. "I knew right away I had to cast her." Even though her resume revealed little experience, she was irresistible with big brown innocent eyes and an engaging gap-toothed smile. Betsy saw in Marga a sexy androgynous quality that afforded her the power to charm anyone. She won the role of Greg, Kate's skirt-chasing boyfriend.

We were adamant that the performing ensemble remain all female. This was essential to our mission. The three male characters—Lawn, Jeff, and Greg—were "real" guys, not the broad and satirical males we had portrayed in the past. Our goal was to impersonate these guys in drag without looking like girls in men's clothes with fake moustaches.

The following day's audition, Jane brought in her friend Mary Valentino. Mary stood squirming in front of the group. "I've never done this before."

"That's okay," said Betsy. "Just be yourself."

"I laughed hysterically when I saw Les Nickelettes at the Mabuhay Gardens," Mary gushed. "It was like watching little kids playing dress-up."

Jane nudged Betsy's elbow and whispered, "Mary *is* a Nickelette—you have to cast her."

But Mary's audition faltered. The weight of scant performing experience bore down on her, and she came across as flustered and distracted. On the positive side, she demonstrated noteworthy Nickelettes charm. Planting a hand on a thrust-out saucy hip, she signaled an exuberant sexuality while smiling innocently like a nice girl. Still, Betsy hesitated to cast her.

After Mary left, Jane rallied on her behalf with a personal story. One day, she related, out of the blue, Mary called her. "I don't have any women friends to talk to," she sobbed. Mary's boyfriend, Robin, was one of Jane's best friends. "Robin didn't come home last night," wailed Mary, "and he hasn't even called."

"Come over to my house right now," replied Jane.

By the time Mary arrived, Jane had stocked up on enough beer and snacks to indulge in an all-day gabfest. "He ditches me for a couple of days and doesn't care how I feel," Mary cried into her beer.

"Robin's a cad," declared Jane. Mary cheered up, and after a couple more beers they were both giggling and singing old show tunes. "You should audition for *Curtains!*" Jane told Mary. "You have the Nickelettes spirit, and you can sing."

Jane turned to Betsy and asserted, "Mary has natural talent."

"Yeah, but doesn't she still live with that drug-dealing cad?" Betsy asked. "That could make her unreliable."

"Don't worry, I'll babysit her," promised Jane.

So Mary was cast as Linda Lake, the daughter in *Kafka Knows Best,* and understudy to Greta Samsa. It was an important role because Linda takes over the starring role after Greta—in a cockroach costume—is murdered. "I was ecstatic when I got the part," Mary said. "The only performing I had done was a musical in Catholic high school. I always wanted to sing and act, and here it was. I felt like Cinderella."

Betsy and I were taken aback when fifteen-year-old Tara Moss bounced into the audition studio flashing a naïve, guileless smile, and shaking her shoulder length golden brown hair. She was too young for any of the roles, but we were impressed with her courage to audition. Instead of dashing her ambition, we created a couple of small parts in the script for her. Tara's parents consented to her being in the play, but Betsy had to step in to buffer the classic teenager-parent conflict a few times. In the end, Tara's internship in Les Nickelettes was like a three-unit course in Feminism 101.

The auditions left a big gap in casting. Our script called for three mature female characters, but no one older than thirty tried out. We rejected the idea of having young women in age makeup for the roles—we wanted the real thing. Our mission was to integrate older, wiser women into our world. We did this despite fearing a rift. The "generation gap" clashes with our own parents left us wary of elders' opinions. And, further, what if these mature women couldn't adapt to our anarchistic philosophy?

Betsy consulted with me about an older woman who had done a cameo in a play Betsy did a few years earlier. I met the six-foot, big-boned Jean Taggart Born and was struck by her youthful sense of humor. "I'd like to cast Jean as Marjorie Metaberg," said Betsy. "She has the look of a seasoned producer."

"I agree," I said. "She's funny, and she's got the commanding presence needed for that role."

Jean was thrilled to get the part. "I took drama at Oroville Union High School," she said, "and tried out faithfully for every play that came along and never made one of them." Now, in her late fifties, she would get her chance.

After attending a production of *Arsenic and Old Lace*, Betsy called me and whooped, "I found our Frances!" The role was crucial to the comedy of the play. In the scene where Greta shows up at the breakfast table as a huge cockroach, Frances/Grandma, shouts, "Where's the Raid?" Furthermore, this eccentric, addled character spouts Shakespearean prophecies at relevant moments in the mystery. Yvonne O'Reilly, a perceptive sixty-five-year-old actress with a lengthy theater resume, had long, silky, white hair that she braided, twisted, and pinned around her head like a crown that shone above her twinkling eyes. I congratulated Betsy on this lucky find.

Greta Samsa, the unfulfilled housewife turned cockroach in *Kafka Knows Best*, was the final part to cast. The character's offstage persona, Barbara Beacon, was an over-the-hill ingénue who rubbed everyone the wrong way, and thus became the murder victim. Rosalie suggested her friend Mary Kearney. In her early forties, Mary Kearney looked the part with a comely face and shoulder-length blond hair. And she nailed the audition.

Finally, casting was complete, thirteen actresses in sixteen roles. "And a cast that runs the gamut in age from fifteen to sixty-five," said Betsy.

"This is exciting," I added. "We're sending the message that feminism is inclusive to all ages." Thus, the project took on an added purpose: the opportunity to learn from the experiences of older women and at the same time nurture the younger generation.

But the jolt of expanding from a cozy club of five friends to a group of thirteen age-diverse strangers caused friction. Betsy gathered the cast together. She instructed everyone to sit cross-legged in a circle. "To start things off," she said. "I want to go around the circle and have everyone state their reasons for wanting to be in this play."

Marga and Debbie expressed appreciation at being cast in the innovative project. Shelley and Mary Kearney liked the idea of having a say in the process. But Yvonne bristled, "You don't need to examine why you're here, you just need to get on with it."

"It is a little silly," concurred Jean. Squirming next to her, Mary Valentino murmured under her breath, "Sitting in this circle feels like being in kindergarten."

After an awkward silence, Ellin told the assemblage, "Les Nickelettes are not only a women's group, we are a feminist group, and our creativity springs very much from the feminine principle. In this play you'll get the freedom to combine elements of experimental theater, underground collective, and razzle-dazzle chorus line all in one."

I added, "The beauty and power of a women's group is that together we can be unafraid to express our unique voice."

"And you don't have to worry about the toilet seat being left up in the dressing room," joked Jane. Everyone laughed, and the mood shifted.

❧

Betsy stuck to our "get serious" agenda by introducing exercises before each rehearsal that focused our energy and promoted group unity. But the inexperience of the cast soon became evident. Jean had so much trouble with her character's solo prologue scene that we cut it from a full page to only a few lines. She also struggled in her duet with Jane.

"I'll sing harmony, you do melody," Jane told her.

But the minute Jane started harmony, Jean went into harmony; the minute Jane did melody, Jean went back to melody. "I was such a slow study," confessed Jean. "At the time I had a dream. I was at rehearsal and was in trouble: Les Nickelettes threatened to lock me into one of those medieval stocks. Maybe the dream was telling me I'm too old for this."

Betsy also had to exercise extreme patience with Mary Valentino. Mary teetered on an emotional cliff. She'd start off happy-go-lucky and then burst out crying when she couldn't remember her lines. On the first night working with the cockroach costume, Betsy waited an agonizing three minutes for Mary's character to enter her scene as the bug.

"Mary, what's the matter?" called Betsy.

Mary walked out half-dressed and flustered, "I can't get this damn costume on."

"Don't worry," Betsy assured her. "Rosalie, could you help Mary with the costume change?"

"Sure," said Rosalie.

Mary's experience with other women had always been competitive, so she wasn't used to the positive reinforcement. Later, she would reflect, "In Les Nickelettes, I made the best friends I ever had in my whole life."

And then, life imitated art when Mary Kearney staged a real-life backstage drama. Mimicking the fading ingénue character she portrayed, she sat in front of the dressing room mirror and examined her crow's feet. "I'm getting old," she moaned. Here was this gorgeous woman lamenting about wrinkled skin. She brought everyone down.

It got worse. She flaunted her superiority to other cast members. "She considered herself an actress," said Jean, "as opposed to the rest of us." She even put herself above the director.

"She was very condescending," said Betsy. Mary Kearney's holier-than-thou attitude went against Les Nickelettes "all for one and one for all" philosophy, and it pushed Betsy's patience over the limit a number of times.

In contrast, the oldest cast member, Yvonne, turned out to be a sweetheart. She loved her part and came to appreciate that she had a say in the overall production. Yvonne shaped the Frances/Grandma character by adding an age-wise depth that the playwrights didn't yet possess.

In the middle of all this were fifteen-year-old Tara and ten-year-old Rebecca Valentino. Rebecca, Mary Valentino's preteen daughter, hung out at rehearsals and assisted with selling refreshments during intermission after the show opened. "Telling my friends what my mother did was totally bizarre," recalls Rebecca. "Weird, but it was cool, too." The teen and preteen soaked up the scene and fit in with our notion of nurturing a love of theater in young girls.

Our experiment with a large age-diversified cast was bumpy, messy, and joyful all at the same time.

～～～

Jill Rose became our first ever-female musical director, and composed six of the eight songs in the play. "It was the first time I felt that writing music was my craft," beamed Jill.

But two songs called for a Broadway style that Jill didn't feel comfortable with. I had coaxed Sharon McNight to take time out from her blossoming cabaret career to help us with choreography. Now, I asked her to lend her expertise with these genre songs. "Suspicion" comes at the point in the plot where all the characters are looking at each other with mistrust.

Suspicion . . .
I'd tell you whodunit but I'm certain
I would get the final curtain.

A critic would later state that the song was "good enough for Broadway."

Sharon's other song, "Wasting Your Breath," contained one of the best lines in the show. During the song, Greg, the three-timing stage manager, tries to hit on ace detective Diana and fails, so he asks her, "Where did I go wrong?"

She replies, "Puberty."

The metaphor of an American housewife wishing to break out of her dreary kitchen existence metamorphosing into an insect called for a cleverly constructed cockroach costume. I called on ex-Nickelettes and costumer extraordinaire, Ann Rudder. Ann constructed a bulbous bodysuit covered with a muted brown glitter fabric. Attached to the back were thick foam black velvet wings. An invisible string linked two stuffed gloves to long black gloves worn by the actress enabling all four appendages to move together and for six legs to stick up in the air—an essential detail in the scene where Greta winds up dead and prone on the kitchen floor, after the murderer places a poison-dipped hatpin in the bug costume.

But Ann didn't do masks, and a bug head was a must. Ann brought in her friend, Ernesto, who was a mask artist. Ernesto created a cockroach mask that covered the head and face to just above the mouth. It was painted dark brown with gigantic gold, glittered eyeballs. Attached to the top of the head were two long, flexible antennae with bells on the ends that tinkled when the bug moved her head. Ann and Ernesto constructed a perfectly creepy, glamorous, cockroach costume, which we considered a Kafkaesque/Nickelettes masterpiece.

Publicity photo for *Curtains!*:
Mary as Greta Samsa in the cockroach costume

Curtains! debuted on May 4, 1978, and I waited with a mixture of excitement and anxiety about how our new direction would be viewed by critics. Ellin arranged a pre-opening interview with Bernard Bauer printed in the *Berkeley Barb*. Headlined "Franz Kafka Meets Agatha Christie," the article chronicled Les Nickelettes' "former outrageous" history and described *Curtains!* as the group's new "toned-down incarnation." Ellin made sure to point out: "Women have a right to be funny, to make trouble, to express their whole personalities."

But subsequent reviews stayed within the same predictable lines of conflicting male/female views. First, Bernard Weiner in the *San Francisco Chronicle*:

A Weak Musical Murder Mystery

Unfortunately, the murder mystery they scripted has not much going for it, and is played too straight. . . . Les Nickelettes are lovable because they are unafraid to be different, going their own wacky, amateur way in the San Francisco theatrical world.

Next, the female point of view from Margo Skinner from the *San Francisco Gazette*:

A Surefire Winner!

Curtains! *is a neat title for a "musical murder mystery"—and the play is a lot of fun at that! As campy and amusing as earlier Nickelettes offerings,* Curtains! *is more structured . . . and the ensemble has learned a lot through experience. . . .* Curtains! *is full of echoes of good old (bad?) movies, musicals, and mysteries, and it is a total delight.*

Poster for *Curtains!*
Design by Trina Robbins

The message I got from these opposing critiques was that the male view advised us to go back to our wacky, amateur ways, and thus, stay lovably marginalized. The female view encouraged us to continue taking risks.

∽ ⁊

Another kind of shift happened during the run of *Curtains!* For the first time we had a lesbian in the group. Marga Gomez ushered the group into the emerging era of an openly gay community in San Francisco. Marga was enjoying the freedom of being out of the closet in her newly adopted city after claiming to have run away from her straight family in New York City. In 1978, disco was queen. Top *Billboard* songs like "I Will Survive" by Gloria Gaynor, "Last Dance" by Donna Summer, and "YMCA" by the Village People thumped through stereo speakers everywhere. In New York, Bianca Jagger and Liza Minnelli breezed into the premier disco club Studio 54 while riffraff patrons lined the street begging for entrance. In San Francisco, hipsters got high and did the Hustle all night long at the I-Beam and Trocadero Transfer. Gays and lesbians were front and center at these bass-heavy, hedonistic dance-a-thons.

We wanted to get on the disco diva bandwagon, too. So Jill threw private dance bashes every weekend after our shows. This led to a big backstage romance. Jill had mostly been into guys, but Marga flipped her AC charge to DC.

"I had a major crush on Marga," confessed Jill. "It was the first time I had feelings for a woman that were so unbelievably physical." Acting like a goofy teenager, Jill fell head-over-heels in love during their fling. "The affair went on for a couple of months, and then she dumped me for a dancer," reported Jill after the breakup. "My heart was broken, but it was worth every second. I didn't have a clue about sex with a woman, and probably wasn't very good."

For the straight women in the troupe, Marga was our first open encounter with a lesbian. Even during the fling with Jill, Marga used her exuberant charm to shamelessly flirt with all the women in the cast. Greg, Marga's character, was so cute that Ellin left the stage panting after their romantic scenes. "It was funny," said Ellin, "because she was playing a male lady-killer onstage." And backstage, she was acting like a kid in a candy store.

One night, I drove Marga home from one of our disco parties. During the ride we laughed and joked around. I pulled up in front of her place; she looked over at me with those big brown eyes, seductively smiled, and asked if I wanted to come in. I was stunned, not only by the invitation, but by the butterflies in my stomach. Flattered, I still declined. I didn't see her register any rejection. She seemed amused and turned on by the chase.

With two weeks left of the summer run, Betsy announced she was leaving to join a performing troupe traveling down the Mississippi River. It was an exciting opportunity for her, but I groaned inside. That meant I would have to fill in the gaps left by her absence.

At a going-away party, the cast and crew surprised Betsy with a wristwatch. The parting gift had a special meaning; at every rehearsal Betsy would ask, "What time is it?" over and over. After she gleefully strapped on the watch, we had fun ribbing her all evening: "Betsy, what time is it?"

As the party wound down, I asked her, "So are you coming back?" It was more of a plea than a question.

"Of course," she laughed. She assured me that the river gig was only for the summer, and she would be back in the fall.

The future of *Curtains!* was already in question before Betsy left, but Lynn Gamble dispelled all doubt in her review for the *San Francisco Bay Guardian*. First she noted the overall intent:

> *The sheer lunacy of* Curtains! *and the spirited enthusiasm of the cast make for an amusing evening. If you've had your fill of women's theater groups, rest assured that, as Featherstonehaugh puts it, this is not another "feminist turkey."*

But then she pointed out the weak spots in the script and cut to the chase: "If the first act were shortened and the mystery reworked, many of the problems would be resolved."

The critique confirmed what we already knew, but at this point we were too bored to rewrite *Curtains!* On the other hand, collective restlessness left little patience to spend another whole year writing a new play.

We had submitted the script of *Peter Pan: A Rock Fairytale* to the New York American Playwrights Theater hoping it would be accepted for a New York staging. It was rejected. They responded that although they liked the story, it was too crude for them. On the other side of the coin, our experiment of dropping bawdiness from *Curtains!* engendered the opposite audience feedback. Friends liked the show, but complained that it was too tame. Fans preferred the off-the-wall, raunchy stuff to this new subdued approach.

I gave this conflicting criticism some hard thought. The *Curtains!* script avoided our usual comic innuendo and outrageous puns, but the process of writing it had strengthened our skills as playwrights. Why not use those skills to revise *Peter Pan: A Rock Fairytale?* The establishment wasn't buying our brand either way, so why shouldn't we just do our thing and let them catch up? We desired legitimacy and grant money, but if we lost our identity, what was the point?

❧

This getting serious stuff was no fun; so fuck it. Les Nickelettes reclaimed our social anarchistic reputation with a smoky, sweaty, jungle-juiced disco party: The Fifth Annual Salmon Awards. Filet of Soul and Tuna Turner sang, "Embrace the Swim Upstream." Red Snapper and Marlin Brando urged participants to experience, "Spawn Fever." We danced all night to the music of the Teenage Fakes and even threw in a cockroach striptease.

Sandra Rider from the *Theatre Bay Area* newsletter *Callboard* chronicled the event:

> *Les Nickelettes are a theatrical anomaly. . . . The presentations were in keeping with Les Nickelettes' tradition for frivolity and silliness. . . . I loved it! But Les Nickelettes are not for everyone. Described by one critic as "juvenile," they readily admit, "He may be right."*

I was jarred out of my adventures in Les Nickelettes by an alarming family event. My mother, a force of unstoppable energy even in her late fifties, was diagnosed with a brain aneurysm that required immediate surgery. I was scared. But Mom told me not to worry. "It's nothing dear, just a little brain surgery."

I took her at her word and went into such denial that I decided to wait until the operation was over to go to the hospital. I deluded myself by envisioning popping into the recovery room post-surgery for a cheery visit with Mom. But as the surgeon attempted to repair the delicate aneurysm, it burst, and she almost died on the operating table. The doctor saved her life by quickly clamping the artery, but the rupture caused a major stroke. My spunky, workaholic mother was left with a partially paralyzed body, so weakened on the left side that her left arm was rendered almost useless.

My sister, Ruth, told me that before they wheeled her into the operating room Mom looked afraid and vulnerable like a little child. My family thanked God that she survived, but with weeks of hospitalization and months of rehabilitation ahead, we dared not think about her future. At first she couldn't talk but slowly gained a slurred speech. The first question she asked was, "When can I go back to work?" The doctor informed her she wouldn't ever be able to return to work as a nurse, a profession she loved.

My mother eventually regained the ability to walk with a cane, but the feisty, independent woman who raised me was now disabled and helpless. I could only allow the physical and psychological changes in my mom to permeate my consciousness a little at a time, but they had a profound effect on me. Back in 1973, when she attended Les Nickelettes' *Mother Show,* I failed to grasp her influence as my Nickelettes role model. Now, five years later, I realized that her brazen, off-color sense of humor lay beneath my own comic sensibilities.

As a child I had observed her speaking her mind freely, even if it differed from male opinions and embarrassed everyone in the room. Her bantering was brash and sometimes a little raunchy. And she talked incessantly, carrying on conversations with anyone and everyone. It didn't do any good to tune her out, as my father, a man of few but succinct words, often tried to do. During my teenage years, as I inherited my father's quiet, reserved personality, I sometimes wanted to yell at my mom, "Shut up!" But I never did.

Mom was no Harriet Nelson or Donna Reed, the iconic 1950s housewives I saw portrayed on TV. The only figure she resembled was Lucy Ricardo on *I Love Lucy.* Mom was a schemer like Lucy, always hatching a new plan or two. And like Lucy, I think she had a dream of breaking into show biz. Shortly before she became pregnant with me, she had a professional portrait done hoping to launch a modeling career. This beautiful, airbrushed studio photo captured her in a low-cut bodice with a hint of cleavage, dreamy eyes cast out to castles in the clouds, and golden-blond-highlighted hair cascading over a creamy bare shoulder. Whatever hopes she invested in this headshot derailed after she became pregnant with me.

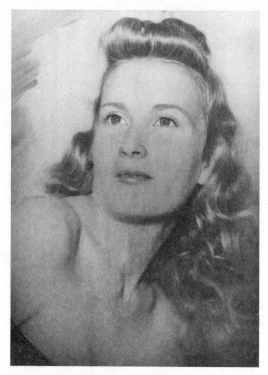

Portrait of Dorothy, my mom

Also, like Lucy, she was the wife of a musician, sort of. My dad managed and played in the Melloaires, a small band that gigged at local high school dances. Like Ricky Ricardo, he was a handsome devil, but whether he actually played the big stand-up bass fiddle was debatable. He ran the fingers of one hand up and down the strings and strummed with the other, so it looked like he was playing.

We lived in the Los Angeles suburb of Torrance, just a hop, skip, and jump away from the fame and fortune of Hollywood. When I was a toddler, Mom's grand scheme switched to getting her kids into show business. But I wasn't the one groomed for stardom. My nine-year-old sister Ruth became the designated singing and dancing protégé. Tom, my seven-year-old brother, was next, and at three, I trailed at the back of the pack (my

I'm three years old wearing the
acrobat costume that Mom made

two-year-old brother, Steve, was too young). Mom enrolled
Ruth, Tom, and me at the Betty Thomas Dance Studio for tap
dance, acrobat, baton, and singing lessons. Ruth's signature
song and tap dance number was "Put Your Shoes On, Lucy."
She and I teamed up in an acrobat act, each of us wearing an
identical funky two-piece sequin costume that Mom sewed.
Tom sang "I'm Little But I'm Loud," and he and I did a duet
tap dance to "The Bells Are Ringing." Our family troupe performed at amateur nights, state mental hospitals, and if there
was a supermarket opening, we were there.

My parents befriended local celebrity hillbilly singer
Walkin' Talkin' Charlie Aldrich on the pancake breakfast circuit where we were doing our acts, and he was singing his local
hit single, "Walkin' the Guitar Strings." Charlie had a weekly
show on country-western television station KTTV-LA called
The Walkin' Talkin' Charlie Aldrich Show. Television in the
early 1950s was in its infancy, so daytime hours featured more

local programing than today. Charlie invited us kids to be on his variety program. Shows were live with no tape replay, so we didn't get to see ourselves on TV; only a few grainy photos snapped directly off the screen of a tiny black-and-white set survived as proof of our debut.

Following this appearance on TV, and right before my fourth birthday, I experienced the biggest show biz event of my life so far. "Here's little Denise Larson, the youngest person ever on a float in the Santa Claus Lane Parade," Walkin' Talkin' Charlie Aldrich breathlessly announced to the crowd. I was tied to a pole on the front of a float and told to hold the pose of a majorette: left leg raised and bent, baton cradled in the right arm, and left arm reaching for the stars. "Smile, Denise, smile," Mom continually prompted me as she ran alongside the float the entire three-and-a-half-mile parade route, carrying my two-year-old brother on her hip. She cheered me on and made sure I was okay.

Our show-business life continued with Mom driving Ruth tirelessly around the Los Angeles area to dance concerts and contests. Although I was too young to participate, she often took me along, too. Mom watched over Ruth's performances as I sat alone in the theater wings transfixed by the backstage scene: performers going on and off stage, unlit set pieces resting against the back wall, a dusty curtain that got hoisted up over-head, and a crew silently moving props in the dark. I even recall the alluring musty smell. These backstage images were etched in my memory as one of my earliest childhood remembrances.

By the time I started kindergarten, Mom had to go back to work because of money problems. The lessons and performing tapered off. There was also some adult dispute with the Betty Thomas Dance Studio that I was too young to understand. On top of that, Ruth moved into her preteen years and, although she still loved to do her tap dance routine, concluded that per-forming at pancake breakfast shindigs in supermarket parking lots was no longer cool. Like many show biz dreams, ours fizzled out.

During my mother's convalescence, for the first time, I connected these early family experiences to my current life as a theater performer. I understood where, when, and by whom the seed had been planted. It took almost losing her for me to link my show biz aspirations to my mom.

~~~

Betsy returned from her summer adventure. She liked the idea of reviving *Peter Pan: A Rock Fairytale* but itched to do something new. "Let's do a camped-up version of *The Women*."

The Women was a 1936 Broadway play, and a 1939 movie, written by Clare Boothe Luce and featuring an all-female cast. The story revolved around bitchy, gossipy women stealing each other's husbands. The part that tickled Betsy the most was that much of the play took place at a dude ranch in Reno with the New York socialites waiting out the six weeks necessary for their divorces. In an effort to bolster this proposal, Betsy told us of a visit to New York City after her Mississippi River experience: "In New York, Charles Ludlam's Ridiculous Theatrical Company do campy takeoffs of well-known stories. And it's very popular. We could do *The Women* and make it hysterically funny."

I disagreed. "We shouldn't copy the Ridiculous Theatrical Company. If we're going to do something new, we should develop our own original material."

"Okay," said Betsy, "then let's do our own story with cowgirls on a dude ranch."

Still skeptical, I said, "If we do a new show, it will delay working on *Peter Pan*. This is what we always do, jump into a new project and present it before it's ready."

Betsy didn't back down. "We can still rewrite *Peter Pan*. But at the same time, we just sketch-out a quick outline for a soap opera serial, and then do a live improvisation with an audience."

"It could be fun," interjected Jane.

"And we do need to have some fun," seconded Ellin.

I agreed that getting back to our roots with newly acquired writing skills would be an interesting experiment. "But not cowgirls—something more topical."

Star Wars had opened the previous year, but it was still all the rage. Fans lined up to see the movie four, five, ten times. George Lucas revealed that *Star Wars* was the first in a trilogy, and there was speculation about what would happen in future episodes. Lucas further disclosed that he based his sci-fi adventure on ancient Western myths.

"Yeah, the age-old story of good versus evil with the male hero saving the world for the beautiful princess," I commented. "*Star Wars* has just one major female role, what's up with that?"

"Yeah, and her hairdo is a pair of cinnamon buns, what's up with that?" cracked Jane.

"Maybe we could create a new sci-fi myth starring a woman," said Betsy.

"Space cadet heroines flood the universe!" Ellin chortled. "Oh, maybe throw in one token male."

We all laughed.

"But let's not make it trite," I continued, "with the man being the bad guy. It would be juicier to have a real villainous woman."

"Les Nickelettes take on the cosmos," declared Ellin. "First there was *Star Trek*, then there was *Star Wars*, and now . . . *Spaced Out!*"

I dove into researching ancient mythology. Other myths existed before the Greek and Roman hero adventures depicting a young male on a quest to prove his strength and manhood. Prehistoric European cultures had matriarchal myths that revolved around the Great Goddess or Mother Earth as the creator of all things. The Great Goddess had a triple aspect that represented the cycle of life: birth (the virgin), love and maturity (the mother), and death and rebirth (the crone). Each aspect had myths and rituals associated with it. Starting around 4300 BCE, patriarchal imperialistic peoples invaded the peaceful agricultural villages of Old Europe and destroyed or assimilated these early cultures.

This research took root deep in my subconscious. I pulled out a well-worn copy of *Archetypes and the Collective Unconscious* by psychologist Carl Jung. "In 1971 I studied Jung when I played the role of the virgin archetype in a play called *The Rites of Passage*," I explained to Betsy.

Betsy, in turn, shared her experience with the writings of Jung. "My parents always had a copy of *Man and His Symbols* on the coffee table, and Jung was like a priest to us. It was our religion as much as anything. So I grew up knowing about archetypes."

"Jung's theories help me to understand the personification of myth in the virgin and mother aspects of the Great Goddess," I said, "but the crone baffles me. She's wise and kind like a benevolent grandmother, but then causes havoc with death and destruction."

"Yeah, like Mother Nature at her most vicious."

"An archetype that destroys life to create new life."

I did more research. The folklore told of a powerful crone who was both revered and feared. The invading patriarchal tribes seeking power had to annihilate her to seize control of the ancient matriarchies. Betsy and I were so intrigued by this enigmatic archetype that she became the star of the new show.

We outlined a feminist sci-fi story with an evil megalomaniacal crone threatening the human species. Fighting this menace was a heroine rebel figure who, with the help of the Great Mother spirit, vanquished the villainous crone and gave birth to a female child (the virgin) destined to save humankind. We placed *Spaced Out*'s satire in the action of space cadets battling the over-the-top vile shrew. "You can't take megalomaniacs too seriously," commented Ellin.

Betsy's day job was as an artist-in-residence teaching theater to elementary school children. One evening, at a brainstorming session, she recounted a story about her second-grade students. She had assigned them to create their own play. "Of course, they wanted to do *Star Wars*," she explained. "And one kid came up with a character for the play: Ella Vader, the ex-wife of Darth Vader."

"We *have* to use that name for our megalomaniacal crone!" I exclaimed.

"We're not above ripping off juvenile second-grade puns?" asked Betsy.

"Absolutely not," replied Ellin.

"The ex-wife of Darth Vader, we'd never have come up with that." I laughed.

"Ella Vader. Pure genius," concluded Jane.

We wrote a rough draft for the serial—divided it into six sections—and then each week, we more or less winged it in front of an audience. Betsy got the plum role of Ella Vader. "Playing a vile megalomaniac was the most fun I ever had," mused Betsy. Everyone had a blast. We hammed it up in silly space battles using silver spray-painted hair dryers as laser guns. It was like old times letting our imaginations go wild ad-libbing on stage. Although I had resisted doing this impromptu project, in the end, I conceded it revved up our creative juices.

1978 saw the explosion of home video technology. Personal video cameras were expensive and cumbersome, but Les Nickelettes saw a whole new potential for low-budget video production. We couldn't afford to buy one of the new cameras, but Betsy's friend Steve Christiansen possessed one. She coaxed

Me and Jane battle aliens with
our laser hair dryers in Spaced Out

him into making a recording of Les Nickelettes. *The Camp Performance*, a compilation of Nick skits filmed in a couple of hours, provided us with a twenty-minute video that could be used to promote the group.

Betsy also had another motive for initiating this project. "I was so in love with Steve Christiansen," she confessed, "I could hardly see straight. But working on *The Camp Performance* was an experience in semi-unrequited love. Pining after Steve, I asked him, 'What do you think of the show?' He replied, 'Why do you need my approval?' Even though I was in charge, I wanted a man to validate me." Being a feminist didn't inoculate you against being a fool for love.

I saw friends like Betsy struggling to find satisfying relationships, but I was secure in mine. Vince and I were happy together, and he continued to support my work with Les Nickelettes. Despite my evolution as a woman's libber, I liked having a man to validate me.

CHAPTER 8

PETER PAN CATCHES
A NEW WAVE

"Groupies in Bondage"

I t was time for me to take charge and direct the new production of *Peter Pan*. If Betsy could do it, so could I. The
courage I'd gained from being in an all-women group helped to
shut out the nattering inner voice placed in my head by college
theater professors: "Directing is men's work." Also bolstering
my confidence was the anticipation of a continued partnership
with Betsy as we reversed the roles of producer and director.

But Betsy had other plans. She was off to Oregon to work
on a theater project with her heartthrob Steve Christiansen.
Les Nickelettes couldn't compete with impulses driven by
blind lust. Before she left, I picked her brain—faithfully scrib-
bling down notes she passed on to me from her experience
directing *Curtains!*

Next, I turned for advice from the only other woman director I knew, Sharon McNight. Sharon and I not only shared a
college experience, but were also both influenced in high school
by Central California culture: she in Modesto, and I just twenty
miles south, in Manteca.

"The only directing I've done was at age fourteen," I told Sharon. "I didn't get cast in the plays at Manteca High School, so during the summer, I organized the neighborhood kids to perform in a play I wrote. But the directing was a means to an end. The whole point was to create a starring role for myself."

Sharon laughed knowingly at my story and shared that her theater calling also started as a teenager in Modesto, writing and directing plays for children. But it was a college production of *The Wizard of Oz* where she cut her teeth on directing.

I asked her, "What guidance can you give me as a first-time director?"

"They don't expect a woman to be in charge, so at first they don't take you seriously," she advised. "When I started out, I learned real fast how to swear and smoke and be tough."

"And then they took you seriously?" I asked.

"That's right. They're not used to a woman knowing what she wants. Even now when I walk into a gig for my cabaret act and tell the tech guy that I need a stage light moved, they just stare at me like I don't know what I'm talking about." She let out a guffaw. "So I order them to get the ladder, and tell 'em I'll do it."

"Ha! So then I suppose they call you a troublemaker and a bitch?"

"Right. But when you're the leader of the pack, you gotta take the heat if you want to get the job done."

After talking with Betsy and Sharon, I recalled a favorite childhood book, *The Little Engine That Could*, and visualized that determined little train puffing its way to the top of the mountain. Then I sat down and organized a methodical plan of action to make *Peter Pan* the best Nickelettes show ever.

My first step was to upgrade Les Nickelettes' professional profile by moving our administrative operations from my apartment to an office in the Women's Building. In 1979, the San Francisco Women's Center, founded to nurture grassroots women's projects, fulfilled their dream of creating the first women-owned and operated community center in the country by purchasing a four-story stucco building on 18th Street between Valencia and Guerrero and naming it the Women's Building. We rented fifty square feet of office space in a large, open room shared with four other women's groups for a mere $25 per month. It wasn't much, but it was a legitimate address.

I wasn't sure Les Nickelettes would be accepted by the other tenants, but after performing our specially written sketch, *Off-the-Women's Room Wall,* at the official opening celebration, we were warmly welcomed by this diverse cross-section of the women's community, and it made us feel all warm and fuzzy inside.

So, when we were invited by the Fort Mason Foundation to take part in *Perspectives on Women in the Performing Arts*: *Women's Use of Humor in Art,* we were stoked. Advertising for the event promised that three feminist theater troupes ". . . will perform scenes and analyze women's use of humor and political satire." The fact that *three* all-women's performing groups thrived in San Francisco was a radical political statement in itself.

First to perform was It's Just a Stage, representing the perspective of an emerging lesbian voice. Next, Lilith presented the viewpoint of the political feminist theater movement. Last, posturing as glam punks for women's liberation, Les Nickelettes performed a politically incorrect skit gleefully poking fun at current cultural trends including feminists and lesbians.

The only response to our antics from the predominately female audience was an embarrassed chuckle here and there. During the post-performance discussion, we were asked, "Why are you perpetuating female stereotypes that only make women look silly and frivolous?"

"We're having the last laugh, on our own terms," I responded.

"Our motive is to explode out of a marginalized compartment by deliberately mocking female stereotypes," added Ellin.

The members of the other performing groups shook their heads in disgust. It seemed our feminist sisters wanted to pigeonhole female humor into a tight box.

~⁓⁓

If you can't get no respect from your peers, there's always reality TV. Before *America's Got Talent*, before *American Idol*, even before *Search for the Stars*, there was *The Gong Show*.

In 1979, *The Gong Show* was one of the most popular programs on television. Chuck Barris, the shrewd but goofy creator and host of this talent contest presented performing acts ranging from very good to deliberately awful. A panel of three judges rated each act from one to ten and awarded the act with the most votes a cash prize. The gimmick of the show was that unforgivably bad routines were eliminated from competition mid-act by a judge banging on a gigantic gong with a large padded hammer. The reverberating gong-tone cued corny rejection music, and the performer either wilted or loudly protested. If Chuck Barris Productions was seeking quirky and outrageous acts, Les Nickelettes had a leg up.

After sending in our videotape, we were invited to audition in Los Angeles. Jane, Ellin, Mary, and I hopped on a plane heading south, a day ahead of the tryout. LA resident and ex-Nickelette Debby Marinoff met us at the airport and whisked us off to her cozy bungalow. As a La La Land native, Debby expertly navigated the streets of LA and soon had us in stitches as she expertly mocked pretentious Hollywood.

Besides letting us crash at her apartment, Deb also graciously offered her artist's studio space to rehearse our audition piece. We worked the song and dance until we could do it in our sleep. "No Nose Nanook," originally written for the Cockettes by Scrumbly Koldwyn and Martin Worman, was an upbeat Cab Calloway-style number. We chose it because of its brevity (they only give you ninety seconds), and because it was not likely to be gonged. "It's cute," Ellin pointed out, "always a crowd-pleaser. And most importantly it's one of the few numbers in our repertoire that won't offend the men who run the show."

The next day, we ventured out on the streets of Southern California in a rental car and were beset by a barrage of honking horns. Driving in La La Land was like jumping out of a warm, safe fish bowl into a cold shark tank. "The meek may inherit the earth," chimed in Ellin, "but they will never make a left turn in LA."

On a rundown street off Sunset Boulevard, we parked and hunted for the address. On one side of the street was a hofbrau—that's not it. Could it be the peepshow across the street? No. Then we spotted it—a low wooden building with the faded words "World of Imports" still visible across the front.

"Yep, this is the place where all our dreams of stardom will come true," I snidely observed.

In a tiny bathroom, we changed into our Alaskan arctic winter costumes. Jane, singing lead, wore a black fur coat, woolen scarf, and carried a white fur muff. Ellin, Mary, and I, as the backup chorus, were dressed in leotards, black mini-Danskin skirts hemmed with white fur, and matching bellboy hats. Waiting for our turn while sitting on plastic folding chairs—in a room devoid of decor, under the flat glare of fluorescent lights—felt more like hanging out at a Greyhound bus station than the start of a big Hollywood break. We were called in, did our ninety seconds, and that was that. No smiles, no chuckles, no reaction, nothing. Good-bye. Next.

Much to our surprise, after returning to San Francisco, we got a call that we had been selected to be on the show. "But for consideration you have to come to the Barris Productions office in two days for a callback audition. It's just a formality."

We'd just finagled time off from our day jobs to make the first LA trip, but hey, sometimes the desire for stardom forces you to call in sick. This time, the instructions were to appear at a small corporate building on Sunset Boulevard. The show's musical director, Milton DeLugg, impressed us by playing our song perfectly the first time through. Two women sat behind a table and timed the song at exactly a minute and a half on a huge digital timer—so far, so good.

But then the head matron of the production staff told us we couldn't sing "Too much snortin' / Too much cavortin'." "No drug references," she explained and suggested, "too much sportin'."

Yuck. Furthermore, she nixed the lyric "In the land of the Midnight Sun / There're six months of midnight fun," because, "People will think it refers to fucking."

So? We were brusquely dismissed before we could protest. On our way out, we got some good news from the receptionist. We scored a slot on the nighttime version of the show, and win or lose, we would be paid union scale.

On Sunday, August 12, at eight in the morning, we signed in for our *Gong Show* taping. Not used to being anywhere so early, we stumbled bleary-eyed into a large warehouse studio, only to learn that the grueling all-day schedule involved taping three shows back to back. Morning: rehearsal for thirty acts in order of appearance. Break for lunch. Afternoon: tape the three shows—ten acts each, bam, bam, bam. A production assistant informed everyone that no one could leave the waiting area except for rehearsal or taping. Even if we had to use the bathroom, one of the assistants needed to tag along.

"We're inmates," I complained. "If we don't get scheduled until the third show, we'll be incarcerated all day."

"How will I keep my glitter eye shadow fresh?" fretted Mary.

"Does anyone have any drugs?" asked Jane.

At nine a.m., the lineup for the three shows was posted, and Les Nickelettes were at the top of the list. "We're number one, we're number one," we softly chanted. An assistant led us to the soundstage for rehearsal. Half awake, we could barely fathom that we were about to kick up our high heels before ten in the morning.

After the run-through, Chuck Barris nixed the middle part of our number, saying, "It's too long."

I looked at Jane, rolled my eyes, but said nothing. Backstage, after being dismissed, I fumed, "First we have to cut a three-minute song to ninety seconds, then they make us change the lyrics, which changes the whole meaning of the song, and now they cut it down to sixty seconds."

"Choreography changes at the eleventh hour," moaned Ellin. "It's too early in the morning for this."

"Well, what are we going to do, walk out?" asked Jane.

"We can't walk out on a chance to be seen by millions on national TV," said Mary.

I groaned. "So this is what they call selling out."

After they served the performing inmates lunch, the taping began. We were the first act escorted out of the warehouse studio. We wouldn't return. Hidden behind the curtain we could feel the palpable electric atmosphere emanating from the boisterous throng of three hundred audience members. Chuck appeared center stage in his trademark top hat and whooped, "First up is a phenomenal act from San Francisco, California—Les Nickelettes." And we were on! For one minute, we give 110 percent. The audience cheered, and Chuck cut to a commercial break. Mary bounced up and down, "I want to do it again! I want to do it again!"

Chuck turned to Ellin and asked, "Was it worth the trip?"

"Wait till we see the score," Ellin replied.

Back on air, Chuck introduced the judges: George Lindsay, Joanie Summers, and Pat McCormick. We'd never heard of any of them, but they each gave us a ten for a total of thirty, the best possible score. In response we grinned, clapped like crazed over-the-moon contestants, and skipped offstage.

After our hearts stopped pounding, we settled in to watch the competition. We applauded Punkenstein, a white-faced mime/dancer with sunglasses—the judges not so much. We snickered at Joe Dynamite, a plastic kind of Las Vegas lounge act, who sang "Please Release Me." Joe was followed by a jazz singer performing "The Lady Is a Tramp," and she scored a thirty. "She's really good," commented Jane. Next up was a male disco band, the lead singer adorned in a silver lamé outfit with flashy fringe. They got the audience cooking in their two-minute set, and also earned thirty points. "This is the one to beat," muttered Ellin.

In the event of a three-way tie, the judges determined the winner. The acts were brought back onstage for the big reveal of who would be awarded the cash prize of $712.05. With a flourish, Chuck announced, "Let's find out the judges' decision. The winner is . . . the disco band!" Balloons and confetti descended as we glued happy grins on our faces, and danced up a storm as instructed earlier by the backstage crew. Chuck cozied up to Mary and gave her a friendly pat on the butt. The curtain came down, and it was all over.

Freed at last from *Gong Show* incarceration, we walked out into a glum late afternoon rain. As we trudged through the gate, we passed the disco band. "I thought those girls were going to win," Ellin overheard one in their group say.

"Didn't the judges get the memo that disco is dying?" I lamented.

My sister, Ruth, lived in the LA area, and she and her family came to the taping. They were waiting for me in the parking lot. I planned to spend the night with them before flying back to

Me, Ellin, Mary, and Jane in our *Gong Show* outfits
Photo © Tom Copi

San Francisco. As I put my suitcase in the trunk of their car and crawled in the backseat, my five-year-old niece, Heather, told me, "You should have won." Later that evening, Heather followed me into the bedroom and made a beeline for my glitter high heels. Picking them up reverently, eyes shimmering with performance lust, she whispered, "They're beautiful."

We lost the big cash prize but didn't leave empty-handed. No siree, folks. We received consolation prizes in the mail. Jane hit the jackpot with $25 worth of TDK cassette tapes. Mary won $25 worth of shampoo, enough to wash her hair for a year. Ellin's prize of a full-year supply of Turtle Wax was turned into a gag gift at our next Salmon Awards Raffle. And lucky me, my envelope contained twenty-five $1 coupons for Cup O' Noodles, a windfall so pathetic even we wouldn't stoop so low to use it as a gag gift. We also received a SAG union scale check from Barris Productions for our appearance. Real money, but after taxes, it barely covered expenses for the three trips to LA.

Our *Gong Show* episode aired on November 1, 1979, but was preempted that night in the Bay Area, so we didn't see it until the rerun on March 30, 1980. Our friends agreed we were robbed, but by then Les Nickelettes had moved on.

<hr>

Peter Pan: A Rock Fairytale needed to be updated. *A Disco Fairytale* was proposed, but disco was dying a slow and painful death. The new rage was punk. Punk had bolted out of the UK and kicked everyone in the arse. It was raunchy and cocky, with half-naked sweating bodies leaping onstage, swearing in raw loud voices, "Up yours!" *A Punk Fairytale* sounded trendy, but our female spin on it didn't gel. Meanwhile, a new genre caught our ear. New wave was an experimental fusion of disco and punk-pop-synthesizer music. The sound was irreverent, arty, and appealed to us more than punk. I took out the *Peter Pan* poster from 1976, crossed out ~~Rock,~~ and wrote *Punk*, crossed out ~~Punk~~ and wrote *New Wave*; *Peter Pan: A New Wave Fairytale*.

Revisions to the *Peter Pan* script began with the writing collective rooting around for a stronger climax to the Battle of the Bands scene. "Peter singing 'Don't Grow Up, Baby' still works," I stated. "It exposes him as an ego-inflated rock star."

"Yeah," said Ellin, "it's deliberately awful, so he comes off as washed up."

"V. D.'s song is too tame," added Jane. "We need the Pirate Queen to come on strong."

"A new wave song that blows the competition away," continued Ellin.

We silently contemplated her proposal, but our imaginations stalled.

"Hey, did you see that Jello Biafra is running for mayor?" Ellin said, diverting the conversation to city politics.

"Only in San Francisco could you have a punk singer from the Dead Kennedys run for mayor," I laughed.

"And a drag queen," added Jane. "Sister Boom Boom from the Sisters of Perpetual Indulgence is also in the race."

"Not to mention Dennis Peron," continued Ellin. "He's probably the least ultra-progressive—he only wants to legalize marijuana."

"Unreal," I commented.

The press was having a field day with the shenanigans of these candidates. But the 1979 mayoral Democrat incumbent and front-runner Diane Feinstein, was not amused. Feinstein's reelection committee circulated a flyer that called the contenders "kooks."

"Look," I said, and pulled a flyer from my purse promoting Peron's campaign. The flyer had a photo of Diane Feinstein next to one of Dennis Peron under a banner of bright red letters that blared: "Is San Francisco becoming Kook City?" Under Dennis's image, in small letters, the campaign added: "Yes, and we are the kooks."

Ellin laughed, "What chutzpah."

"Kook City is a good nickname for San Francisco," chimed in Jane.

"It's also a great title for a song," added Ellin.

Within days Ellin wrote the lyrics for "Kook City," a terrific new wave song for V. D. to introduce in the Battle of the Bands scene. And it made Peter Pan's performance look like a dirty old sock:

I used to live in a little town
The people stared and put me down

I wasn't what they thought I should be
So I went to where they were more like me
I went to Kook City—It's got lots of hills
Kook City—The home of cheap thrills
Kook City—Where the weird people play
It's kind of strange, but I like it that way.

An homage to our beloved berg, it would go on to become Les Nickelettes' signature song.

~⁓~

After the script was completed, I plunged into my new role as director by holding auditions. Casting was half the battle, so I carefully weighed each candidate for individual strength, ensemble composition, and overall look of the production. From the many aspiring Nickelettes who showed up for the tryouts, I cast five.

Rhonda Zirkle bounded into the audition exhibiting super high energy. That, along with her athletic build and short brown androgynous haircut, assured me that I had found our Peter Pan.

A statuesque Lauren Cloud with long, thick blond hair commanded the stage and made her an easy choice for V. D. the Pirate Queen.

Virginia Lombard, physically squat with wild, black hair and a broad expressive face, was the visual antithesis of Lauren, and together they made an interesting pair of lovers. Virginia stepped into the role of the Pirate Queen's manager and partner, Sylvie Snatch.

Monika Gurney was young, just eighteen. Her clean-scrubbed youthfulness and buoyant personality put her on a fast track for the role of Wendy's prepubescent sister, Tammy.

Amy Ryder became an immediate shoo-in for the Tinkerbell part when she belted out her audition song. She was a hefty ball of spunk, and a singer strong enough to pull off the show-stopping

"Fairy's Lament." Jane had been a candidate for this part but chose to reprise the role of the rock impresario, Crock.

Although I had the last word in casting, I consulted with the collective core group on the choices. Ellin lobbied for Mary Valentino to play Trendy Wendy, the part Ellin originated in 1976. Mary read for the part of the hippie-dippy groupie flawlessly, and I agreed with Ellin's assessment. The last casting decision wasn't easy. Tiger Lily, a Native American activist, inexplicitly besotted by Peter Pan, represented the Nickelettes political viewpoint in the play. None of the other candidates from the audition had the right qualities for the character.

"Let's take another look at the audition resumes," I told the group, "to see if we missed anything."

Ellin uncharacteristically burst into tears, "There's no part for me!"

In my zeal to be the perfect director I had forgotten to cast Ellin. A glance at Jane confirmed my blunder. Ellin had given up the role of Wendy, and I should have immediately slotted her into another part. I had violated the sisterhood. Ellin was cast as Tiger Lily, and as things like these often turn out, she was excellent in the role.

Initial cast meetings were always a bit nerve-racking. I broke the ice by leading a series of non-threatening theater games. At the end, I announced that rehearsals would begin the following week after our annual fundraiser, the Sixth Annual Salmon Awards. I told the new cast, "If you want to see what you've gotten yourself into, you're invited."

"Can we perform?" asked Monika. "I could do a tap dance."

"Sure," I said taken aback by her boldness.

"I could sing a song," said Amy.

"Okay." I made a note to cross off "bashful" on my list of adjectives to describe these newbies.

Les Nickelettes kicked off the Sixth Annual Salmon Awards with our traditional number, "Come to the Salmon Awards," playfully teasing the audience with the lyric: "Could it be that this is art?" Amid the wafting odor of marijuana and the potent jungle juice for sale were dynamic performances by our performing friends: The Distractions, Ral Pheno, and Jane Dornacker as Leila the Snake.

The 1979 Martyr of the Year award went to Jane. I had won twice, Ellin once. Jane had campaigned relentlessly throughout the year and deserved the highly coveted satirical award. When her name was announced, Jane hammed it up by falling to the floor and crawling on all fours to the microphone in mock submission. Her acceptance speech was short: "It's about fucking time."

But the highlight of the evening was the first ever Fan of the Year award. We had begun to notice a heavyset man dressed in T-shirt and jeans with a long grey beard sitting front row center at every Nickelettes event. No one in the group knew him, but he always showed up. We found out his name was Art Grant, a quirky artist from Marin famed for his conceptual sculptures made out of ice, food, and repurposed junk. As he sat in his usual front row center seat enjoying the show, he had no idea of the honor coming his way. "And the winner of the Fan of the Year is . . . Art Grant!"

In a delighted daze, Art stumbled to the stage to claim his glitzy decorated secondhand trophy. "Thank you so much, Les Nickelettes," he mumbled.

Catherine Wurdack from *Boulevards* attempted to describe the Salmon Awards scene:

It's not punk. It's not Las Vegas. And it's not the Andrews Sisters. Les Nickelettes, an all-women's satire musical comedy/theatre group, almost defies description. Is it entertainment? Is it art? Is it Dada? Is it for real?

To our mind the Salmon Awards represented our true artistic statement. And, for the first time, we had a visual record of our "art." Vince had purchased a home video camera and inaugurated a new role for himself—Les Nickelettes' in-house videographer. Now, we got to rewind and view the spectacle for ourselves.

I got down to the business of directing the play and was pleased to watch the bright, energetic, and talented actresses develop their characters and bring everything to life.

Amy came on like gangbusters as bossy Tinkerbell, and Rhonda matched her intensity with a cocksure portrayal of Peter Pan. The pair took every zany direction I gave them in stride. But Rhonda balked at wearing a stuffed white athletic sock in Peter's crotch.

"I wore it when I played Peter in 1976," I pointed out, "and it worked. It's a vital, satirical symbol in the play."

"Yeah?" she replied.

I could see she wasn't convinced. "Yeah." I insisted.

At the next rehearsal, Rhonda showed up with a metal slinky stuffed in a knee-high sock. She clipped it to her crotch and when she unzipped her pants it bounced down to her ankles. The cast cracked up.

"Okay, sure," I said, still afraid it would undercut the satire.

One night, at the end of Peter's finale song, Rhonda let the slinky-sock drop to the stage floor then picked up the tip and extended it to her mouth using it as a mock microphone. As Peter sang the final line, "And remember baby, don't grow up," Ronda pantomimed a shuddering orgasm. It notched the parody up to another level and was outlandishly funny.

Mary's confidence soared in the role of Trendy Wendy. "I didn't have any problems with being an airhead," she explained. But there was one joke in the script she didn't get.

Ditzy Wendy explained her devotion to Peter Pan: "It's our karma to be together. The I Ching said, 'Walking through tall grass, male swinger desires golden showers.'" "What are golden showers?" Mary asked me.

I started to explain, "It's when a girl . . ."

Mary cut me off, "No, no, don't tell me." She understood ditzy.

Sometimes I felt more like a mother to teenager Monika than her director, but she had a natural talent. Monika's precocious, preadolescent character Tammy needed to tower over Wendy and Peter Pan, so, with Monika already fairly tall at five foot seven, I costumed her in three-inch platform shoes. But she clomped around backstage when she was supposed to be quiet. Mary told her repeatedly, "Walk softly, the audience can hear you." Monika ignored her. "Why won't you listen?" Mary persisted.

"I dropped out of high school because teachers like you tried to tell me what to do," replied Monika.

This was my first inkling that she was younger than I thought. The confirmation came when she invited the cast to her sweet sixteen birthday celebration. "Sixteen?" I said. "You told us you were eighteen."

"Oh, just a little white lie," she smiled.

Oh my God, we had cast a fifteen-year-old runaway. She bragged that she left home to become a professional actress. No wonder she convinced me she could play a fourteen-year-old going on twenty.

"My mom knows I'm living on my own in San Francisco," she assured me. "She says I'm too much to handle." Later, Monika reflected, "I was stridently independent and occasionally naïve." She was sixteen.

Jane, reprising the role of ruthless rock impresario Crock, and Ellin, in the role of Native American activist Tiger Lily, were doing the best work of their Nickelettes career. My only problem was the new wave pirates. Virginia's portrayal of Sylvie Snatch was coming along, but Lauren as V. D. the Pirate Queen was weak and Virginia expressed frustration with her partner. Lauren looked the part and had done a great audition, but she failed to grasp the feel of Les Nickelettes' underground fairytale style.

I scheduled extra rehearsals for the pirates. Lauren had majored in theater in college, so I gave her homework in character development, explaining that even though V. D. was an exaggerated cartoon character, she still needed to build the role in the same way as any other acting assignment. At the next rehearsal, her actions still came across as false posturing. Virginia took me aside, "She doesn't connect with me. There's nothing there."

With only two weeks of rehearsals to go, I crossed my fingers and promised Virginia, "We'll keep working on it."

A picture is worth a thousand words. And a video is worth dozens of directorial notes. I used Vince's video camera to tape a preview and played it for the cast the following evening. The pirate scenes stood out like a Jack O' Lantern on Christmas Eve. V. D. stepped onstage, and the play's energy sank like a rock.

The next day my phone rang off the hook. "This one actress is bringing the whole show down a notch," Ellin said. Jane echoed the sentiment, "Everything clicks except Lauren." Virginia called me three times. "I'm jumping through hoops, but Lauren still makes me look bad. You've got to get rid of her," she repeated, in case I hadn't heard her the first two times.

With less than a week before opening night I couldn't just snap my fingers and have a new actress ready to go. Complicating matters was the fact that Lauren and Amy were tight friends, and Amy's loyalty could lead to a showdown. I didn't want to risk losing a terrific Tinkerbell.

I scheduled an emergency cast meeting hoping to clear the air, but instead the atmosphere turned as smoggy as a toxic alert.

"My friends who came to the preview told me I was good," Lauren said defensively.

"You're ruining the show," Virginia replied, not hiding a seething desire to ax her.

"Virginia that's unfair," Amy said, sticking up for her friend. "She just needs a little more time. Give her another chance."

"No. She isn't cutting it," Virginia shot back.

"Enough," I cut in. "There's no time for a change, so let's pull together and do the best show we can. Lauren and I will work nonstop until opening night to make the character work." This bought me some time, plus an uneasy truce.

No more pussyfooting around. It was time to show Lauren exactly how to play V. D. I stepped into the critical "Groupies in Bondage" scene to model for her. With comically evil relish, I tied up the groupies and threatened: "Wendy, I'll force feed you Twinkies and Ho Hos, and you'll get so fat you'll be known as Good and Plenty Wendy, ha, ha, ha! As for you, Tammy, I'll put male repellant in your feminine hygiene spray!"

I finished, and she got up and played the scene like a one-dimensional cardboard cutout. I'm optimistic, but not stupid. All I could wish for was some kind of miracle.

Opening night the place was packed, and the crowd laughed and applauded with feisty vigor. The performers were ecstatic with this audience feedback. But it didn't alleviate the problem with Lauren. Instead, things got worse. Rubbing everyone the wrong way, she put on a prima donna show backstage. Why couldn't she transfer that performance to her role?

I had put my heart and soul into this project, and one person was ruining my joy. I tended to avoid confrontation, but I faced Lauren and said, "This role is not a good fit for you. I think—"

She cut me off, "Don't worry, I'm quitting after next weekend." What a relief.

Rhonda and Mary as Peter and Wendy

Photo © Tom Copi

The first review came from Barbara Graham of the *Bay Guardian*:

> Peter Pan *is outrageous, dirty, and very funny. Denise Larson has directed with vitality and freshness. . . . The right-on pop humor derives from the trendy and the timely and is positively superior.*

I was thrilled to get a shout-out for my first-time as a director in this positive review. At the cast party, I was flying high until Lauren waltzed up and told me she might change her mind and stay with the show. My mood plummeted, but I said nothing. Still my mind was made up.

A few days later Bernard Weiner from the *San Francisco Chronicle* put in his two cents:

> *Les Nickelettes' updated version of* Peter Pan . . . *exhibits the best and worst of this silly, wacky, delovable troupe of all-female amateurs . . .*

Here we go again; he insisted on describing Les Nickelettes as "amateurs." What will it take to break through the professional glass ceiling? This time, we pushed back. Ellin and I dashed off a protest letter to Mr. Weiner, scolding him for this persistent sexist put-down. We gave Bernard examples of our recent "professional" growth to bolster our argument: becoming a nonprofit corporation, producing successful original productions, and engagement in community activities. To our surprise Bernie replied. He admitted that using the term "amateurs" was ill advised, and wrote, "I shall endeavor to be a better boy in the future." I gave kudos to Bernard for a sense of humor.

Mr. Weiner's critique notwithstanding, we got our best reviews to date. Every show was standing room only with people begging for tickets, a problem I could live with.

～

I brought in Liza Kitchell (the piano player from the 1976 *Peter Pan*) to be musical director in the summer when I started rehearsals. She worked with the singers, added scene transition music, and wrote an overture that introduced the audience to the show's musical themes. But she had to return to the University of California at Santa Cruz in the fall to continue her classical music studies. I needed a piano player for the run of the show. Virginia volunteered her boyfriend, Ed Drake, and Liza taught him the music before she left. Ed was a laid-back mellow kind of guy who played the piano and didn't try to butt into the group dynamics.

On the Friday afternoon of Lauren's last weekend, I got ready to leave for the theater, looking forward to the fact that after Sunday night I wouldn't have to deal with her any more. The phone rang. Virginia's voice was frantic, "There's been an accident! Ed got hit by a car; he's in the emergency room at San Francisco General Hospital."

"What? Are you kidding?" I lamely sputtered.

"Both of his legs are broken and his pelvis is fractured," she cried.

"Oh my God, this is not happening," I replied in disbelief.

"It's true, it's true," screamed Virginia. "I'm at the hospital."

"Okay, okay," I said. "Calm down and tell me what happened."

Virginia took a deep breath, "Ed and I were crossing Guerrero Street and the stoplight changed to red and we got stuck on the strip between lanes. A speeding car came out of nowhere, jumped the median, and hit Ed. It just barely missed me." Virginia's voice shook with psychological shock. "I have to go, they're taking him to intensive care."

I had no other choice but to cancel the show that night. The trauma shifted me into a slow motion time warp. I couldn't stop thinking stupid thoughts like, *This is a joke, right?* The cast and crew freaked out.

"This is too real and grown up," commented Amy.

The following morning Virginia called to say that Ed had slipped into a coma and she was keeping a vigil at his bedside. I had to face the dilemma of what to do about that night's show. The age-old theater axiom kicked in that "the show must go on," but how? Our tiny theater company didn't have the luxury of understudies or backup musicians. There was only one person who could play piano for that evening's performance. I enlisted Ellin to contact Liza and beg her to come up from Santa Cruz, "Tell her we're desperate. Tell her she has to do it."

And there was only one person who knew Virginia's role well enough to take over at a moment's notice. I grabbed the script and frantically began memorizing Sylvie's lines.

Ellin called back and said Liza could do it, but she had no way of getting to San Francisco. I told her to find someone to drive down there and pick her up. I set up an emergency rehearsal with Lauren to go over the pirate scenes. Even as my adrenaline ramped up and I went into laser focus mode, I understood, after all the animosity and squabbles, the irony of having to step onstage and pretend to be Lauren's lover.

Going onstage with only a few hours preparation was the edgiest and scariest experience of my entire career. Acting face-to-face with Lauren clearly illuminated why Virginia was unhappy. It wasn't just that she wasn't right for the role—she wasn't on the team. Onstage, she made no effort to support me. In contrast, the others encircled me in collective solidarity. Even Amy assured me after the show, "You were perfect."

I held Lauren to her final week notice—sorry, no changing your mind. I had already set up an audition to replace her and eagerly anticipated the casting call. But when no one showed up, I despaired.

"Why not give Marga Gomez a call and ask her to take the part?" Ellin suggested.

"Good idea, Ellin."

Much to my relief Marga (from *Curtains!*) was available and came onboard. She stepped into the role and within a week captured dead-on the wickedly funny and cartoon satirical essence of the character.

Virginia was overjoyed to be working opposite Marga when she returned to the show. The other good news was that Ed was out of the coma, although he faced a long and arduous recovery.

Liza's piano playing was a perfect fit for the show, and I wanted her to stay until the end of the run. But she was ambivalent: "I was terribly nervous playing the piano for *Peter Pan*. I never felt like I had the chops." She told me to find another piano player. I made a halfhearted effort, but it didn't work out, and I talked Liza into staying. "I started coming up to the city on weekends on the Greyhound bus," said Liza, "and playing the *Peter Pan* show and then going back to school during the rest of the week. School began to suffer. I didn't like UC Santa Cruz, and I didn't like my classical piano teacher. I was having more fun in the city doing the shows with Les Nickelettes." It wasn't long before Liza dropped out of college.

With Marga in the role of V. D. the Pirate Queen and Liza on piano, everyone's spirit brightened. It was like Tinkerbell had sprinkled fairy dust over the whole production. The fun of performing returned. The show was a hit, and my dream of creating the best Nickelettes show ever had come true. People came back two and three times. The large crowds put the ledger in the black. We were so flush, we even gave the actresses a stipend.

"It was a big deal," said Mary. "Everybody was running around, saying: 'We get paid, we get paid!' We all got twenty-five bucks."

There's a saying: "Life is what happens to you while you're busy making other plans." Just as I was basking in Les Nickelettes' success, I got a disturbing call from my mom. My older brother, Tom, was in the hospital, diagnosed with terminal lung cancer. "The doctors said he has only a few weeks to live," my mom sobbed. Tom was thirty-six years old. Shock and denial hit me like a sledgehammer. I didn't cry, I didn't believe it—couldn't believe it. I put a pillow over my head and tried to zone out of this unreal reality.

I hadn't seen or heard from Tom in nearly a year. He had been severely shaken after our mother's brush with death and had disconnected his phone. Dad told me he was also struggling to hold on to his menial job. The family knew he was troubled. Several years earlier, he had been arrested for throwing bricks on a busy boulevard. His justification was that a car had recently struck a child on that street, and he was just trying to slow down traffic. On Christmas, he gifted my parents with four archery arrows, with the explanation: "You have four straight-arrow children." No one understood his odd behavior. Finally, a diagnosis of paranoid schizophrenia with manic-depression (now called bipolar) gave the family some clarification. But at the time, I had little understanding of this mental illness.

Tom came in and out of my life depending on his mood. One time, he showed up unannounced on my doorstep and stayed up all night, pacing the floor and discussing politics, community action, and history. The next morning he took off. Later, I phoned to see how he was doing, and he mumbled a few incoherent words and hung up. After his diagnosis, my parents urged him to follow the drug regimen prescribed by the doctor. But like many manic-depressives, he took the pills when depressed but stopped when the manic high set in. Tom also didn't take care of himself. He smoked three packs of cigarettes a day and ate only junk food.

I drove from San Francisco to San Jose to visit him in the hospital. I didn't know what to expect as I approached his bedside. The depth of his illness was disquieting. The meaning of "terminal" hit my senses like a nauseating whiff of rotten garbage. I put on a cheerful smile, but the visit became agonizing.

I visited as often as I could. Sometimes he would be his funny, sardonic self, making me laugh in spite of the situation. Other times he would be disoriented and delusional—ranting that the FBI was coming to take him away. Tom died ten days after he entered the hospital, and I was overcome with grief. The last time I saw him in intensive care, I sensed that he wasn't fighting anymore. He looked me in the eye and said, "Forget about me." My heart broke. I assured him that I would always love him and added the lie that everything would be okay.

It was the first time I'd lost a close relative. Through the funeral and months of grieving that followed, I struggled to grasp this enormous emotion of loss. Staying focused on the responsibility and commitments of Les Nickelettes kept me from being swallowed by the heartache of my brother's untimely death.

On the day my brother died, the saddest day of my life, Les Nickelettes received jubilant news. A letter from the California Arts Council announced that we had been awarded a grant of $1,000. Our first grant! I suspected that the reason this application had been successful was Betsy's letter of support to her friend Peter Coyote who was serving on the Arts Council. It was just a measly $1,000, but it gave Les Nickelettes a legitimacy that we hoped would buy us a ticket on that elusive government gravy train.

In an effort to master the corporate game needed to secure government grants, I took on the puffy title of administrative/ artistic director and attended workshops, symposiums, and conferences to get the hang of how to write winning grants. I was like a fish out of water at these predominately male seminars. And my eyes glazed over during long discussions of "boiler plates" and three-year projected budgets. Getting this CAC grant with a little insider help made me smarter about how these things really worked.

With renewed optimism for a National Endowment for the Arts grant, Ellin invited West Coast NEA representative, Mr. Robert Gordon, to a performance of *Peter Pan*. Unfortunately, his calendar was full during the play's run, but he did offer to meet with Ellin and me at his downtown hotel suite to discuss our pending application. I vowed not to blow it. I reminded myself that I had just directed a successful play and deserved to toot my own horn and not clam up like I had done in the past. It helped that I wasn't alone. Ellin was good at articulating the group's mission.

Mr. Gordon greeted us with an amiable smile and a warm handshake. He had a middle-aged salt-and-pepper moustache, and was dressed business casual in a blazer and shirt with no tie. Ellin broke the ice by chronicling Les Nickelettes' accomplishments. I bragged about *Peter Pan: A New Wave Fairytale*: "The message of the play is that a narcissistic rock star indulges in the juvenile notion of never growing up."

"And because he's a famous rocker he convinces his groupies to follow his lead," continued Ellin.

"The symbol of his out-of-control machismo is a large phallic sock in his crotch," I tittered.

"This large dick personifies the male dominance in our society and especially in the hugely influential culture of rock and roll," added Ellin.

"But we take it even further with a slinky inside the sock

so that it falls to his ankles and makes his bouncy male endowment look foolish."

I laughed. Ellin laughed. Robert Gordon didn't. Not even a smile.

"But our message is often misunderstood," Ellin quickly backtracked.

"Or misinterpreted," I added.

Mr. Gordon replied that he could see why people would think ridiculing big dicks was not funny.

We were our own worst enemies. Our inability to reframe our satirical feminist message with phony government babblespeak betrayed us once again. No NEA grant again this year.

The 1979 annual board of directors meeting had a roster of new faces. Ron Turner remained, but Bill Wolf, Jeffrey Tar Genza, and Sharon McNight resigned. Newly elected was Jean Taggart Born, from *Curtains!* Much to her delighted surprise, she was also chosen to be president. "I wanted to be in the zany Nickelettes whether I was cast in productions or not," Jean said as she accepted. The board also recruited and elected four new members: Michael Rudman, Rosalie Schmidt, Stafford Buckley, and Paul Reinhardt.

Ellin, Jane, and I informed the new board that we wanted to book an extension of our hit *Peter Pan: A New Wave Fairytale* after the holiday break. But there was a problem. Les Nickelettes, Inc. had received a cease and desist letter from Linden and Deutsch Attorneys at Law, London, England. The letter stated that they represented the Hospital for Sick Children, the copyright and royalty proprietors of *Peter Pan* willed to them by author J. M. Barrie. Apparently a patron at one of our performances had snitched on us. The attorneys demanded we stop production of the play and provide them with a complete statement indicating all previous productions. The board contacted

Bay Area Lawyers for the Arts (BALA) to assist with this legal crisis. BALA referred us to Mr. Bushnell, an attorney specializing in copyright infringement. He told us flat-out that we had infringed on the copyright and should capitulate to Linden and Deutsch's demands. We argued that it was a parody. Mr. Bushnell countered that it was too close to the original, but agreed reluctantly to call the attorneys in London on our behalf. He reported back that they stood by their original position. How hard he really tried was up for debate.

The board of directors deliberated about what to do next. Ron related his experience with the Air Pirates Case where Disney sued Dan O'Neill and Ron's company, Last Gasp. Dan had drawn a cartoon parody of a randy Mickey Mouse in an underground comic book that Last Gasp published. Ron settled out of court. Dan went all the way to the Supreme Court—who refused to hear his appeal—so, the judgment against him by the Ninth US Circuit Court of Appeals held. But, in the end, he never paid a dime. Ron cautioned, however, that with our nonprofit status, Les Nickelettes, Inc. would be a different case. Individual board members could be liable for a judgment against the organization. It was a lose-lose situation. If we settled, we could never do the show again. If we fought and lost, the board members could be held accountable.

Ellin consulted her father, Madison Avenue lawyer Monroe E. Stein, and he advised us to write a letter to Linden and Deutsch claiming the work was permissible parody under the rule of fair use, that we made no profits from the show, that our financial limitations precluded us from incurring legal fees, and that we had no intention of doing the show again. This strategy worked. But we had to sign a letter promising never to do the show again or use the title *Peter Pan* or any of the character names and send them all the copies of the script to be destroyed. We were off the hook legally, but our plans to re-launch the show were extinguished. Our mistake was not

changing the names of the characters. But this was Peter Pan—
that was the point. Caught and punished by the art police.
Ellin researched the copyright and learned it expired in 1985.
Well, screw them; we could still do the play after the copyright
expired. We surrendered the scripts, but they had not asked
for the videotape.

Les Nickelettes vowed that our next project would only
contain original material.

CHAPTER 9

SPACED OUT:
A SCI-FI MUSICAL

"She's mad! She's bad! She's Ella Vader!"

T he '80s. No one knew what to expect. The decade kicked
off at the 1980 Winter Olympics in Lake Placid, New
York. The United States hockey team pulled off an incredible
upset by snatching the gold medal away from the Soviet Union.
Mt. St. Helens, a volcano dormant for 123 years, unexpectedly
erupted in Washington State. *Star Wars Episode V: The Empire
Strikes Back* broke box office records with the startling revelation that Darth Vader was the father of Luke Skywalker. And
who could have predicted that the United States would elect
Ronald Reagan, a sixty-nine-year-old ex-Hollywood actor, to
be the nation's fortieth president? Sometimes the unexpected
is a gift from heaven and sometimes it's a goddamn kick in
the butt.

Les Nickelettes took advantage of the mania surrounding
The Empire Strikes Back to dust off our original sci-fi improv
sketch from 1978 and turn it into a full-length satirical musical.
This new production of *Spaced Out* adopted a 1980 motto:
"Expect the unexpected."

I phoned Betsy in Oregon. "Remember that improvised outer space show you talked us into doing a couple of years ago?" I asked.

"Yeah, I loved that show," answered Betsy.

"The Nicks are going to revise and expand it into a full-length musical to stage this fall."

"What a great idea! And guess what? I'm coming back to San Francisco in April. I would love to direct it."

"That makes sense—it was your baby."

"And I think you should play the part of Ella Vader."

"Wow, cool. I've been itching to perform again. I learned so much about acting from being a director. Playing Ella Vader will be off the charts."

What an unexpected turn of events. I couldn't wait for Betsy to return to the group.

Spaced Out, Les Nickelettes' tale of outer space romance, revolution, and kelp, was rooted in female myth. An archetypical evil crone, Ella Vader, ruthlessly controlled the citizens of Califia, a planet she received in her divorce settlement from Darth Vader. Califia came from a legend we read about on how California got its name. In the folktale, a Black Queen Califia ruled a society of female Amazons on the Island of California. The Amazons occasionally sailed to other islands to mate with males and become impregnated. If the child was female she was nurtured and welcomed into the tribe. If the child was male, he was killed. This practice prevented a male takeover. Whoa, don't mess around with these Amazons. Thus, the plucky heroine we invented to defeat Ella Vader's repressive regime on Califia was named Amazonia.

206 ★ ANARCHY IN HIGH HEELS

Cataclysmic floods devastated Califia, and when the waters receded, the sole food source for the population was kelp. Ella controlled the kelp farms. She sprinkled her newly invented powdered male contraceptives on the seaweed to insure compliance with her ban on all human reproduction outside her notorious insemination banks. When Ella got wind of an insurgency, she additionally dosed the kelp with a mind control drug. Things looked bleak. But Amazonia, invoking the vulva salute, conjured up the mama seaweed spirit, Yerba Buena. Yerba Buena inspired Amazonia and her intrepid Space Cadets to overthrow Ella and make Califia safe for human, plant, and mutant alike. After toppling Ella Vader, Amazonia gives birth to a female child, a fusion of human and plant life. The Kelp Child gave hope to a new beginning: "I'm a plant, but I'm going places!" Peace and balance were restored to the universe.

Being precast as Ella Vader gave me an inside edge on the development of the script. The others in the writing collective argued that they deserved the same advantage. I pointed this out to Betsy, and we collaborated over the phone on casting decisions. Core members Jane, Ellin, and Mary, plus two newbies from *Peter Pan*, Virginia and Monika, were precast.

Ellin fit the mold of the Space Cadets' fastidious electronics expert, Garleeka Mundane.

Jane snagged the role of the vitamin-strength B-12, a Space Cadet android.

Virginia took on the dual role of Dede Day-Glo, the proprietor of the Intergalactic House of Kelp by day, and Amazonia, the secret leader of the Space Cadets by night.

Mary begged to be cast as Reggie Von Veggie, the male illicit lover of Amazonia. "I played airhead Trendy Wendy and now I want to stretch," pleaded Mary. Betsy hesitated. It was hard to imagine Mary, the quintessential female archetype, in the role of a man, but she finally acquiesced.

Monika wanted the part of W-2, Ella Vader's android

henchman. This became sticky. Monika was sixteen years old. Betsy didn't think she was experienced or nuanced enough for the role. After a back-and-forth debate, plus intense lobbying by Monika, we decided to let her do a try-out in the planned spring workshop presentation, and afterwards Betsy would make the final decision. That left just two parts to be cast at later auditions: Barbi Cue, chief medical officer for the Space Cadets, and Yerba Buena, the mythical spirit of seaweed.

Betsy returned in April, and we staged the *Spaced Out* rough draft as a work-in-progress in front of a live audience. We had no music yet, so Betsy brought in Liza to view the play in anticipation of writing and arranging the music. Then, in a brilliant move, Betsy sweetened the pie by asking Liza to perform in a few walk-on parts, despite the fact that she had no acting experience. "I wanted to, strangely enough," said Liza. "It just sounded really fun."

Putting Liza inside the action helped her pinpoint the places in the story that could be told in song. And she admitted, "Being in the show made me more committed to Les Nickelettes." It also nurtured musical collaboration. All the actresses contributed to writing lyrics, but Liza and Ellin developed a special partnership during the process. "I liked working with Ellin," said Liza. "But we really could get in there and slug it out."

Ellin loved to spar, and their clashes produced good songs. One of the most powerful was sung by the Space Cadets, "Twenty-Fifth Century":

We're not going to be kept down
We won't always be underground
We are going to break the chains,
We don't want no chains on our brains.

Ellin's journalistic career had been building since 1977. Her first job was as a theater critic for the *Berkeley Barb*. Recently her reviews appeared in *Boulevards*, an alternative newspaper in San Francisco. In early 1980, she heard that the theater critic for the *San Francisco Chronicle* was leaving and jumped at the chance to interview for the job. She was on cloud nine the day she was hired. I congratulated her on the coup. But the position created a conflict of interest as a performer with Les Nickelettes. Ellin was forced to drop out of *Spaced Out*.

As director of our new project, Betsy represented Les Nickelettes in "An Evening with Bay Area Women Directors," a forum cosponsored by *City Arts* and Theatre Communications Center of the Bay Area. In a *City Arts* article, "Five Women Directors on Power, Sexuality, and Art in the Theater," preceding the forum, Hal Gelb talked to the five directors: Terry Baum, Alma Becker, Joy Carlin, Stefani Priest, and Betsy Newman. He noted in his introduction that the Bay Area theater scene was unique in that there were "any number of companies run wholly or in part by women."

This portion of Gelb's interview with Betsy stuck with me:

> *Newman's growth as a director is one she gauges in terms of a difficult progress towards confidence. . . . Confidence, for Newman, is the source of creativity. "It's not a matter of your having a million good ideas and being afraid to go with them. The ideas don't come if you don't have the confidence."*

I reflected that it was hard for a woman to slog it out alone in a man's world. My confidence, thus creativity, came from being in an all-women's group. The sisterhood built the moxie.

Jane, Monika, Virginia, Me, Mary, Ellin,
and Amy posing as Punk Girls
Photo © Tom Copi

After the forum, Betsy took off again, returning to Oregon for a couple of months to fulfill a prior obligation to the Oregon Repertory Theater. "Don't worry," she assured me. "I'll be back in plenty of time to mount the production and oversee the rehearsals."

I sighed, suppressing my annoyance. I didn't have Ellin around to do publicity, and Jane had recently cut back on doing Nickelettes production work after joining the Distractions, an eight-part harmony group headed by Scrumbly Koldwyn. Jane deserved this opportunity to showcase her incredible voice, but it meant the burden of doing preproduction tasks fell entirely on me. I had been looking forward to focusing all my energy into taking on the biggest acting role of my career.

But then, some of the weight was lifted off my shoulders. The board of directors allocated the $1,000 California Arts Council grant to hire me as the organization's part-time administrator. I cut back on my hours at Macy's to concentrate on this new paid position. Even though the paltry part-time wages covered three full-time jobs rolled into one—fundraising, preproduction, and the company's day-to-day operations—I was elated. Every day, I headed off to our tiny office space in the Women's Building in my funky gold Ford Pinto, happy that, at last, I was earning part of my living in the career of my choice.

Our swim upstream shifted into glide mode. The Seventh Annual Salmon Awards were presented with the precision of a well-oiled machine. This crucial fundraising event provided us with the seed money we needed for the show. With this funding goal accomplished, my spirits were high as the Salmon Awards party wound down.

After we cleaned the theater and packed up all our gear in a borrowed van, I said goodnight to everyone and hopped into the driver's seat, eager to get home. The van wouldn't start. Damn! Why was I always the last to leave? Even Vince had driven off, saying he would see me at home. I turned the key again. The engine refused to kick in. I pounded on the dashboard of the feeble vehicle, screaming, "Motherfucking machine!"

It was past two in the morning—my day had started eighteen hours earlier, and I had been going nonstop ever since. Not to mention the past five hours of merrymaking, performing, guzzling goblets of jungle juice, and consuming any mind-altering drug offered. I turned the key again: *click, click, click* . . . followed by dead silence. I deserved that goddamned Martyr of the Year award I'd just won.

I leaned against the steering wheel and sobbed, tears smearing glitter eye shadow and mascara down my face. I had to do something. I didn't want to spend the night in this steel wreck. I opened the creaky door, gathered my party gown up to my knees, and stumbled up one block to Haight Street. The bars were already closed. There was not a soul to be found. With the aid of a guardian angel, I found a working pay phone and scrounged in my purse for a dime. I dialed Vince with a teary plea to be rescued.

A Cinderella story in reverse: one moment I was Queen of the Ball, and the next a helpless maiden in a rusty, broken-down van waiting for my prince to come. I vowed in the future to expect the unexpected and never be the last to leave the ball.

One unavoidable production task needed to be completed before Betsy returned: auditions. Five of the seven parts had been precast, and the role of Yerba Buena went to Virginia's friend Pat Ramseyer, who took on the role in the workshop version. Pat owned a popular lesbian bar called Wild Side West in Bernal Heights. She was in her fifties and off-the-wall funny. That left just one opening, the character of Barbi Cue, at least until Ellin dropped out; now we also needed a new Garleeka Mundane.

I never knew what to expect when I called an audition. Arriving on a motor scooter, Content Knowles, a blue-eyed, solidly built Scandinavian blonde with a deep voice, strode into the room, and said, "Hi, my name is Content." My first thought was, *Who names their child "Content"?* During her audition, she never stopped talking and came across as anything but peaceful. However, she knew how to belt out a song. I pegged her for a good fit in Ellin's vacated role as the Space Cadet technology specialist.

Of the seven candidates, only three stood out to me: Content, O'Clair, and Judith. Then Virginia, playing Amazonia in the audition scenes with the perspective Space Cadets, took me aside and said, "Watch that one, her comic timing is perfect." I hadn't paid much attention to the reserved, nondescript Valerie Helmold. She had thick chestnut hair, a pale complexion, and a blank expression. I took Virginia's advice, and she was right.

Valerie's timing was pitch perfect, and her face transformed from a blank slate into a variety of comic emotions when she acted. "I'd been auditioning forever and not having any luck," recalled Valerie. "So I was very taken aback when Les Nickelettes all laughed after I finished my reading." Valerie got the role of the Space Cadet's resident doctor, Barbi Cue.

Betsy hadn't committed to keeping Monika in the major role of W-2, Ella Vader's male android. Her lack of maturity kept Betsy on the fence, and the option remained open to possible recasting. With her husky voice and muscular body, I began to envision Content in the role. But Monika wasn't going down without a fight. Before casting decisions were set in stone she showed up with a killer song for W-2, "On Assignment":

On assignment, Ella said.
Your ideas and thoughts are not good
Listen to Ella, as you should.
Mind Control. Now I see.
Absolute power corrupts absolutely.

She presented the song in a stylized robotic staccato voice. It was good. Monika earned the role of W-2, and Content got the role of Garleeka Mundane.

Casting was complete, but expect the unexpected. One day, five weeks prior to opening night and five days before Betsy returned, Virginia called me. "There's a lot of things going on in my life, and I don't want to make a three-month commitment. I have to drop out." Two days later, Virginia's friend Pat also dropped out. Yikes!

Virginia's Amazonia was a major character in the play, and Pat, as Yerba Buena, was a small but pivotal role. I rushed to review resumes from the previous audition. Judith and O'Clair had been promising, so I invited them to a callback audition.

Judith Rain had tawny brown skin, black hair, and brown, almond-shaped eyes. I couldn't place her ethnicity. I guessed mixed-race African-American, or possibly Asian fusion? Adding to the racial intrigue was the surprise of a full-mouth of metal braces when she sang. I could see her in the role as Amazonia, but hesitated, not because of her ethnicity or braces, but because her demeanor was so serious, so not Nickelettes. Judith didn't seem to be picking up on the tongue-in-cheek style. "It was the first time I auditioned for anything outside of college," recalled Judith. "So I concentrated on being real professional."

I asked her to read from one of the key scenes to gauge her reaction to the off-the-wall material. The scene takes place in the secret hideout of the Space Cadets after they rescue Amazonia's clandestine boyfriend, Reggie Von Veggie, from Ella Vader's clutches. Ella had done the dastardly deed of freeze-drying Reggie, and now he was the size and texture of a rag doll.

"We'll just bring Reggie back to life by mixing him with a little water . . ." Amazonia proposes.

"No, Amazonia," warns Garleeka, "reconstituted vegetables come out soggy, mushy, and squishy."

"I don't want Reggie to be squishy." Amazonia replies, "I want him to be like a little brick!"

When Judith read the line, she blasted out an uproarious guffaw. *Okay, she gets it.* I cast her as Amazonia.

I called Judith with the news. "Oh my God, I got the lead?"

she exclaimed. She told me to call her Judy, and asserted that her heritage was Filipino/Polish.

O'Clair put in a decent audition as Yerba Buena, so I cast her in the role. A few days later Betsy returned, and I was freed from dutifully filling in as director. I turned my energies to creating the twisted character of Ella Vader.

One day, unexpectantly, I got a call from Ellin: "The *San Francisco Chronicle* fired me!" she screamed, totally freaking out. She had held her journalistic dream job for six weeks. The reason for the dismissal seemed unclear; all I could make out was that she and the editor didn't see eye to eye. "I'm through with San Francisco," she angrily told me. "I'm going back to New York."

"Don't leave yet," I pleaded, "At least stay until the opening of *Spaced Out*. We need you to help with the music."

"Okay," she said, "but after that I'm out of here."

Liza and Ellin came up with the idea of recording the music rather than relying on live musicians. "Taped music is a cost-effective and more reliable option," Ellin pointed out.

"And it will add a fuller sound," said Liza. It was true our meager budget only allowed for a couple of musicians, and it was difficult to get the necessary commitment from the players for every performance.

Liza secured Jeff Roth's Focus Studio to record the music. "At the time," said Liza, "Jeff just happened to have a bunch of name jazz artists recording there. So I asked if they would play on the *Spaced Out* tapes."

"Yeah, sure, we'll take the job," they assented. Liza on piano led a well-known lineup of Bay Area session musicians: Austin de Lone (guitar), Jim Eschliman (bass), Eddie Marshall (drums), and Tucki Bailey (saxophone). "It was really easy to do," said Liza. "The drummer, Eddie Marshall, was fantastic.

It was great showing him these simple punk songs. I had fun, and they all had a great time, too."

Top-notch musicians for peanuts—had we died and gone to heaven? Criticism arose because we didn't use live musicians, but every night when I heard that wailing sax in my song, I was ecstatic.

Evolution continued with costuming. I created Ella Vader's overt sexual look with two pieces I found on a clearance rack in the trendy Fiorucchi store during a visit to New York City. A neon-green, strapless, skin-tight halter-top, matched with a hot pink, spandex miniskirt. For an out-of-control evil effect, I accessorized with green gloves featuring sharp red plastic fingernails, and a fuchsia spray-painted wig decorated with pink Easter grass for kelp.

But, for the first time, a costumer designed the other costumes. The San Francisco Costume Bank was a free service for nonprofit art organizations. Pam Minor ran the project for the San Francisco Art Commission's Neighborhood Arts Program. Betsy and I outlined the story to Pam, and she began pulling out materials, "Okay, so leotards and metallic breast ornaments for Space Cadets, silvery fabric and foam pieces for androids, and green chiffon for the seaweed spirit—I like that one, I'll do that myself." All the materials were free, but we pitched in with the sewing and construction.

~~~

Ten days before opening night, O'Clair (Yerba Buena) unexpectedly quit. Betsy had recruited Amy Ryder (from *Peter Pan*) to do choreography for the show, and now begged her to step into the role. Amy declined due to prior commitments, but suggested her roommate, Debra Jean.

Debra Jean Pollock had recently relocated to San Francisco from Denver. After burning out as a theater major in college, she sought a change of pace. "I vowed not to do any theater for at least a year," she said. "So, a couple of weeks after I get to San Francisco, my friend Amy asked me, 'Do you want a part in a show?'"

At a hastily scheduled audition, Debra Jean stood in front of a sink in the kitchen of the church where we were rehearsing and did an impressive reading of the part for Betsy and me.

"Thank you," said Betsy. "Just give us a moment." Betsy beckoned me to follow her into another room.

"She was great," I said.

"I don't know how serious she's going to be," replied Betsy, "with purple hair and a diamond-studded nose piercing. Plus, she's only nineteen."

I chewed on that, "Monica's only sixteen."

"But we've worked with her before."

Betsy called in Debra Jean, "Are you sure you *can* and *want* to do this?"

Her bow-shaped lips broke into a smile as she cited a lengthy resume of theater experience, adding, "I've been in theater for a bajillion years, I know what it's like the week before a show opens." She joined the cast the next day.

Betsy also brought in Sue Ferreira to be assistant director. It seemed a little late to bring in someone new, but I was too busy to give it much thought. And any extra help was welcome as I juggled publicity tasks, day-to-day operations, and fitting myself into the evil mind of Ella Vader. Amid all the hustle and bustle, I missed the significance of Betsy telling me, "The assistant director keeps an eye on things in case the director isn't there."

On September 4, 1980, *Spaced Out: A Sci-Fi Musical* debuted at the Summer Eureka Experimental Theatre Festival. The Eureka Theater was a major player in the San Francisco theater scene, and Les Nickelettes being invited to take part in their second

Poster for *Spaced Out*

Design by Trina Robbins

annual festival was significant. I took it as validation for the group as we fit right into the festival's stated purpose of choosing underground artists with, "a flair for the wild in mind."

During the opening weekend, I pulled off a couple of publicity coups. John Stanley hosted KTVU's late-night Saturday program *Creature Features*. The gimmick in this stoner underground series was to run bargain basement horror movies from the 1950s and '60s and then, during commercial breaks, John Stanley delivered wry in-jokes about the plot and actors. Sometimes, he had guests. Our creation of Ella Vader, ex-wife of Darth Vader, amused John, and he invited her to make an appearance. I reenacted Ella's scene where she barks into her red patent-leather high-heel shoe phone, "For God's sakes, Darth, stop that heavy breathing or you'll get no more alimony out of me."

John cracked up, and we got free TV publicity.

Waking up the next morning, I opened the arts section of the pink-hued Sunday "Datebook" of the *San Francisco Chronicle* to a near full-page photo of myself staring back at me. Everyone in Northern California interested in the arts read "the pinkie." This publicity photo caught Ella Vader in a moment of megalomaniac rage: face painted in ghastly extreme makeup, teeth bared, with wild kelp-infested hair. Subsequently, every mainstream and underground newspaper in the Bay Area printed this iconic image of Ella. Trina Robbins used it as a model for the cartoon drawing on the poster, flyer, and program along with the quote, "She's mad! She's bad! She's Ella Vader."

And then, perhaps just a coincidence, there was this three-dot item in Herb Caen's *San Francisco Chronicle* column: "If Ella Hutch married Darth Vader would she be Ella Vader?" Ella Hutch was a San Francisco city supervisor, so Herb was making a City Hall joke. No mention of Les Nickelettes; maybe creative minds think alike?

Me portraying an enraged Ella Vader

The reviews were as usual mixed. Robert Chesley from the *San Francisco Bay Guardian* weighed in as a fan:

> *[Les Nickelettes] are nutty, messy, flashy, trashy and very funny . . . Go see and go stoned.*

But Robert Hurwitt of *City Arts* missed the point:

> *It's a witty show, sometimes hilarious . . . But I found it disappointing. It just doesn't add that much to the basic fun of the movie. It adds sex, and we can revel in the raunch; and it adds sociopolitical assumptions we can all share. But it's only a spoof, sharing the basic*

individualism vs. totalitarianism simple-mindedness of the original movie.

This time, all the reviewers were male, and what they failed to recognize was that *Spaced Out* wasn't based on the traditional Western male myths portrayed in the *Star Wars* movies, but a comedy based on made-up female myths. The two female foes fight to the finish in a "babble battle" rather than guns and starships. Salvation comes in the form of a female kelp child, the result of a fusion of human and vegetation, rather than a conquering heroine. Maybe the message wasn't conveyed assertively enough. Or perhaps our campy comic book style distracted so much that it was overlooked. Or maybe it just went past them. Board member Ron Turner provided some insight: "The problem with being so innovative is that what Les Nickelettes did had no rules, and so the expectancy wasn't there for the audience. It was entirely driven by Les Nickelettes themselves and by how they interpreted the world."

～

Ella Vader was my Lady Macbeth. She was a crone's crone, the worst of Mother Nature unleashed. I dug deep to portray this arrogant, sinister woman intent on controlling or destroying everything. In her depraved solo song, "Satisfied," the audience learned that she was unable to be sexually satisfied by human, machine, or android: "Got an itch that I can't scratch, / A libido made to match." The music ended in a lone saxophone note as Ella attempted to satisfy herself on the edge of a lab counter.

Her insatiable sex drive led to a quest for total sexual control of the planet's population. All men on Califia were required to submit daily sperm specimens to her insemination banks where she personally conducted quality control tests. Audiences gasped when Ella drank with gusto huge test tubes of sperm.

"Every night, it was so striking," commented Betsy.

"It was shocking to me to be in a show where women were onstage talking about sex and their desires," said Debra Jean. "But I loved Ella Vader's line, 'Lunch, smunch, where's my sperm?'"

I don't think audiences or reviewers fully took in the implication of a megalomaniacal woman controlling all the male sperm. In a different era, she would have been burned at the stake for heresy.

The most difficult scene was Ella's meltdown. W-2, Ella's loyal android, fell wildly in love with the female android B-12, and defected to Amazonia and the Space Cadets. This led to a denouement with Amazonia in the form of an epic babble battle. Having completely lost her grip, Ella attacked with gibberish. Amazonia countered with truisms. In final desperation, Ella spewed her nemesis with a mind control drug, but Amazonia spit it back into Ella's mouth, which caused her to disintegrate into a blithering mess, muttering, "Ella Vader going down."

Ella Vader was a caricature of evil, but I had to play her authentically to make it work. This exhausting, emotional intensity consumed me, and I struggled not to let it seep into my personal life. For better or worse, I removed myself emotionally from my relationship with Vince during the run of the play.

As I was occupying this alternative universe of Ella Vader onstage, Betsy announced that she was leaving to return to Oregon—and Steve Christensen. "I was restless and in love," Betsy later explained. "And I was poor. I was living at a friend's apartment—not paying any rent and hardly had enough money to eat. My diet was one burrito a day."

The news that Betsy was leaving *again* made my blood boil. I hadn't taken the hint when Betsy brought in Sue, but now I understood the need for an assistant director. Looking ahead to three more performing venues with an inexperienced assistant director didn't sit well. My rational self told me to stay calm—everything would be okay. But my alter ego, Ella Vader, occupying space in my psyche, sent me into an agitated rage. How dare she leave the show for a guy?

This time Betsy would not return.

I went home and crashed into a deep sleep, but woke in the middle of the night and violently threw up. I didn't know if the cause of this illness was a virus, a discomfort between my true self and Ella Vader, or my reaction to Betsy leaving. I was bedridden for three days. The following weekend I performed with a fever, and to make matters worse, a vertebra in my neck went out of whack. Offstage, I lay flat on my back willing myself to continue on to the next scene.

"You were on a mission," observed Debra Jean.

With all the last-minute cast changes setting off a dizzying sprint to opening night, we hadn't had time to catch our breath. Now, as we settled into our second venue, new connections began to bloom.

"It was hard to get to know people," Debra Jean said, "I definitely felt like an outsider."

"We all felt like outsiders," recalled Valerie.

Mary brought everyone together over the makeup kit. The kit was stored in a large tackle box stuffed with jars of glitter eye shadow, eyeliner pencils, face powder, black mascara, eyelash curlers, brushes, lipstick, and plastic pots of rouge. With nine actresses using all the cosmetics, it was in constant disarray. Not able to tolerate the chaos, Mary became the "Mistress of the Makeup Kit." She fussed at everyone like a mother hen, "to return everything to its proper tray." She also doled out makeup tips. She taught Valerie how to put on false eyelashes, and showed Liza, who had never worn makeup before, how to apply blush. "The blush made my cheekbones stand out," said an enlightened Liza.

Judy and Debra Jean bonded over cereal. During pre-performance preparations, Judy would whisper to Deb, "What kind of carbohydrates did you bring today?"

"Judy took me under her wing," recalled Debra Jean. In return Judy sought advice about her struggle to play the dual role of Dede Day-Glo/Amazonia. "Dede was a meek and mild waitress, and I didn't connect with her. I was much more comfortable being Amazonia. As Amazonia I had nipples made of steel."

This became a Judy and Debra Jean in-joke. The mention of rock hard nips had them rolling on the floor. They transferred this playfulness onstage in their portrayals of Amazonia and Yerba Buena.

Content proved to be a real-life Space Cadet. She missed rehearsals, forgot her lines, and showed up late. Then she'd rush in and suck up all the energy in the dressing room, and spew it back out in a loud, obnoxious voice. But she came through for Judy. "I wasn't getting the seaweed spirit song," said Judy, "And Content, who had a Baptist background, taught me how to sing gospel." Teamwork can develop where you least expect it.

Valerie proved to be a rock solid performer onstage, but lay low backstage. However, that didn't stop her from coming out of the closet to the cast. Debra Jean confessed, "The fact that Valerie was a lesbian was incredibly intimidating."

And Judy admitted, "Becoming good friends with a lesbian was a whole new experience for me." But before long, they were all cracking jokes together.

As mad, bad, Ella Vader, I sat in a far corner of the dressing room avoiding all the preshow levity.

On the eve of Ellin's departure for New York, she threw a going away party in her now empty apartment. The party added to my unsettled feeling that things were out of kilter. No furniture, no clothes hanging in the closet, and no decorations on the walls gave the revelry a hollow feeling. I bid Ellin goodbye amid a tumble of emotions.

The following night, the performing group convened to discuss future plans. Ellin and Betsy were gone. Then the third strike was thrown over the plate. Jane announced that after *Spaced Out*, she was dropping out to devote all her time to the Distractions.

Feeling a hole in the pit of my stomach, I retreated from the discussion about the future. Betsy, Ellin, Jane, and I had been the creative core of the group for five years. The four of us had transformed Les Nickelettes from a loosely formed art performance troupe into a theater company. Together, we developed a unique form of female musical comedy and learned collectively how to write, produce, and direct plays.

Mary, Monika, and Liza enthusiastically chattered on and on about possibilities for a new project. The new members of the group—Valerie, Judy, Debra Jean, and Content—looked to me for a response, but I remained mute. I was in no mood to be a cheerleader.

After a successful run in Haight-Ashbury, the show moved to the quirky San Francisco Tenderloin District, where street drug dealing, peep shows, and prostitution butted up against the city's distinguished theater district. I booked a dirt cheap, beautiful though neglected and rundown art deco theater housed in the rear of the YMCA. This YMCA didn't fit the vision of gleefully dancing young men portrayed in the song by the Village People. It housed a mental health facility and was where you went if you were desperate. The new members of the group questioned the location, and I explained, "We produced a couple of very successful fundraising events here."

But the setup at this funky theater didn't bode well. The ancient lighting system crashed, and Sue knew nothing about theater lighting. I spent the next day tracking down and installing the appropriate fuses and adaptors for the light board. I barely had time to scramble into my Ella Vader costume before show time. I figured something like this would happen after Betsy jumped ship. To say I was resentful would be an understatement: I seethed.

This was supposed to be the point in the run that put the ledger book in the black, but it was a disaster. Audiences didn't show up. We pumped up publicity, but nothing worked. At one performance there were only three people in the audience.

Taking the weight of this catastrophe entirely on my shoulders, I shrank even further away from my usual leadership role in the group. The other acknowledged leader, a grumpy, burned-out Jane, similarly projected a "don't bother me" demeanor. She showed up, did her job, and chalked it off as one day closer to her departure. That left the rest of the cast, unfettered by any oversight, to do whatever they pleased.

Monika, having just turned seventeen, took the lead by hijacking her scenes. She'd barge onstage and do anything that struck her as funny. Her ad-libbing didn't throw Jane and me, as we had taught her the art of riffing off the written script. But the others were caught off balance. "She was outrageous on so many levels," said Valerie. "She had a confidence that exceeded her age."

"In other shows you had a script," said Judy, "and there was no deviation from the script. The script was the Bible and you didn't change it, and here she was changing the Bible." But it didn't take long for Judy and the others to join in the spontaneity.

"I'd been in other shows," observed Valerie, "where if things were in a downward spiral, and morale was low, you just end the run and everyone goes off. This was different. We started coming together."

"We had such chemistry," chimed in Judy, "that all our periods coincided with each other."

I enjoyed the impromptu gags onstage but didn't let it alter my martyred state of mind. I played an authoritative megalomaniac, but I felt powerless. I moped through all the fun and offstage bonding.

I was already dreading the move to Berkeley for the end of the run. Two weekends at two different theaters meant two tech setups and myriad possibilities for things to go wrong. I wasn't disappointed. At the first tech rehearsal, the dimmer board blew out. I dashed across the bridge to San Francisco where I knew I could locate the appropriate fuses. Speeding back to Berkeley in my trusty gold Ford Pinto, after also picking up half the cast, I got a ticket. I tried to laugh it off, but my alter ego, Ella Vader, flared up in a wild fume of fury.

But I did have a laugh that evening when, in the middle of a Space Cadet scene, a giant red cockroach that had hitchhiked in a costume bag from the YMCA scampered across the stage. Breaking character as fearless Garleeka, Content screamed like a helpless little girl. Jane, maintaining her B-12 character, robotically shuffled over and squished the offending insect. Turning to Content, she ad-libbed in her android voice: "Garleeka, Space Cadet headquarters is cleansed of the invading bugging devices of Ella Vader."

The second weekend was redemption. No tech glitches, and an enthusiastic audience packed the Berkeley Live Oak Theater. After the final performance, the cast went out to mingle with the crowd, but I retreated alone to the dressing room. I stared at the pathetic visage of Ella Vader in the mirror, and wiped off the makeup with cold cream for the last time.

The following day, Judy invited the cast and crew to a party at her apartment. Her gala "pasta party" was held to inaugurate a recently purchased pasta machine. I awoke that morning with my ragged, exhausted brain only registering that I was done with Ella Vader. Playing this villainous egomaniac had zapped every ounce of energy from my being.

Did I really want to get up and drag myself to a party just to eat pasta? Then the phone rang. "So are you coming?" asked Judy.

"Okay. Yeah, sure," I mumbled. I took my time getting myself together, intending to make a late and brief appearance.

By the time I arrived, pasta was strung up everywhere to dry, and everyone was in high party mode. Despite my miserable mood, I slid into the groove. I even liked the pasta. I sat, slurping up my last noodle, when Judy and Debra Jean trumpeted a ceremonial pageant and declared, "By the order of Les Nickelettes, we now declare Denise Larson above and beyond martyrdom, having now attained sainthood." They placed a glittery decorated cardboard crown on my head and handed me a "Saint" certificate.

Caught totally off-guard, I felt tears welling up, and my heart flooded with gratitude. This overwhelming flow of emotion flashed a message to my brain: Les Nickelettes were being reborn! In my dark grief about lost collaborators, I had been unable to visualize the dawn just over the horizon. Judy, Debra Jean, Valerie, Content, Mary, Liza, and Monika were signaling to me, "Hey we're in."

I didn't know what was in that pasta, but Amazonia, the Spirit of Seaweed, and the Space Cadets saved Les Nickelettes that day.

"I don't want it to be over," said Valerie.

"Well, what's next?" asked Judy.

"We're going to write a new show," I replied.

"What a bold thing to do," said Debra Jean, "to say we're going to write a show."

"That's what Les Nickelettes do," I reminded her.

"I've never written anything," said Valerie. "I don't know what to do. I don't even know if I have the ability to do it."

"Well, here's an opportunity to find out," I told her.

"I guess we just have to claim it for ourselves," added Debra Jean.

"Until Les Nickelettes asked for my opinions, I didn't think my thoughts mattered," added Valerie. "This group makes me feel like I belong, it just feels natural."

The newbies would need to evolve. Judy, Valerie, and Debra Jean were recent theater major college graduates. I had learned, in college, that men were the leaders. But eight years as a Nickelette had transformed me. "This will be a different experience," I told them.

"I've never been in a situation where women had all the control," admitted Valerie.

"It's not the same," I explained. "No men making all the decisions; no men to hide behind or run away from."

"Sounds good to me," said Debra Jean.

"When you work with men," mused Judy, "you get caught up in the male-female games, and you have to hide your tampons and Kotex."

"Hide your moods," added Mary.

"Maybe pretend not to be too smart," chimed in Valerie.

"Maybe not lift so much," continued Judy.

"Don't worry," I assured her, "you'll get to do as much heavy lifting as you want. Maybe more."

But before we could truly come together, the newcomers needed to embrace the female satire doctrine that was at the heart of Les Nickelettes. "And they did convert," said Liza. "Everybody who has joined Les Nickelettes has become converted."

"Or perverted," I joked.

"Yes, including me," replied Liza.

"If you don't get the joke you might as well leave."

Not everyone stuck around. The initial planning meetings were conducted as theatrical producing and writing seminars, as I laid out the nuts and bolts of running a nonprofit organization. I also explained that we had applied for grants without much success.

"My mother is a professional grant writer, and I'm sure she could help out," offered Content. "When she writes a grant it's a slam dunk."

Until that moment I considered Content a bit flaky, but this was big. I gave her copies of all our past grant applications, budgets, and organization statements for her mother to take a look at.

At the next scheduled meeting, Content didn't show up. She didn't call, didn't return my phone calls. Then her phone was disconnected. She disappeared. We never saw or heard from her again. Sometimes, you never know what to expect.

○~~~~○

Leaving Ella Vader behind, I was able to restore my relationship with Vince. One evening in early December 1980, I was preparing dinner while Vince watched Monday Night Football. It felt good to just be at home having dinner together. The game was suddenly interrupted, and Howard Cosell announced the unbelievable news that John Lennon had been shot and killed in New York City. What?

In January 1964, I fell in love with the Beatles after hearing "I Want to Hold Your Hand" on the radio for the first time. Their music was so exciting, so alive, like nothing I'd ever heard before. On February 9, 1964, I sat transfixed in my parent's living room as the Beatles appeared on the Sunday Ed Sullivan Show and swept America into a frenzy of Beatlemania. My avid lifetime fan status was signed, sealed, and delivered after I won tickets in 1965 from a local radio station to attend a Beatles concert at San Francisco's Cow Palace. The screaming girls prevented me from hearing much of the music, but the impact of seeing the band play live electrified me. At sixteen, I declared that Paul was my favorite because he was "the cute one"; secretly, I thought John was the coolest. As my devotion deepened, I came to realize that the reason they were so remarkable was due to the synergy of all four. Like a mandala, you couldn't have a whole without all the elements. It made me love them all equally. I owned two complete sets of Beatle records because the first one wore out from constant use.

John hadn't put out any new music in five years, and I was looking forward to the new *Double Fantasy* album he and Yoko Ono had just released. Now, John was gone. This incomprehensible murder hit me as hard as if an immediate family member or close friend had been killed. I joined fans worldwide in a stunned and devastated spasm of grief. What did the assassination of a rock star say about our culture? In 1980, sadly, expect the unexpected.

CHAPTER 10

"I'D RATHER BE DOING SOMETHING ELSE"— THE DIDI GLITZ STORY

"I'm utterly fabulous, honey."

Enthusiasm to write a new show was high, but a collective concept failed to bubble to the surface. The moment of inspiration occurred after Ellin walked into her last Les Nick-elettes meeting before she departed for New York. She was wearing a bright pink T-shirt emblazoned: DiDi GLITZ—HOT PINK. The cartoon figure on the shirt was a provocative woman decked out in high-heeled mules, hip-hugging zebra-skin pants, and a blond bouffant hairdo, sitting with one leg crossed over the other and hoisting a cocktail to her lips.

"Wow, Ellin, what a cool shirt, where did you get it?" I asked.

"From cartoonist Diane Noomin," explained Ellin. "Her DiDi Glitz strip is in *Twisted Sisters*, an underground comic book."

"I want one," chimed in Mary.

"We all want one," I said.

Ellin not only got us T-shirts, but also copies of the comic book. The cartoonists in *Twisted Sisters*—Aline Kominsky-Crumb, Krystine Kryttre, Phoebe Gloeckner, and Carol

Tyler—told salacious and hilarious female stories. But Diane Noomin's strip particularly piqued our interest. Her DiDi Glitz cartoon laid out the story of a single mother with limited resources from Canarsie, New York. Her perfect life is envisioned in an illustrated "Priority Pie." The "Pie" was sliced into all the marvelous things she desired: delicious bubble baths, yummy golden Cadillac cocktails, onion dip, vacations in Miami Beach, lavish interior design schemes for home redecorating, shopping for utterly gorgeous outfits, and fabulous financial status. The largest piece of the pie was allotted to fascinating, devastating love affairs with men, followed by the tiniest slice—sex.

We all donned our hot pink T-shirts, took a group photo, and declared DiDi Glitz an honorary Nickelette.

"DiDi seems like a character in one of our shows," I said.

"Maybe this DiDi Glitz story should be our new play," said Deb. (Debra Jean was now just Deb.)

A meeting with Diane Noomin was set up. She was the last to arrive. I nervously sat waiting with the others as we speculated about what this cool cartoon artist would think of us. I was taken aback when Diane walked through the door. She looked nothing like flashy, trashy DiDi Glitz. She had long, straight, brunette hair and was dressed in a librarian-worthy black outfit with Coke-bottle thick, black-framed glasses perched on her nose.

"A lot of people are often startled when they meet me," Diane later recalled, "because they confuse the cartoonist with the character, and they expect some wild and crazy person to appear. Cartoonists are introverts who hunch over drawing tables."

We eased the awkwardness with shared comedic riffs, and it didn't take long to discover we were all off the same wall. "What Les Nickelettes want to propose is that we collaborate with you to create a musical comedy based on your DiDi Glitz Story," I said to Diane.

"Utterly fabulous," she replied, using a favorite phrase from her cartoon alter-ego.

Having broken the ice, we were soon laughing at prospective ideas, and sketching out the details of working together. But I had another pressing issue on my mind.

"Who's going to direct?" I blurted out, leading to an uncomfortable pause. "I guess by default, I'll have to do it," I added with just a hint of martyrdom in my inflection, "but I'd really rather act." I hoped Valerie or Judy would raise their hand and volunteer.

"I'll direct," said Deb.

Her matter-of-fact tone took me my surprise, "Are you sure?" I hadn't even considered Deb. To me, this was too big for a twenty-year-old novice.

"Yeah, I'd love to do it," answered Deb.

"Do you have any directing experience?" I challenged.

"I started as an assistant director in college," she answered, pitching her resume, "and then directed two productions— *Women Behind Bars* and *The Killing of Sister George.*"

"That sounds impressive to me," said Diane.

"Okay, yeah. Why not?" I said, dazed, but relieved.

That evening I wrote in my diary, "Amazing! It looks like this thing is going to work out. And it was so easy."

Les Nickelettes' campy style had always been akin to a live cartoon, but teaming up with a visual artist to make a comic strip come to life would be a new adventure. Both Les Nickelettes and women's underground comics emerged and thrived in the anything-goes experimentation of 1970s San Francisco. The meshing of the two was a natural fit.

Diane's career as a cartoonist began in 1972 when she moved to San Francisco from New York. In 1973, she dressed up for Halloween as a housewife from Canarsie, inspired by the women she'd observed as a teenager in the southeast Brooklyn neighborhood where she grew up. Sashaying around in a faux leopard skin mini-dress and bubble blond wig, her friends called her "Didi." She turned this alter ego into a cartoon character. Since then, her DiDi Glitz comic strips had appeared in *Wimmens Comix* and *Twisted Sisters*.

For me, heading up this group of novices writing their first play, Diane brought to the table a strong grasp of storytelling and a take-charge attitude. Most importantly, Diane and the group gelled around the same outlandish, risqué style of comedy.

The outline of the script came together with lightning speed using Diane's settings, characters, and scenarios. Our plot blended two of her comic strips: *I'd Rather Be Doing Something Else—The DiDi Glitz Story*, and *She Chose Crime.*

DiDi was a single mother with a precocious twelve-year old daughter, Crystal, whom DiDi dolled up in crinoline-lined baby doll dresses and Shirley Temple curls. DiDi's priorities were bubble baths, love affairs, and redecorating. But her life changed after she got fired from her job at a movie theater for taking it upon herself to redecorate the lobby.

Unemployment left her at a loss about how to pay the mortgage and her daughter's Girl Scout dues. With her flamboyant best friend, Loretta, she attempted a variety of get rich schemes: a Rubberware party, sweepstakes entries, and becoming a contestant on the game show *Go for Baroque*. But these schemes failed to line her pocketbook with cash. In desperation, she tried a loan company but was turned down. Even her retired mother in Miami rebuffed her plea for money.

At the end of her rope, DiDi chose crime; she robbed a bank and then fled with her daughter, sister, and best friend to her mother's home in Miami. But after failing to hook up with the Rubberware salesman ("Trashed by a man I thought would be true"), she rebounded by buying a dive bar with her illicit cash and redecorated it into the Leatherette Lounge. The bar became a springboard for her daughter's success as a punk star, but DiDi, approaching forty, was left with only wrinkles. Nevertheless, she danced off into the sunset with a chorus line of male escorts.

The outline was easy—fleshing out the lines was not. To write the dialogue, we employed the same improvisational/workshop technique used in *Spaced Out*, but this time the actresses took turns playing different characters. Diane watched over the process like a hawk, and it took on the tense quality of an audition.

"I couldn't let the work or the characters be compromised," confessed Diane. "I was very protective."

Diane was also fastidious when we sat down to the nitty-gritty work of shaping the improvs into a script. She hesitated to compromise on even the smallest detail. I loved the writing process. I even enjoyed sparring with others about which element or line worked best. But with Diane, the battles got brutal. "We have to put the word, 'jeez' at the end of the line, not at the beginning," stated Diane.

"It really doesn't matter," I argued. Back and forth we bickered until I concluded with, "It will all come out in the wash during the rehearsal process anyway."

Deb weighed in, "Sometimes the words aren't as important as the gestures. I can direct the actress to show the attitude."

At the end of each debate, only Diane, Deb, and I were left to thrash it out. "Everybody else would just shut up and let us fight it out," recalled Diane.

"The creative disagreements got very emotional and vehement," observed Valerie, "and then everyone just moved on. I was an apprentice. I saw the others as these real hip artist types. So I sat back and watched the big girls go at it."

Fusing techniques of a visual artist with that of theater artists proved challenging. Diane's process of drawing and creating a story involved a neatly laid-out page on which she could manipulate every aspect. An actor's method of interacting with a director and a group of other actors in interpreting and developing characters was messy and unpredictable. Diane pushed us to polish the material in a way that we had never done before, but we understood that written dialogue and spoken dialogue were two different things.

"It was very hard to make a transition from being someone in complete control," said Diane, "and learning to trust Les Nickelettes enough to accept input." Trust was built one bouffant hairdo at a time. It wouldn't be until opening night that Diane fully trusted Les Nickelettes' theatrical instincts.

Deb announced open auditions, and anxiety levels tensed up tighter than an aerialist walking on a high wire without a net. Members of the group would have to compete with outside candidates. No one was guaranteed a role. "I finally felt part of the group," said Valerie, "and then I had to audition." Deb would make final decisions in consultation with Diane.

"Everybody wants the part of DiDi Glitz," I confided to Deb. "And everyone's trying to impress Diane."

I was no exception. I had just played the lead role of Ella Vader. I didn't want to be greedy, but I joined the others in the fierce competition. Monika openly lobbied Diane in her best New York accent: "I would be utterly fabulous as DiDi."

After three grueling days of auditions and callbacks, Deb and Diane bid us adieu and went off to the Good Karma Café to make the casting decisions. I prayed for good karma to come my way.

"I have Valerie in mind for DiDi," Deb told Diane.

"I wasn't thinking of Valerie. Mary looks more like DiDi." Diane had keyed into Mary's blond locks and sassy demeanor.

"With the wonders of wigs and makeup, we can make Valerie look like DiDi," Deb pointed out. "Plus, Valerie was the only one to nail the Canarsie accent."

"DiDi is the scariest decision for me," confessed Diane.

"I knew in my heart of hearts that Valerie would be DiDi," Deb told me later, "but I had to talk Diane into it."

Valerie had grown up near New York and easily slipped into a Brooklyn vernacular. Mary, Monika, Judy, and I were California girls, and even with Diane's coaching, we never got it right. In California we could get away with most of the characters having half-assed accents. Had we been in New York, "fuggedaboudit."

"The accent wasn't hard for me," said Valerie. "But I had no faith that I would get the role. Deb called me that night to tell me I had the part, and I was so excited. Right after that, my mother called, and I was screaming with joy and she blandly replied, 'That's nice, dear.'"

Valerie as DiDi Glitz

Photo © Ed Kashi

Diane hadn't been the only one who thought Mary was a shoo-in for DiDi—Mary did, too. But her recent hook-up with another drug-dealing boyfriend dampened her chances. Even she admitted, "I was really screwed up and appreciated getting any part." Mary was cast in three minor roles: DiDi's mother, the Rubberware salesman's wife, and a bank teller.

Judy was also cast in three roles, all male: the Rubberware salesman, the loan officer, and the bartender at the Miami dive bar. "When I read at the audition," said Judy, "I soon realized Diane wasn't going to have a little brown girl in a blond wig running around saying, 'I'm fabulous, utterly fabulous!' I played three different cartoon guys, and it gave me a kind of freedom to go wild."

Monika was cast as DiDi's best friend, Loretta, an exhibitionist without a hint of self-awareness. Monika, who thought she deserved the coveted lead, confronted Deb, "Why didn't I get the part of DiDi?"

"Because you're perfect for the role of Loretta," Deb deftly answered.

I was cast as DiDi's new-age feminist sister, Glenda. The character is the reality anchor in the story. A fitting casting choice, I suppose. But being excluded by Deb and Diane as they called the shots was a hard pill for me to swallow. The irony that I had gratefully relinquished the reins of responsibility only to then feel left out wasn't lost on me.

At least they cast everyone in the core group. That left two open parts for outsiders: DiDi's daughter, Crystal, and a dual male role—Brut, a Chuck Barris-type game show host, and Tony, a slimy talent agent.

Rose Bianco caught Deb and Diane's eye. She was Puerto Rican–Italian with big brown eyes, large sensuous lips, and a robust, youthful personality. Short and slim, she fit the physical criteria of twelve-year-old Crystal, but could she pull off the childlike naïveté? "We weren't sure," said Diane.

Rose as Crystal Glitz

"I had to sing at the audition," recalled Rose, "something I generally never did because I wasn't a very good singer and had no training, nor did I have a prepared song. However, I had recently memorized an Irish dirge for an audition for a Brendan Behan play. It didn't occur to me at the time that it was a pretty odd selection for a comedy show audition."

In the end, she was the best candidate so she got the role. Plus, Deb said, "She had to have a sense of camp to sing that absurd Irish dirge."

But there were no suitable candidates for the role of Brut/ Tony. Diane suggested a friend she had recently seen at a monologue reading. Gudrun (Goody) Thompson was invited to audition. "I went to one of those Woolworth photo booths and got a strip of pictures done," said Goody. "I was wearing plaid wool pants and a polka dot sweater. I combed my dirty hair like a guy because it was a guy's part, and I put on weird cats-eye glasses." Goody's nervousness showed at the audition, but Deb and Diane liked her intentional geeky look and irreverent attitude. Additionally, her low-pitched voice convinced Deb she could play a male character, so she was in.

With casting completed, a jolt of charged energy zapped the troupe. "It was the first inkling of things coming to life," said Diane. "It was exciting."

Liza was on board again to write, arrange, and record the music. She was into 1950s music at the time, and the show dovetailed with that style. Diane insisted on being involved in every aspect of the production, and she stepped in to flesh out lyrics with Liza. "Diane had very definite ideas about what she wanted," said Liza. "She wanted it to be perfect."

One song, though, popped fully formed into Liza's head. "I wrote the song during my lunch break," she explained. "Within half an hour the whole thing was done. The song 'Hot Pink' was influenced by a couple of punk bands I was listening to, X-Ray Specks and the Psychedelic Furs."

Hot Pink is a color
Ask your mother 'bout it
They don't teach you colors in school
Hot Pink is a feeling that I've got
They don't teach you 'bout colors in school.

Summing it up, Liza added, "Songs are spontaneous things."

Judy took on the chore of choreography. "It would be cool to see some dances from that 1950s and '60s era," stated Judy.

I invited Judy and the others to watch a bootleg video of the Teenage Awards Music International show from 1964. *The T.A.M.I. Show* was revolutionary because, for the first time, a rock 'n' roll concert featured a mix of white and Black performers on stage. Before this breakthrough, audiences didn't see an act like the East Coast "Godfather of Soul" James Brown sharing a stage with the West Coast "Surfing Safari" Beach Boys. The civil rights movement made it possible to undo this musical segregation. *The T.A.M.I. Show* event, filmed in front of an audience of mostly white Santa Monica teenagers, blended the classic rock of Chuck Berry, the hot rods of Jan and Dean, the Motown sounds of Smokey Robinson and the Miracles, and added a dose of British Invasion with the Rolling Stones. But what I wanted to show Judy was the crew of energetic go-go dancers romping to the infectious beat of the music with '60s dance moves like the hitchhiker, the monkey, and the pony.

Judy jumped up and danced the pony, singing along at the top of her lungs. Soon DiDi, Loretta, and Glenda would be a hoppin' and a boppin' with these distinctive '60s moves.

Pop star Lesley Gore came on in the middle of *The T.A.M.I. Show* and sang "You Don't Own Me." We watched in silent awe. Lesley's song announced to the boys of her era an uncompromising declaration of freedom. Hard to believe this feminist anthem had been recorded almost twenty years earlier.

⌒〜ꝰ⌒

We went back to Pam Minor and the Costume Bank for costumes. Pam referred us to her assistant, Jan Edwards. Jan's personality was effusive and chatty.

"I've had a lot of theatre experience," she informed us. "I've acted since I was five, but I don't want to act anymore. I want to become a costumer."

Les Nickelettes provided the opportunity for Jan to costume her first show. Deb explained to Jan what she wanted, using Diane's drawings of DiDi: "Big, bold cartoon designs."

"Okay, I get it," replied Jan. "I don't have to be subtle."

Jan clad the cast in eye-popping bright colors, polka dots, tasteless patterns, and garish paisley. But Jan's biggest coup was the wigs. The hair had to be big like in Diane's drawings, but the budget couldn't be stretched to purchase the more than a half-dozen expensive real hair wigs we needed. So Jan concocted cotton wigs. She arranged cotton batting around a wig form, fashioned it into a hairdo, and then spray-painted it.

Initially, the actresses thought these cotton-candy wigs were ludicrous. "It's a comic book look," Jan reminded us. "I think it will work."

She was right. In fact, the wigs became a signature element to the look of the show. And Jan became more than just our costumer; she became part of the group.

The one area where Diane wanted absolute control and perfection was the sets. She meticulously drew the set designs and insisted the scenes look exactly like her drawings.

Deb and I grappled with how to transfer those illustrations onto to a viable theater backdrop. "First we'll need someone to build a structure," I said.

"No problem," replied Diane. "My uncle Bernie's a carpenter."

Bernie built two freestanding double-sided panels that could swivel and accommodate four different settings. Deb and I viewed the finished product in Bernie's workshop, as he beamed, and Diane expressed delight. I didn't want to critique this gift of in-kind construction, but I was worried. Uncle Bernie was a carpenter, not a set designer, and the backdrops were made of heavy, solid plywood instead of stretched muslin over a wooden frame. Deb and I hadn't explained the details of lightweight theatrical flat construction to Uncle Bernie or Diane, so we had to suck it up and live with these bulky sets.

The next obstacle was how to transfer Diane's detailed, nine-by-eleven-inch drawings onto the set pieces so they could be painted. Diane came up with the idea of making slides of the drawings and then projecting the image onto the wooden panels. But getting the correct proportion required a room a hundred feet deep with no impediments. The free rehearsal space that Vince had finagled for us in a China Basin industrial building was too small. But one night we snuck the plywood sets into an unfinished drywall space next to our studio, pulled the slide projector back, and it worked. Diane feverishly sketched the drawings onto the wood. We held our breath for a few days hoping our unauthorized use of this space would go undetected. It did.

Next was painting the designs. Diane was obsessively protective of her artwork, but there was no way she could paint them all by herself. So she turned to the comic community. "I roped in every cartoonist I knew to help paint those sets."

The group of talented graphic artists Diane prevailed upon included Bill Griffith, Becky Wilson, Kim Deitch, Michael McMillian, Diane Balter, Joel Goldstein, and Joyce Zavarro. As a result, the finished sets looked like they had been ripped out of the pages of a DiDi Glitz comic strip.

Just as things were rolling along, Deb took me aside and said, "The ending sucks. How am I going to stage DiDi hiring a dozen men from an escort service to dance kick-line style off into the sunset?"

She had a point—the gimmick worked as a funny ending gag in a comic strip, but not in a play. "You're right," I said. "There's no way you can stage that, plus it lacks any character growth or resolution for our protagonist."

"No one leaves until we come up with a dynamite ending," Deb declared at the beginning of an emergency writing session. We started in the morning with bagels and orange juice, broke out the booze at lunchtime, and at sunset—opened a packet of cocaine. During the marathon meeting, we turned ideas up and down, inside out, over and sideways, and then circled back to the beginning. People bailed. "Only the hardcore went to the end," said Deb.

At the end of the play, our protagonist is at a crossroads. DiDi assumed Tony, the talent agent, wanted her to redecorate his hotels in Las Vegas, but he wanted to sign her young, hip daughter, Crystal, after he saw her perform "Hot Pink." This situation set up DiDi, who was pushing forty, into the classic female fear of being cast aside once looks started fading. But how could we portray DiDi overcoming this societal bias? Finally, after twelve hours, the light bulb went off on a simple resolution through a song, "I'm Pushin' Forty but Forty's Not Pushin' Me":

You know what they say, about being over the hill
That a girl loses her power to thrill
I'm not gonna worry 'bout how old I am
I'm fabulous, honey. I don't have to pretend
I'm pushing forty, but forty's not pushin' me

A get-the-job-done team was forged of Deb, Diane, and me. Between us as director, designer, and producer, we worked nonstop to bring *The DiDi Glitz Story* to the stage.

"It was a time of power for me, collective women power," said Deb. "We were there a hundred percent for each other."

"In the morning I jumped in my gold Pinto," I elaborated, "and headed off to the Women's Building to work on publicity, then dashed off to do a radio interview, after which I picked up Diane and Deb, and we'd go to China Basin and work on the sets till six in the evening."

"And then before rehearsal we'd smoke a giant joint," said Deb.

"And after rehearsal we ended the evening with a production meeting," I said.

"It was fanatical," added Diane. "We never had normal meals. I would leave home in the morning and not be home for supper." Diane lived on a late-night microwaved baked potato diet for weeks on end, and fretted about never getting to see her husband, Bill.

The frantic schedule also took a toll on my relationship with Vince. He continued to understand and support my steadfast commitment to Les Nickelettes, but the prolonged absences caused a kind of disconnect. Even my efforts to steal a few moments to be together here and there fell flat. And truthfully, when he went out socializing with our friends without me, I was jealous. I missed being part of the crowd. "It won't be forever," I reassured him, as well as myself.

~~~

The soft-spoken, unpretentious Valerie had to be eased into the role of the loud and vulgar DiDi Glitz. "I had to learn to walk in high heels," she said, "and dance in them."

"I bombarded Valerie with girly stuff, and I painted her nails." said Deb.

"Eww, my fingernails can't breathe," howled a panicked Valerie.

"You take the polish off once a week and let them breathe."

Jan costumed DiDi in gold lamé stretch pants and a hot pink, frilly, low-cut blouse. To complete the look, Deb coerced Valerie into a push-up bra to give her cleavage.

"Do I *have* to shave my legs and armpits?" Valerie pleaded.

"It's part of your character, honey, so get over it."

Valerie's biggest test was the double-headed dong in the Rubberware party scene. "Whip out that rubber dildo and wave it in Glenda's face," directed Deb.

Valerie cringed. "Oh my God, I'm a lesbian. I'm not supposed to touch this stuff."

Along with other sex toys for sale, DiDi introduced "The Incredible Prolong—with constant pulsating power. Guaranteed to produce pleasure, even after organism." This line got

Me, Valerie, Monika, and Mary in
final pose of the "Rubberware Song"

a huge laugh from the audience, and after that, Valerie had no problem flinging around the wobbly dildo.

Valerie was also going through a transformation in her personal life. Things were heating up with a new girlfriend, Sandy Starkey. Sandy, a heavyset woman with black, close-cropped hair, was falling hard in love with Valerie. Sandy wanted to spend every minute possible with her new love.

"Why do you devote so much time on this DiDi Glitz thing?" she challenged Valerie.

"Les Nickelettes gives me an identity," replied Valerie.

It finally came down to an ultimatum. "It's either me or Les Nickelettes," demanded Sandy.

"No way in hell. This is what I'm doing, and you're just going to have to tag along."

Taken aback by Valerie's uncharacteristic assertiveness, Sandy mumbled, "Okay." So instead of walking out the door, she joined the club. She became our follow-spotlight operator.

Les Nickelettes would also lead Sandy to a personal transformation. It shocked her to witness the play's open display of female sexuality. "I was just a little Midwestern girl who went to Bible College," she said.

Having grown up in Kansas City, Sandy clung to a muted persona, dressing only in black, brown, or hunter green. One night Liza asked her, "You never wear any colors, do you?"

The remark stopped Sandy cold in her tracks. "No, I don't." After that Sandy discarded her drab clothes for a more colorful wardrobe.

Mary continued in a downward spiral of unreliability and emotional outbursts. Her latest druggie dreamboat enticed her to consume massive amounts of drugs and stay up late partying every night. But that wasn't the worst of it. As a child, Mary had contracted juvenile diabetes, and her current lifestyle interfered with adequately monitoring the disease. It not only caused her to be unhealthy physically, but also emotionally.

One night, after she disappeared in the middle of rehearsing one of her scenes, Deb and I found her crying in the bathroom. "I can't get the dance step right," she sobbed hysterically.

Deb rolled her eyes in disgust, "I'm done with this, I'm sick of it. We can't depend on you, Mary."

Mary collapsed in a pool of intense wails. Deb threw up her hands and walked out.

My patience was wearing thin as well. Usually I just shrugged, but this time I warned, "Mary, if you don't get your act together, Deb is going to replace you."

"I can't, I can't!" she shrieked.

"Snap out of it, Mary," I said, as I planted a soft slap across her face. And just like in the movies, it worked. Mary pulled herself together, rejoined the rehearsal, and buckled down for the rest of the run.

Deb proved her mettle as a director, but sometimes youth tripped her up. One scene had her stumped. The script called for a nightmare/dream sequence where all the people in DiDi's life swirled around her demanding top priority. "I want to bring in my theater friend Michael to help," Deb told me.

"Absolutely not," I said. "You can't bring in somebody else, especially a man. You have to do it yourself."

I knew from the past that once a man comes in, no matter the intentions, things changed. I pressed Deb to trust herself and forced her to take ownership of the show. But I also supported and assisted her, as did the other actresses, while she worked out the action of the scene. In the end, it turned out great.

"It was just fear," admitted Deb. "When you're twenty you don't want to admit a level of immaturity."

❧

Three weeks prior to opening of the show, the Eighth Annual Salmon Awards were held in the ballroom of the Women's Building. I turned the task of producing the annual extravaganza

Poster for *The DiDi Glitz Story*

Design by Diane Noomin

over to board of directors vice president Stafford Buckley. The first thing he did, after taking on the role of head honcho, was to give the event a theme—"A Return to the Fabulous Elegance of the Early Sixties"—and proceeded to team up with Jane Huether to write a real cheesy award show with inane scripted dialogue—that, he instructed, "must be delivered deadpan."

Caught up in a whirlwind schedule of rehearsals and production chores, I welcomed Stafford and Jane taking charge. The newbies in the group were inaugurated into our annual party celebrating the ongoing swim upstream and the satirical joy of spawning. Judy and Deb grooved on the kitschy concept of handing out faux Hollywood awards. Rose delighted in having an event to wear her new secondhand Jackie Kennedy dress. And Diane, who had become increasingly anxious, discovered that gluing feathers, sequins, and rhinestones on secondhand trophies calmed her nerves.

On July 9, 1981, the World Premiere of *I'd Rather Be Doing Something Else: The DiDi Glitz Story* took place at the Performance Space. The site was a small auditorium behind the All Saint's Episcopal Church near the infamous intersection of Haight and Ashbury Streets. The space was a multiuse facility, not a theater, so each night, in addition to acting, singing, and dancing, the actresses also scrambled to position the set in place and put up the audience chairs. To make matters worse, the dressing room was a tiny, dank hole in the basement that could only be accessed by a rickety ladder, and had no toilet. Once the audience arrived, we were forced to pee in a jar. The things we do for love.

In the days leading up to the opening, Diane was nearly jumping out of her skin. On the brink of publicly displaying her artistic brainchild, she demanded perfection. Deb, more versed in theatrical openings, knew that wasn't going to happen. But

Diane's pre-opening demands and jitters caused Deb to be wound up as tight as a rubber band ready to break. "Do it again, and do it right!" she barked at the actresses.

After final dress rehearsal, because of the cramped space, Deb was forced to bend like a pretzel at the top rung of the steep dressing room ladder to give her feedback notes. It was the last straw; she lost it and stormed out of the theater. Thirty minutes later, she returned and called the cast up onstage for a "girl yell." The "yell" or "scream" would go on to become a pre-performance ritual that served to bring everyone together.

"It was *the* most liberating thing I'd ever done in my life," stated Deb. "To stand in a circle with my arms around eight other women and start out with a real low, quiet sound and then slowly accelerate into a scream was so empowering, so invigorating, to just let that fire come up from deep down inside."

Girl power.

Despite Diane's anxieties and Deb's melt down, it was clear we had a hit on opening night. Tim Lewis from *The Spectator* confirmed this impression:

> *DiDi Glitz, underground [comic] heroine . . . has come to everlovin' life! . . . Valerie Helmold is classic as the dizzy DiDi, from her New Yawk accent to the "wild and crazy" schemes she has under her polyester plush-pile hairdo.*
>
> *. . . There's really not enough superlatives for this show. Les Nickelettes have performed a major coup in camp theatre.*

Tim Lewis raved about every aspect of the production: the cast, the script, the set and costume designs, the songs, and Deb's debut as a director (". . . keeps the production at an energetic, rollicking pace"). Plus, his description of Valerie's performance attested to Deb's vision of her in the lead role.

Valerie looked and sounded like DiDi, but there was more to it. "Many actresses would have only played a one-dimensional DiDi," observed Rose. "But Valerie imbued the role with vulnerability and hurt and goodness at the core, without sacrificing the comedy and camp."

"I'm fabulous, honey!" Valerie crowed with DiDi's signature line. "It was easy . . . well, not easy. I worked on it, but it was a good fit."

I played Glenda, DiDi's politically correct, feminist sister. Diane described the character as, ". . . the only one that was my real voice. She was the grounding element. Without her, there would be no contrast."

"Glenda was the only character that I could personally relate to," added Deb.

Decked out in jeans, vivid tie-dye, and the only one to wear a natural hair wig, Glenda also looked more like a daytime version of Les Nickelettes. I got to say corny lines, like: "DiDi, your materialistic energy is stressing me out."

But my favorite bit came in the scene after the bank heist. Watching the TV news about the female suspect in the crime (and not knowing it was her own sister), Glenda commented, "Don't you love it? More women are robbing banks!" It was such a comfortable part, I didn't give it much thought. Besides, I was too busy producing the show.

But a week before we opened I panicked. "You haven't given me any direction," I complained to Deb.

"You're doing so well on your own, I didn't feel you needed a lot of direction," explained Deb.

"Why didn't you push me?"

"Because you're an accomplished performer."

It wasn't Deb's fault; it was mine. My tantrum was akin to a lazy college student blaming the professor for having to cram the night before an exam. The truth was that I adopted a throwaway attitude toward acting, and it alarmed me. My urge to perform had always been the engine that kept Les Nickelettes moving forward. Now my preoccupation was with writing and producing.

A defining aha moment happened onstage. In one scene, Glenda was supposed to be listening to DiDi, but I broke character and mentally put on my producer hat. While my co-performer was acting, I visually did an audience count and checked up on the lighting technician. On reflection, I was shocked that I had violated the first rule of acting: stay in character at all times. At that moment I grasped how my primary role in Les Nickelettes had evolved from an actress in search of a great part to that of de facto Head Nickelette.

"You were the matriarch," said Deb. "The ultimate person of responsibility, the default person."

"And we needed you to be that," added Diane.

"You were our guiding light, so to speak," said Rose.

In this revamped group I had matured into a mentor, and I was the glue that kept everything together.

In the gay newspaper, *The Bay Area Reporter*, the accolades continued with a tongue-in-cheek endorsement by Dan Turner: "Les Nickelettes make drag look like it was invented by women. . . . DiDi sticks to you like hair spray." Word of mouth sold out the six-week run with fans returning two or three times and bringing their friends. Who can complain about such success? But an observation from reviewer M. J. Lallo in *Coming Up!* caught my attention:

. . . if there is a political perspective in this play amid all the craziness, it's that single mothers are doing hard times, and their children are even worse off. However,

Les Nickelettes, a company formed to offend every-body, embellishes their plot to the point that political commentary is lost.

Many scenes are hysterical, but in our laughter we tend to forget to ask the question, "So what?" . . . I wouldn't harp on this matter so much, but Les Nickelettes do define themselves as a theatre company dedicated to a "unique sense of humor that celebrates an evolved female consciousness."

M. J. Lallo zeroed in on a problem I had with the limp message that DiDi delivered at the end of the play: "I'm pushing forty, but forty's not pushing me." This rebellion against society's disposal of aging women was not as punchy as it could have been. Unfortunately, I had no brilliant solution to spiff up the finale, so I kept these misgivings to myself. Plus, whenever my mind wandered to this problem, my inner Brooklyn DiDi loudly dismissed the unease: "The audiences are raving, and the house is sold out; what's not to like?"

～✦～

High from having a hit show, we were like addicts craving a bigger dose. Confidence breeds creativity. One day, Judy came in with a proposal to jazz up "Don't Just Relocate, Redecorate" by turning it into a tap dance number.

Incredulous, I said, "Let me get this straight. You want us to change the set from a dive bar into the Leatherette Lounge, sing, and *tap dance* all at the same time?"

"Do you think we have it too easy?" added Valerie.

"There's no way we can learn to tap dance during the six-week break between runs," I said, hoping to end the conversation.

"Sure you can, no problem," Judy assured me. "I'll teach you. The tempo of this song just has a soft shoe feel to it."

"I took tap lessons as a kid," chimed in Monika. "I could do a solo; I still have my tap shoes." Valerie and I bought tap shoes, and every night Judy gave us lessons. And voila! DiDi Glitz met Busby Berkeley. The difficult part of the set change took place during Monika's front and center solo. "See, no problem," repeated Judy. A string of four revved-up dances in the second act would become like the last grueling miles of a marathon for the performers, but a highlight for the audience.

The Julia Morgan Theatre in Berkeley was twice as large as our San Francisco venue, but we still packed the joint. Valerie's parents, visiting from Arizona, came to one of the shows. "I was really nervous," said Valerie. "But they absolutely loved it. I think they were so happy that I looked all femmed-out."

"They never mentioned the rubber dildo you were waving around?" I asked.

"No, my mom just thought I looked wonderful. My dad did talk about the monk in the audience. Berkeley was like another universe to them."

Berkeley was also a different kind of heaven for the performers. We had a real stage with a proscenium arch and permanent seating, plus best of all, a dressing room with a toilet. The fans became an extension of the show, like a family. The Sisters of Perpetual Indulgence showed up in full nun drag and white-face makeup. Rose welcomed the Crystal Glitz Fan Club. The club was apparently formed to celebrate the blossoming of preadolescent Crystal Glitz into Crystal "Hot Pink" Blitzkrieg swathed in a tight pink sheath, and sporting a fuchsia Mohawk singing, "I love hot pink; nails are pink, hair is pink, shoes, belts, gloves, mink, everything can be hot pink . . ."

Mary, as DiDi's mom, Irma, in an aqua crushed-velvet muumuu, blue wig, and big fake butt to give her body an aged look, went out to greet audience members after the show, "Hi, how are ya? I'm DiDi's ma." She repeated the sage advice that Irma delivered to her daughter in the show: "You win some—you lose the rest."

Overseeing it all, Diane beamed like a proud mother, reporting with glee, "People are giving DiDi Glitz parties."

From the start, the identifying brand for Les Nickelettes had been tons of glitter adorned on eyelids, cheeks, and lips. We stocked our makeup kit with small jars of the sparkly specks of plastic in every color of the rainbow.

When you wear "tons" of glitter several nights a week it invades every part of your existence. No matter how thoroughly you scrub it off, a few shiny flakes stick like glue. This generated a running joke about the weirdest places we discovered traces of glitter.

"I found glitter in my armpit," I said.

"In my belly button," said Monika.

"In the creases of my panties," said Mary.

"In my bed," said Deb.

"In my pubic hair," said Judy.

"On my boyfriend," said Rose.

"On my girlfriend," added Valerie.

"You're not a Nickelette until you have a total glitter infestation."

"Hell, you're not a Nickelette till you shit glitter."

This priceless phrase became a Nickelettes motto.

At the closing cast party, Deb gifted everyone with red T-shirts emblazoned "You're Not a Nickelette Till You Shit Glitter." We applied glitter to our lips and licked it off as proof that we'd earned this badge of honor.

Diane campaigned to extend the run, but the performers balked. Working nonstop for a year—writing, rehearsing, producing, and doing thirty-eight performances, while holding down day jobs—had left us exhausted. "I'm excited just to have dinner at home," sighed a fatigued Valerie. I understood Diane didn't want to let it go, but I missed sleeping. I also missed being with Vince; we needed to reconnect. We hadn't spent quality time together in months.

The DiDi Glitz Story was Les Nickelettes' most successful and profitable show to date. Harboring a hope that this success would lead to bigger things, we clung to the fantasy that a visionary producer would materialize to offer us a mainstream theater run, a spot on the newly emerging cable TV, or a movie deal. But this elusive dream failed to emerge, so we banked our profits and contemplated our next move forward.

As we mulled over our options, Judy announced that after she got her braces off, she was moving to New York City. It had always been her dream to make it in the Big Apple. As I digested this news, it occurred to me DiDi Glitz hailed from Brooklyn. What if we took her back where she belonged? An East Coast tour of The DiDi Glitz Story would be a great way to expand our credentials. And what better place to be discovered? It was time to make a bold move. Have you ever seen salmon swimming up the Hudson River? Nothing ventured, nothing gained.

CHAPTER 11

NEW YAWK

"You can't get rid of us."

The aspiration to take *The DiDi Glitz Story* three thousand miles cross-country caught the wind of destiny. When Judy relocated to the Big Apple, she would join two other ex-Nickelettes who had lived there for about a year. Betsy Newman and Ellin Stein had even teamed up to do a couple of shows under the banner of the New York Nicks.

Ellin, who was freelancing as a journalist in New York City, contacted me about an article she was working on for the *Village Voice*. She explained that the piece—"Rhinestone Politics: Bay Area Experimental Theater. How Far Off-Broadway Is San Francisco?"—would include Les Nickelettes, and asked me for a current photo of the group. I quickly set up a photo shoot featuring *The DiDi Glitz Story* characters and dashed off a picture to her of Les Nickelettes playfully looking the world straight in the eye while brazenly sticking out our tongues. That image was prominently displayed under the title in the lead-in to the article.

Ellin argued in this March 1982 article that New York experimental theater had nothing on San Francisco. She

Valerie, Betsy, Diane, Monika, Judy, Me, Jean, Debra,
and Rose sticking out our tongues
Photo © Victoria Rouse

sketched out the San Francisco underground performance art
scene and included this take on Les Nickelettes:

> *The serious themes of their thickly plotted musicals are
> buried beneath a barrage of puns, visual jokes, cheap
> laughs, plot complications, and every melodramatic
> cliché in the book. They circle around the message,
> approaching it in an oblique "feminine" way in contrast
> to the more overtly feminist companies who dramatize
> similar issues in a "masculine," i.e. direct, way.*

The photo and a mention in the *Village Voice* provided
us with great advance publicity. "Go East, young ladies," the
universe whispered. To make it happen, we only needed two
things: a booking and lots of cash.

We jump-started an aggressive fundraising drive by first
reviving our newsletter *Nick News*. Using a bit of satirical

blackmail, we appealed to our fans and followers for money: "Help us swarm to New York. We've been pestering you with our smarmy antics for ten years now; isn't it time New York finds out how it feels? How can you get rid of us? Simply send money. It's easy. It's *tax deductible*. For those of you who have some kind of perverse moral objection to simply paying someone to leave you alone, we offer other ways to hit you up. Clean out your closets and donate to our super garage sale. Having a party? We'll perform for a small fee. Own a club? Our services are available for hire. And if you want something tangible for your buck, we have super-duper raffle tickets available for purchase. Grand prize $25! Still holding out? Surely we can weasel money out of you for a ticket to our Tenth Anniversary Bash." Coaxing, cajoling, begging; we weren't above any of it. (Selling our firstborn? Okay, maybe that's going too far.)

In 1982, Les Nickelettes had survived ten years of swimming upstream. To celebrate a decade of campy shenanigans, we organized a Tenth Anniversary Bash as an extravaganza/ fundraiser featuring Les Nickelettes. We also enlisted a cohort of underground performers and an extraordinary all-girl band, the Contractions, who rocked so hot and hard they epitomized cool.

As I reflected on this milestone, it hit home that I was the only one who had been with the group since its inception. Year after year, I maintained a stubborn quest to keep the collective chugging along. So, for the big gala, I was assigned to compile a biography of the group: "1972—1982: The First Ten Years," a blow-by-blow retrospective chronicle sprinkled with an archival vault of "greatest hits" performed by the others in the group. Standing behind a podium onstage, I gave this description of the formative years: "There were no entrance requirements, no leaders, no structure, no rules; it was anarchy in high heels." I recited how the accidental creation of the group had led to urban guerrilla performances, then shifted to structured skits, and finally evolved into a fully functioning theater group with scripted plays and original music. I concluded: "Les Nickelettes have proven to the world, despite a display of unparalleled tackiness coupled with unbridled feminine satire, that we can survive and still have fun at it."

The phrase "anarchy in high heels" struck a resonant chord with the others in the group. I had inadvertently hit on not just a characterization of the early days, but also an essential core concept of Les Nickelettes. Anarchy in high heels wasn't a state of dress; it was a state of mind. All the women who had been in the group had shared in this form of female revolution. The current group was different, yet the same.

And there was always room for new recruits. On the morning of the celebration, I arrived at the Mission District Capp Street Center and spent the day leading a Nickelettes crew in setting up the stage and equipment. In the late afternoon, we called a dinner break, and everyone disappeared.

I grabbed a sandwich, but as I was eating, I noticed one big task left undone. No one else was around. I bent over the lip of the stage, and, heaving a heavy sigh, I began to pull out from the dusty alcove a hundred folding chairs to seat the audience. I felt a tap on my shoulder and looked up into the face of a woman in black-rimmed glasses. "Do you need some help?" she said.

She introduced herself as Annette Jarvie, manager of the Contractions. But in that moment, I saw a tech angel with a halo around her curly black hair. "Sure," I replied. She grabbed chairs, and in nothing flat we had them all set up.

⁓⟡⌒

The Tenth Anniversary Bash launched a four-month, all-out assault to raise money. We performed at cabaret clubs and private parties and held garage sales. But in June, we stumbled upon the biggest moneymaker of them all: the Twelfth Annual

Lesbian/Gay Pride Parade. This festive event celebrated gay rights and attracted massive crowds of people from all over the world to San Francisco. We discovered that, as a nonprofit organization, we could rent a concession space, get a one-day liquor license, and sell booze. In the spirit of the glitter glam occasion, we opted for a booth to sell champagne and strawberries. We set up our funky bare-bones stall consisting of a table laden with baskets of juicy, ruby red strawberries and a sign in front advertising our wares. Propping up the sign were plastic ice coolers stocked with bottles of cheap champagne. We christened the new venture with quality control tests, toasting our cleverness: "Can't sell it if you don't try it."

An hour later, the San Francisco Health Services inspector arrived. He informed us that because we were selling food our booth had to be covered.

"Aw, come on, it's just strawberries," I pleaded.

The official fruit police was having none of it, "You're out of compliance, and if you don't remedy the situation within one hour, you will be shut down."

I rushed to the Nickelettes storage basement and returned with cardboard panels and colored bed linens. We arranged the flimsy freestanding set pieces around our table and used clothespins to attach the pink and blue bed sheets over the top. From a distance the makeshift booth looked like a gay Bedouin tent—but it was a Health Services–compliant tent.

The parade ended, and boisterous celebrants swarmed us. As dollar bills stacked up in the cash box, we congratulated ourselves on this shrewd business move. But then—horror of horrors—we ran out of bubbly. I made a mad dash to the nearest liquor store and scooped up their entire stock of low-priced champagne. Next, we ran out of strawberries, but by then the drag queens just roared, "Forget it, honey, more room for champagne."

At the end of the day, we counted up our receipts and were amazed that this eight-hour effort had netted almost $1,500.

Even after expenses, it had been twice as profitable as garage sales, or performing for pennies.

Nevertheless, performing for loose change continued to be a high priority. The tenth anniversary had introduced the new group to old gems: "Birth Control Blues," "Fairy's Lament," and "Slave to My Art." Combining these oldies but goodies with favorites from *The DiDi Glitz Story*—"Rubberware," "Miami," and "Hot Pink"—we created a mash-up cabaret show, calling it *A Touch of Camp*. During the summer, we booked it at every club and party that would pay us.

We even produced a four-week run at the Valencia Rose, a new venue on Valencia Street painted rosy pink. On opening night, I surprised each Nickelette with a kitschy bowling shirt. I had talked Vince into financing the gift and enlisted Diane to design it. The black cotton shirts were embroidered with each member's name on the front. On the back, "Les Nickelettes" was emblazed in hot pink lettering above a champagne glass bursting with bubbles. Slipping on the shirts, we all shifted into faux girl-gang playacting. Next thing you know, a skit about "The Pinks" was added to the show: a bunch of girls all wearing black and pink, and sounding off about "Hot Pink" girl power.

My tech angel from the Tenth Anniversary Bash, Annette, volunteered to help backstage. After the first week of the run, I walked into the dressing room and did a double take as I spied Annette and Deb holding hands and snuggling. Perhaps, they were just good friends? But the next night, Rose and I were standing at the bottom of the old grand staircase in the theater and watched as Deb and Annette waltzed out.

"Deb stopped in the middle, and gave Annette a big kiss," recalled Rose. Rose and I looked at each other and burst out laughing; as far as we knew, Deb was heterosexual. Not any more—Annette and Deb became a hot item. "As it turned out," said Rose, "Annette was much more suited for Deb than her previous male lover."

I, on the other hand, was jolted by a romantic gesture that turned scary during the Valencia Rose run. A dozen roses were sent to the theater by a fan. The enclosed card, addressed to me, was from a guy professing his undying, everlasting love. The next night, he showed up, and sent a note backstage saying he wanted to meet me. Surrounded by a Nickelettes entourage, I reluctantly made an appearance in the lobby. I thanked him for the roses, but after assessing his creepiness, I hastily retreated backstage. This guy was on our mailing list, and my residence was posted as Les Nickelettes return address, so this encounter caused me concern. I shuddered to think that the price of even my small claim to fame in Les Nickelettes could result in this strange guy appearing on my doorstep. I took some comfort in the fact that if he did show up at my apartment, Vince would be there to greet him.

In late spring of 1982, two unrelated events caused a slight shift in the group. It was time for Judy to leave. Rose, Deb, and I went to the airport to see her off to the Big Apple. With no braces, Judy's straight white teeth gleamed in the glare of the terminal's fluorescent lights. We all wept. We didn't want her to go, or we wanted to go with her. "Good luck," I muttered, hugging her, and vowing, "We're going to see you in the fall when we bring *The DiDi Glitz Story* to New York. I promise." We missed her even before the plane departed.

Monika, now eighteen, was set to wed her boyfriend, Mike. The night before the nuptials, Les Nickelettes threw her a bachelorette party. We ate dinner at Enrico's and then surprised Monika with tickets to the Off-Broadway, a lone male strip club wedged among the dozen or so female topless joints on San Francisco's notoriously bawdy Broadway strip.

One by one the male dancers appeared dressed as female-fantasy hunks, cavorted to loud throbbing music, and shed their clothing down to colorful codpieces. It was obvious to us that all these guys were gay, so we chuckled at the kitschy spectacle—seeing it more as high camp than macho turn-on. But the suburban housewives, out on the town for a night of naughtiness, hooted and hollered and seductively slipped bills into the guys' G-string jock straps.

"The Latino guy, Mr. Love, was a swarthy little guy," said Goody, "and he had a huge bulging codpiece. It was pink, and as he danced, he stuck his hand down."

"And the audience started screaming, 'Oh, no! Oh, my God, no!'" I added.

"He turned his back to the audience," continued Goody, "and started to erotically pull something out, and when he turned around—it was a bunny rabbit."

"I guess that's what he thought women wanted," I snickered.

"The best one was the Black guy on roller skates," said Valerie. "He had on a little skirt that shimmied when he spun around." Mary was having such a great time, she jumped onstage, and seductively wiggled and swayed with the strippers.

The bride-to-be's reaction was blasé disinterest. The only thing that mattered to her was getting a ring on her finger the next day. On the morning of the ceremony in Golden Gate Park, the bride's Nickelettes attendants helped her get ready.

"My wedding was special," said Monika. "The Nickelettes bought me real silk stockings, and Deb did my makeup. Rosie cried." After being in the role of surrogate mother to Monika for the past three years, it felt surreal to watch this untamed teenager tie the knot.

Monika's new husband didn't understand her devotion to Les Nickelettes, but tolerated it. Hubby's approval or not, she still harbored dreams of stardom and was determined to go to New York with the troupe. Monika's conflict with her husband caused me to reflect on how lucky I was to have a partner who supported me unconditionally.

The Ninth Annual Salmon Awards followed on the white high heels of Monika's wedding. This was the last big fundraising event of our four-month nonstop assault. The Bossa Nova themed event was fun, but the Ninth Annual Salmon Awards didn't bring in the profit we had come to expect. Maybe we had already wrung out every drop of available cash from our fans, or, maybe, a satirical song sung at the event to the tune of "Blame It on the Bossa Nova" hit closer to home: "Blame It on the Reaganomics."

Maybe, it was just time to get this show on the road.

We intended to take *The DiDi Glitz Story* to New York, but the cost to transport and house performers for six weeks, plus shipping bulky, heavy plywood sets back and forth cross-country, was more than we had in the bank. We considered repainting the sets on lightweight fold-up cardboard, but Diane feared her designs would be severely compromised. She also had reservations about doing the show in New York with our California accents.

"Do it right, or don't do it at all," she told us.

Envisioning being creamed by East Coast critics for our failed attempt to mimic the New York inflection, I concurred with her assessment. "So let's spiff up *A Touch of Camp*, and take it to New York," I proposed. "It has the best numbers from the DiDi Glitz show, and it's totally travel-friendly."

"What other option do we have?" said Deb.

What I didn't see coming was slipping into panic-attack mode. Thinking about how we were going to manage to take time off from our day jobs, fly to New York, pay for lodgings, and put on a show in unfamiliar territory freaked me out.

"It's going to be fine," Deb assured me. "We're going to do this, and that's that. We just have to get on the plane."

It was reassuring to have Deb continue as director and co-producer. She turned our pie-in-the-sky dream into reality by securing the Westbeth Theater Center, an off-off-Broadway venue, for a three-week booking in mid-October. But now, we had only five weeks to get our shit together. We revised the cabaret revue and retitled it *Anarchy in High Heels*. One week prior to departure, we threw a bon voyage party as a try-out in front of an audience.

During the afternoon rehearsal, on the day of the going-away performance, I was seized by a vision of East Coast sharks devouring this California girl in a New York minute. Light-headed and nauseous, I lurched off to melt down in seclusion. Finding a dark vacant room, I curled up in a fetal position, squished my eyes shut, and chanted over and over, "Breathe, breathe, breathe." But the devil kept whispering in my ear: *What if something goes wrong? What if you bomb? What if you run out of money?* I feared my reputation for being the glue that kept everything together was about to be exposed as a fraud.

After fifteen minutes of heart-pounding palpitations, I pretended to slap myself across the face several times, which caused me to laugh. Which reminded me, this was supposed to be fun. Weak and wobbly, I returned to the auditorium. Deb was onstage confidently directing activities. I whispered to her, "Are we really going to do this, Deb?"

"Damn right," she said with a laugh. "We just have to get on that plane."

One song we added to *Anarchy in High Heels* was "You Don't Own Me," snitched from Leslie Gore on *The T.A.M.I. Show*. Our version featured a feminist trio, defiantly declaring their independence dolled up in puffy 1950s-style hairdos and sorority-style prom dresses. We also dusted off the cockroach costume and did a skit about a human-sized radioactive bug from a botched Roach Motel experiment. The ravenous insect warned the masses, "You know you can't get rid of me."

And we ended with homage to our hometown:

In Kook City you're never bored
This burg is the open ward
They don't lock 'em up; they put 'em in the streets
You never know what psychopaths you might meet. . . .

From the stage, after the show, I bid a bon voyage to our fans and congratulated them on contributing to the effort to ship us off to New York. "I guess you *can* get rid of us," I deadpanned.

Someone yelled out, "Are you coming back?" My mouth opened, but I had no response. "You have to," the supporter persisted.

"Of course," I sputtered, not able to come up with a witty comeback. I was disarmed by the fact that even if we bombed in the Big Apple, Kook City would welcome us back with open arms.

The night before we left, Diane, our native New York expert, lectured us on how to stay safe in the harsh city. "Number one: adapt the 'nobody cares' New York attitude. Number two: avoid bad neighborhoods, and watch your back on the subway. And most important, number three: no eye contact." She gifted each of us with metal Cat Defense key-ring devices. If threatened, you inserted two fingers in the cat eyeholes and poked the assailant with the long pointy steel cat ears. Here we come, New York City. Don't mess with us, mister.

The next day, at the crack of dawn, Mary, Valerie, Monika, Deb, Rosie, and I boarded a plane bound for John F. Kennedy airport. Once airborne, my disposition lightened. Deb was right; I just had to get on the plane. Somehow, we had managed to dodge our day jobs for five weeks, except for

Deb. She got a couple of weeks off, but would have to return right after the show opened. "Being in New York will be like a vacation," noted Monika. "We'll be working day and night, but at least we won't also have to hold down straight jobs."

Aloft and heading East, I took a deep breath, relaxed, and drifted off to slumberland. Several hours later, the plane began to descend as we neared our destination. Mary poked me in the ribs. "How can you sleep? I'm so hyped up."

"Me too," echoed Monika.

Deb pulled out her makeup kit to prepare her face for the big city. We all joined in for a pre-landing cosmetic frolic. Even the giggling flight attendants got into the act, offering rouge application tips. In the midst of this fun, the plane banked, and we glimpsed out the window the glorious monstrosity of Manhattan. With lipstick and eyeliner intact, Monika burst out singing "New York, New York." "Sounds like she's ready to take a bite out of the Big Apple," I said to no one in particular. The other passengers looked dubious.

Out of the gate, we hit the ground dancing and giggling with Monika still singing at the top of her lungs. We flagged down a huge, old-time checker cab, and the six of us tumbled in. "We're in New York City, baby," shouted Deb, and everyone laughed like banshees.

"Seventy-Fourth Street between Broadway and Columbus," I instructed the driver.

Finding an affordable place for all of us to stay for five weeks had proved tricky. We had to stitch together three different locales. One was a costly loft rental that we could only afford for one week but which would serve as both a rehearsal and a living space. Second was a three-week sublet apartment. That left the first two days, as well as the last four days of our stay, up in the air. This gap came to light amid plans to save money by booking flights on the cheapest days of the week. Flying on a Thursday saved money, but the loft wasn't available until Saturday. Due to our overextended lodging budget, staying in hotel rooms was out of the question.

These logistic problems threw me in a panic. As I came undone, Vince came to my rescue. A woman he worked with owned a family apartment in midtown Manhattan that was currently uninhabited. He talked her into letting us stay there during the gaps in our rentals. She must have owed Vince a favor. Additionally, Vince loaned us the $1,000 advance we needed to rent the loft. The group presented him with our Knight in Shining Armor award.

To me, the only thing significant about this West Seventy-Fourth Street place had been that it was free. Upon entering the apartment, however, I was impressed by the elegant furnishings and walls covered with expensive artwork. But it was tiny for six people, and I reminded everyone of Vince's instructions: "Don't sit on the antique furniture."

Too excited to hang around in this fragile lodging, we dropped our bags and fled to check out the 'hood. Ignorance is bliss, so my first impression of this posh Upper West Side neighborhood made me think Diane had exaggerated in her scary stories about New York.

At sunset, we hopped on the subway and headed to a party hosted by Betsy. Although Betsy had left the group in 1980, she'd never abandoned "the rebellious spirit of Les Nickelettes." At the Oregon Repertory Theater, prior to moving to New York, she had overseen a successful *Razor Lips Review* based on our 1975 "Ms. Hysterical Contest." Once in New York, she teamed up with ex-Nickelette Ellin to form a group dubbed the New York Nicks (it was supposed to be a pun on the New York Knicks basketball team—I never really got it). The New York Nicks staged *Falsies,* a new rendition of the beauty pageant satire.

"It was a very big hit at the off-off-Broadway Theater for the New City," explained Betsy. "And it could have been a long-term project, but if you're non-Equity, you can only run for three weeks." They followed up with a show called *Feelers* about a giant cockroach based on our 1978 show *Curtains!* But it bombed.

Betsy's party was stuffed with performing artists. How cool was this? Our first night out on the town, and already immersed in the off-off-Broadway New York scene. I enjoyed reconnecting with Betsy and Ellin, a kind of mixing of the old and new guard. But Betsy had a different take: "I felt left out. I didn't know the new Nickelettes. It was such a club feeling, and it was sad for me because I felt like an outsider, not like an insider anymore."

The next day, I discovered that we were staying just two blocks from the Dakota apartment building where John Lennon had lived and was murdered. I made a pilgrimage to pay my respects. The English Victorian building was dark, melancholy, and majestic. Standing on the sidewalk, peering into the arch entryway, I cried as two-year-old TV images of the murder scene and aftermath flashed through my mind.

On Saturday, we moved downtown to the Tribeca neighborhood. The rented second floor loft consisted of a large, sparsely furnished room with brick walls and high ceilings. After being crammed in a tiny apartment for the past two days, the six of us spread out in roomy luxury. Crawling into the swinging string hammock suspended from the ceiling beams, I staked out a private space. I gazed out of this cocoon to the opposite wall where, through three large uncovered windows, I could watch the Hudson River flow by.

As soon as we moved in, we got to work, rehearsing with fierce determination. Judy joined us, and we felt like a complete group again. Spending every day focused only on performing was a luxury. The morning started with an hour and a half of physical and vocal exercises. Leading the physical workout, Monika became a relentless drill sergeant. We groaned and bitched but saw our dancing improve. With bodies and voices

Deb, Me, and Monika in publicity photo
for *Anarchy in High Heels*
Photo © F. Stop Fitzgerald

warmed up, we rehearsed the rest of the day and into the evening, stopping only for meals and preproduction tasks. For the first time, we were living like artists 24/7. "It was fun," said Rose.

On the third day, the guy who owned the loft came by with a couple of friends to pick up some things. They lingered, watching us rehearse, conversing in Spanish. Rose (who spoke Spanish) told us, "They're sizing us up, rating our tits and ass."

"Go bust them," I told Rose.

Strolling over to the doorway where they stood, Rose said, "*Hola. Yo hablo español.*" Sheepishly, they made a quick exit. The empowerment of being in a group of women had allowed us to boldly call out these guys for crossing the line.

We did take breaks to go shopping. Look, people, we didn't travel three thousand miles cross-country to the biggest shopping mecca in America to suppress our female urge to hunt and gather for discounted merchandise. Heading out the door to one of our favorite stores, we chanted like devoted zombies: "Fiorucci, Fiorucci, Fiorucci. . . ."

But one shopping foray opened up a conflict. Monika called her husband every day asking for his approval on her every move. This rubbed the rest of us the wrong way. In contrast, Vince called *me* every day, and we chatted about what was going on. I didn't ask for his consent on anything. On a shopping trip to Canal Street Jeans, Monika found a pale pink, punk-style leather jacket and desperately wanted it as a present for her upcoming nineteenth birthday. But she had to run back to the loft and call Mike to get permission. "Why can't you just buy it?" I asked. "Why do you need Mike's okay?"

"I guess that's what happens when you get tied down," ribbed Valerie.

"Don't let Mike boss you around," added Deb.

"The old ball and chain," I chimed in.

Monika ignored our teasing. Mike gave her the green light, and she raced back to Canal Street Jeans. Upon her return, barely closing the front door, she ripped the coveted purchase out of the bag, shed her clothes, and paraded around in her birthday suit covered only by the waist-length leather jacket. This was the rebellious Monika we all knew and loved.

Mike couldn't hide the fact that he didn't want this silly women's group to undermine his authority. The Nickelettes were never raging, politically correct feminists, but we did support disrupting patriarchy. Discussing the issue of female equality only annoyed Monika. She dismissed the subject with, "That's how it is when you're married."

"Gary was the same as Mike," commented Judy, about her boyfriend. "He'd say, 'When you get with those feminist Nickelettes, you just talk about how you're going to make fun of dicks.'" Judy had left Gary behind in San Francisco when she'd moved to New York, but they didn't break up. I recognized that Gary's point of view echoed the biggest fear in most men: women ridiculing their patriarchy. Maybe that's why men claimed women weren't funny.

It didn't take long after reuniting with Judy to notice that she wasn't the same fun-loving, free spirit we'd said good-bye to five months earlier. *Anarchy in High Heels* was conceived with Judy in the lineup. Deb filled in at the bon voyage party. "I did her part," said Deb, "and I thought, Judy will pick this up just like that. But when we got to New York, her self-esteem was so beaten down I was worried."

This timid New York Judy baffled us. "I didn't feel like the same person. I felt weak," she admitted. "The Nicks gave me strength. I was recognized for my talent, but I also had to pull my weight to maintain respect within the group. And then when I came to New York, I didn't have my support group. I was very alone."

The cruelty of New York had done a number on Judy. She shared a cramped one-bedroom apartment with a roommate who was a talent agent but refused to let Judy try out for her agency. She told Judy to her face, "You're not good enough."

Auditioning also hit her like a slap in the face. "I didn't realize I was a different color until I got to New York," said Judy. "I thought of myself as a character actress who could do almost anything. But the auditions went sour for me because I wasn't the right type. They'd say: 'Are you a little Asian?' 'You're not Spanish looking enough.' 'Can you be Black?'" Being rejected solely because of ethnicity was a bitter pill to swallow. "If I was white, I would have had an easier time." In desperation, she put on an Afro wig and auditioned for *Creamgirls* (a spoof on *Dreamgirls*). "They liked me," said Judy. "But then asked if I was African American and I said no."

"Sorry," they said. "We need somebody Black."

"Why didn't you lie?" asked Deb.

"I knew they'd find out sooner or later. They asked me about my wig, and I said, 'It's my Donna Dumber disco wig.' They didn't laugh."

"They didn't get the Donna Summer pun?"

"No sense of humor."

Seeing Judy reduced to a lethargic and disengaged performer was shocking. "I knew she could do *Anarchy in High Heels*," said Deb, "but it was going to take a while to pull her out of her funk."

Ellin told us about a party to celebrate the reopening of Club 57 (at 57 St. Marks Place). Walking into the club, Ellin introduced us to the host of the evening, Haoui Montaug. Haoui was pitching an upcoming benefit party for Club 57 and invited us to do a fifteen-minute set for the event, describing it as "a cast of thousands to support this legendary East Village institution." We took him up on the offer.

The benefit was held at Danceteria, housed in a four-story building on West 21st Street. We entered the club and ascended a staircase, glimpsing a different scene on each level. On the ground floor was a hip East Village art exhibition. Second floor was music and cabaret live performances. The third floor had a dance floor with DJs playing new wave and funk music. On the top floor was a video lounge with video and film installations. Mingling with the Danceteria crowd, we soon discovered that this was one of the hottest New York scenes—attracting hipsters, fashionistas, musicians, and artists.

We also discovered that our ticket into this scene, Haoui Montaug, was one of the venue's notorious doormen. He turned us over to the benefit's "curators," Andy and Scott, who told us we would go on a little after midnight. Our initiation into how New York cabaret clubs operated was unanticipated: the first performers kicked off entertaining early birds around ten o'clock (the price went up after eleven) and continued through a long list of entertainers until three in the morning. Midnight was about halfway.

After our set, we hung out at the club knocking back drinks and celebrating our first performance in NYC. We snickered among ourselves about Andy and Scott having the grandiose title of curators. "We have to add that to our skit *Slave to My Art*," I chortled. "The pretentious artist, SoSo from SoHo, suffering for her art, can announce in prolonged anguish, 'I curated my performance piece by myself . . . alone in my apartment . . . for three days . . . during my period.'" I was getting into the New York groove.

In the wee hours of the morning, we stumbled out of the nightclub en route to the subway. Diane's dire warning of dangerous streets crept into my consciousness. But we didn't encounter any problems. Maybe, there's safety in numbers. Maybe the sight of six saucy chicks confidently walking down the sidewalk scared the criminals. Whatever it was, we never felt fear. Most of the time people avoided us.

～⁕⁓

On October 1, we moved into our one-bedroom sublet in SoHo. Four of us met with the tenant, Susie, before she left on vacation. She assumed we would be the only ones staying at the apartment, and we didn't contradict that impression. A small deception.

After settling in, we began revving up for opening night at Westbeth. Deb and I had traveled to the West Village to check out the theater. The space was adequate, but the listless managing director had little interest in the group or our show. My gut instinct told me we were on our own. At tech rehearsal, our taped music streaming through the venue's equipment sounded muddy and could barely be heard onstage by the performers. Deb frantically implored the Westbeth tech crew, "Fix the sound!" but was met with an apathetic shrug. It was frustrating to be in an unfamiliar city without access to our usual resources, especially trusted tech people. All we could do was

Poster for *Anarchy in High Heels*

Design by Diane Noomin

cross our fingers and hope for the best. Trudging back to the Hudson Street apartment from the subway, we desperately needed a drink. And, lo and behold, directly under our living quarters was a bustling bar. How convenient—a new hangout.

In anticipation of opening weekend, the crowd crashing at Susie's place grew. Sandy, afraid of flying, traveled three harrowing days on a Greyhound bus to be with Valerie. Diane and Jan arrived to install the travel-friendly fabric high-heel set that Diane had designed and Jan had constructed. Jane Huether came to lend a hand as vocal coach. Annette showed up to be with her girlfriend, Deb. The place was packed to the rafters, and everyone was put to work.

Work hard, party hard. A nightly slumber party followed visits to the bar. Guests came and went. Judy slept over. Inevitably, Susie's place got trashed, and the neighbors complained that we used up all the hot water. Susie later demanded compensation for these indiscretions, and we had to pony up money we didn't have. But at the time, we were too busy to worry about a trivial sublet agreement.

On October 7, 1982, Les Nickelettes debuted *Anarchy in High Heels* at Westbeth Theater Center. Vince sent me flowers and champagne (he's so sweet). Friends in attendance congratulated us on the performance. But the show was brought down a notch by substandard audio equipment, and the Westbeth techie was slow on cues. Deb and I hated not being in control. "When I negotiated with Westbeth, I assumed the equipment was good and normal people could operate it," said Deb. "The light board took four hands to operate, so two people were needed, and we only had one."

Erika Munk from the *Village Voice* reviewed opening night and stuck it to us:

Les Nickelettes are a cheerful, astute, gutsy group of women. . . . They suffer, however, from laziness, or, perhaps too much easy acceptance by their audiences in the Bay Area. . . . Half the time, the singers can't quite be heard, the general technical dishevelment is not so much charming as an insult to the spectators.

Being from San Francisco was a liability. "New York is the worst city-centric place," Diane informed us. "To New Yorkers, everything outside New York, with the possible exception of Paris, is hick or provincial."

The following morning, Ellin called to harangue me about the show, "You don't come to New York with shoddy tech," she scolded.

"That wasn't our plan, Ellin," I said. "The problem is beyond our control." Her main gripe seemed to me to be that she had persuaded the *Village Voice's* Erika Munk to review the show (a big deal) and feared it reflected badly on her. I was tempted to sarcastically reply that I was sorry we'd ruined her reputation, but I held my tongue.

After I hung up, Diane presented me with a laundry list of pressing publicity tasks, followed by specific steps I needed to take to complete them. My head ached. It wasn't bad enough that the weak review and intractable technological flaws of the show weighed me down; now I was caught between the snapping jaws of two native New York pit bulls. I told Diane, "I'll get right on it." Instead, this laid-back California girl took a long walk to clear her head.

Deb had to return to her box office job at the San Francisco Ballet. We threw her an early twenty-second birthday party and celebrated with one last shopping binge. Before she left, she gave me two bits of advice: place a mic in front of the stage to boost the audio, and insist that Jane take over running the sound. The mic helped, a little. Jane delivered cues on target, and the pace of the show picked up, but overall, the sound quality continued to be lousy.

The good news was that, despite the review and the audio problems, audience attendance grew. The bad news was that Westbeth fudged on box office receipts. Our anticipated earnings were coming up short. "I think we're being ripped off," I told the others.

"What's wrong with these people?" Valerie said in disgust. Disappointed with the whole experience, I questioned our decision to come to New York.

⌒〜〜

Haoui Montaug asked us to take part in his roving revue *No Entiendes!* ("Ya don't understand"). The Danceteria ad in the *Village Voice* urged, "DRESS UP! HAVE FUN!"—sentiments we could relate to. The blurb for Hauoi's show announced:

NO ENTIENDES! AN EMERGING CABARET
Featuring
AMAZON SEVEN
LES NICOLETTES
THE SLEAZEBUCKETS

The World Premiere of Sire Recordinng Artist
MADONNA

We were a bit miffed that our name was misspelled, but were pleased to have made it onto the "Featuring" list. We didn't know anything about the other acts. The Sleazebuckets sounded promising. As for the recording artist Madonna—never heard of her.

We dashed over to the club following a Westbeth performance with the anticipation of going on soon after we arrived. Haoui told us we were last on the roster. "Okay, so that means

Danceteria ad in the *Village Voice*

after midnight, right?" Haoui shrugged. He directed us to a basement subterranean waiting area that had the ambiance of a prehistoric psychedelic cave. Every inch of the brick walls were covered with posters and graffiti on top of older graffiti. Brightly colored glossy walls divided the space into semi-separate rooms filled with sweaty performers sitting on grungy couches waiting to be called to the stage. We waited and waited. Midnight came and went. We waited some more, our energy and humor faltered.

At midnight, Madonna went on dressed like a cross between an urchin and Boy George and performed "Everybody" with three male dancers backing her up. Ellin, who was in the audience, told us later, "She was really good, by Danceteria standards."

Buried in the depths of the basement, we missed the momentous occasion of Madonna's first public performance. Not that it would have meant anything if we had witnessed it. In fact, when Ellin told us she lip-synched, we felt superior because we sang live. Maybe if we had been as smart as Madonna, we would have prerecorded our music with vocals and lip-synched as well. "The Nicks didn't go on till three in the morning," said Ellin, "by which time many people had left." A year later, I saw Madonna singing "Holiday" on TV and realized she was that chick from Danceteria.

To usher in our last week in New York, we played Danceteria a third time. Diane asked us to perform a few skits from *The DiDi Glitz Story* for her husband's release party of his new Zippy the Pinhead book, *Nation of Pinheads*. Bill Griffith's comic book character, Zippy, is a polka dotted, muumuu-wearing pinhead who spouts surreal aphorisms. Bill would be signing books, showing videos, and staging a Zippy live appearance. This time, we got to mingle at the party instead of hanging out in the musty basement. Onstage, we performed with the real-live version of Zippy. He asked, "Are you having fun, yet?" Les Nickelettes responded, "Yes, Zippy, take us to your leader."

"Westbeth was lukewarm," said Mary. "But when we went to the East Village clubs, the people raved."

"The clubs were so cool," echoed Monika. Her enthusiasm sparked her to hustle us two late night bookings for our last weekend: Club 57 (a paying gig this time) and the Pyramid Club.

We were ahead of the curve compared to many of the acts in these funky clubs, having already perfected an off-the-wall punk feminist style. This was the heyday of New York nightclubs, and throngs of people lined up to gain entry. The cultural gatekeepers were notorious doormen, like Haoui Montaug, who guarded the entryway and chose who got in. "It was the cat's meow," said Mary, "to saunter past the mob, and say to the doorman, 'We're part of the show,' and waltz in." We felt right at home in these back alley venues.

Our favorite gig was the Pyramid Club. We reveled in the optimal sound system, but encountered a basement dressing room even seedier than Danceteria.

"It was rat city," said Diane.

"Also, smelly and moldy," added Judy.

No use complaining—better to incorporate it into our act. Monika crawled onstage dressed as a bug: "What are you staring at? Haven't you ever seen a cockroach before? Did I mention that I'm ravenous? I didn't get this big by scraping by on Plaza Hotel crumbs. I moved into the Pyramid Club basement a year ago and have been living on vast quantities of rats and mildew ever since." The electric response from the packed audience pulsed an exhilarating rush through our performing souls.

Afterwards, the manager handed us a wad of cash. We made more money on this thirty-minute set than from an entire weekend at Westbeth. Back at the apartment, we spread all the cash on the bed and took turns rolling in the dough.

If we had been based in this city that never sleeps, we would have parked our act in these East Village clubs. Theater in the Big Apple was a tough nut to crack, but this club scene was wide open.

Our final four days in New York were spent back uptown in the tiny apartment on West Seventy-Fourth Street. Closing night at Westbeth was bittersweet. Rose, Judy, and I took on the task of transporting the boxes packed with our huge fabric foldup high-heel sets, wigs, and costumes back to the apartment to await shipment to San Francisco the next day.

A fan had gifted us with a few magic mushrooms, and we thought, what the hell, let's get stupid. By the time we stacked the containers on the sidewalk, we were high as kites. Judy danced back and forth from the top of flower boxes to the sidewalk singing "New Yawk, New Yawk." Rose and I giggled with glee to see Judy as her old self.

We flagged down a cab, and as it rolled to the curb, a billow of marijuana smoke wafted out the front window. Glimpsing the Rastafarian driver, we howled with laughter. Unfazed, he opened his taxi door to three sky-high girls and all our boxes. I underwent a druggie out-of-body experience watching a Marx Brothers style movie scene of four zonked out people tripping over each other to maneuver boxes and bodies into the cab. As he drove us uptown, the driver talked, sang, and shook his dreadlocks, but we couldn't understand a thing that came out of his mouth. Struggling to stifle guffaws, Judy, Rose, and I hid behind the tumble of boxes. Only after we were safely snug in the apartment did we reflect on the folly of our stoned adventure, but that just led to more paroxysms of giggling.

The next day, after our errand to the post office to ship off the boxes, we traveled to Little Italy to stuff ourselves with pasta and cannoli on our last day in New Yawk. Walking down the street to the subway, I saw scrawled on a wall, "Experience is what you get when you didn't get what you wanted." Apropos.

We spent that last night watching TV.

"There's this new MTV channel," said Rose. "It's only available in New York."

We tuned in. Once we started watching the 24/7 musical videos, we couldn't stop.

"This is a revolution," remarked Monika.

"I wish we could get this in San Francisco," said Mary.

"Wouldn't it be cool if we made a video, and it played on MTV?" said Rose.

"Our audience would soar from a few dozen a night to hundreds, thousands," I added. "In no time at all."

My last image of New York was through the back seat of a limo with my face squished against the windowpane by the huge suitcase on my lap. Due to dwindling funds for the return trip home, I rented a limo instead of two taxis to take five people plus luggage to the airport. The driver bitterly grumbled that we needed two limos to accommodate all our stuff, but begrudgingly squeezed us in.

As United flight 765 lifted off the runway, a deep exhaustion set in. The return trip was subdued, unlike the raucous arrival less than six weeks earlier. In mid-flight Rose bonked herself on the forehead and exclaimed, "I forgot my cannoli." The vision of moldy cannoli being discovered months from now in the refrigerator by the owners of our rent-free apartment provided our only moment of levity.

San Francisco sparkled in the bright afternoon sunshine as we drove from the airport. The brisk Pacific Coast air hit my lungs like a long lost friend. Everything looked scrubbed clean and fresh. There's no place like home—there's no place like home. Curling-up in my cozy apartment was like crawling back into the womb. I unpacked and wallowed in home.

Our New York adventure landed us a disappointing $2,700 in debt. I blamed myself for this predicament.

"Nothing's easy in New York," Diane reminded me. "But you managed to put on a show, and that's incredibly impressive."

I still was left with the fact that the highly anticipated breakout moment had eluded us. So now what? Did we want to be a performance art cabaret group or a theater company?

"We could become a rock band and book a tour," suggested Deb.

"Or tour Europe," piped in Valerie.

"Or take *The DiDi Glitz Story* to Los Angeles," said Diane.

"Maybe we should write a new play from scratch," I proposed.

"Let's make a video of 'Kook City' and submit it to MTV," said Rose.

All great ideas, but first we had to return to our day jobs and find a way to pay off our debt.

On Christmas Day, I was alone. Vince was spending the day with far-flung out-of-town family. My parents were in Southern California visiting my sister and her family. I pampered myself by listening to Beatles records and indulging in a long, hot bubble bath.

Wrapped in a bathrobe, I tried to find joy in opening holiday gifts by myself. The hollowness of it made me cry. For the first time in my life, on the eve of my thirty-fifth birthday, I ached to have a family of my own. I had avoided this issue while wrapped up in my busy theater career. Now, I suddenly heard the loud ticking of my biological clock.

Vince and I had been in a committed relationship for eight years, and Les Nickelettes wouldn't have existed without him. But we had slowly drifted apart. I wanted to renew our bond and start a family, but agonized over a major obstacle. Before we met, Vince had undergone a vasectomy after four children in a previous marriage. During our partnership, this meant I didn't have to suffer the birth control blues, but now it stood in the way of what I longed for. I had the baby yearning blues.

On December 31, Vince took me to dinner for my birthday. I was in a sour mood, as all I could hear was the *tick, tick, tick* of the invisible clock. Finally, over dessert, knowing it could end the relationship, I blurted out, "I want to have a baby."

After a long silence Vince asked, "Are you sure?"

"I know we've never talked about it, but I was so lonely on Christmas Day, and I realized what's missing in my life—a family."

Vince avoided looking at me, "You know I can't . . ."

"Of course I do, but for better or worse, I can't hide my feelings anymore."

Vince gazed out the window, and then turned, looking me straight in the eye. "There's a new procedure for reversing these things."

"I know—I read about it in the newspaper," I said, refraining from confessing that I had already thoroughly investigated reverse vasectomies. "Would you . . ."

"It might not work, but I could make an appointment with my doctor."

My mood shifted from depression to elation as he opened the door to this possibility. Clinking champagne glasses, we toasted the New Year, and I glowed with anticipation that 1983 would be the beginning of having it all: a family and a career in a feminist group lauded for shattering the status quo.

CHAPTER 12

ANARCHY IN HIGH HEELS

"Fun is ruining my life."

Vince kept his word, consulted with a doctor, and underwent a successful reverse vasectomy. But the doctor told him, "It will be three or four months before everything is back in working order." I picked up my date book, flipped ahead four months, and wrote a note: "Let the conceiving begin!" This impending date would mark a turning point in my life where my number one priority would switch from theater to motherhood. How this shift would affect Les Nickelettes wasn't on my radar. I wasn't ditching my commitment to push the group forward any time soon, but my sole desire was to have a baby. Whatever happened, I resolved to yield my fate to the universe.

In preparation for this change, I accepted a permanent position at Macy's. During my six years filling in for sales people as an on-call flyer, I discovered that I detested the business of peddling merchandise. To avoid being on the sales floor, I volunteered every chance I got to work in the cashier's office. The cashier job was simple: count up the store's cash receipts, sell gift certificates, and post customer account payments. I also

Program cover for *Anarchy in High Heels*
Design by Diane Noomin

hit it off with the other cashiers. So, when a part-time position opened, I took it. I liked the guaranteed weekly income, but my main goal was to qualify for medical benefits, a must for a forthcoming mother-to-be. And the twenty-five-hour work-week left plenty of time for my performing career.

～ ๏ ～

As I waited for the conceiving to begin, I concentrated on paying off Les Nickelettes' debt. We reshaped *Anarchy in High Heels* and hit the local club scene.

"We decided we didn't have to reinvent the wheel," said Deb. "We could do the material we had and make it better."

We strung together topical skits with adaptability and flexibility to fit the needs of any gig. The structure harked back to the format of our early '70s roots, but the difference in this '80s version was a thoroughly rehearsed and consistent cast. Each performer learned all the songs and dances so we could mix, match, expand, or cut. This versatility made it easy to accept all sorts of engagements, and revamping concepts and reinventing lyrics kept our creative juices flowing.

Judy returned to San Francisco and rejoined the group. She shrugged off her experience in New York as "a bummer." Declaring allegiance to her hometown, she jumped back into our flurry of rehearsals.

Tucked in the basement of the Baybrick Inn was Clementina's, a brand-new South of Market nightclub named after the alley where it was located. Like the inn, the club catered to a lesbian clientele. Les Nickelettes' first gig after revamping *Anarchy in High Heels* was a six-week run at Clementina's Wednesday Cabaret series.

Lea DeLaria, a cutting-edge comedienne and singer, hosted the show. Lea styled herself as an in-your-face '80s butch dyke, slicking back her short black hair in stiff spikes and covering her short stout body in men's clothing.

Lea stirred up controversy by billing herself as "a fuckin' dyke." Even the gay community shuddered at this label. And her raunchy act outdid ours. Les Nickelettes sprang from the same tradition of breaking down barriers, so we saw her as a kindred spirit. But we were pivoting away from using raunch to shock and awe and moving toward using broad comedy to make social/political statements. Over ten years before, we'd blasted our way to thrilling liberation by talking brazenly about female sexuality and saying, "fuck" onstage. Now, our emancipation craved more substance.

"Crying In An Alleyway," DiDi Glitz's sob song about being dumped by a guy, morphed into a lament about the current government attempts to force women into backstreet alleys by scaling back abortion rights: "How can they control me this way / Take all my free choice away?"

In another revision we switched-up the Tanya Hearst tune about an heiress turned ersatz revolutionary robbing a bank to a fed-up feminist toting a gun and demanding a piece of the pie:

The rich get richer, that's how it's gonna stay
The poor get poorer, that's the price they have to pay.
They say crime doesn't pay
But boy it sure is fun
So give me all your money
'Cause I know how to shoot a gun.

"The more I was involved with the group, the more I understood the concept," said Rose. "You didn't have to be militant or do soapbox preaching to be a true feminist. Some so-called liberals misunderstood, and conservatives were outright aghast at our onstage shenanigans."

Still, we weren't above a little bawdiness every now and then. "I was sitting in the front row at the rehearsal before the show at Clementina's," recalls Diane, "and saw Monika beavering the audience."

"She forgot her underwear," explained Mary.

"The consequences of wearing a short tight skirt with nothing underneath never occurred to her," I said.

"And so, she sat on a chair onstage, and spread her legs," said Mary, "and the audience sees this little fur thing."

We got Monika a pair of panties. Maybe if we could have anticipated the notoriety Sharon Stone would get from doing this trick later in *Basic Instinct*, we would have left it in. The ultra-evolved feminists in the audience would have loved it.

We snagged a couple of party gigs with a character named Ed Woods who hosted events for straight corporate singles. One was a Full Moon Celebration held in the Bourn Mansion that had a reputation for hosting wild rock and roll parties. But Ed's party was for the snobbish button-down crowd. We did our most conservative set for this Pacific Heights bunch but still stood out as freakishly offbeat. Afterwards, at the party mixer, we snickered at the faux hipsters but gladly accepted the $200 fee.

But that didn't compare to the weirdest party gig, the Annual Atheist's Convention. Our tailored set included the Rubberware skit, featuring sex toys for sale, interrupted at the end by a church lady barging onstage and launching into a religious rant. We thought the atheists would get a kick out of the satirical message in "Listen to My God" delivered by a woman protected by not one, but three rosaries dangling from her neck:

Death to sinners
Better off dead
Can't separate church and state
Act like me or I can't relate.

Rose, Goody, Mary, Me, Monika, Valerie, Deb,
and Diane in our publicity photo for the San Francisco
version of *Anarchy in High Heels*
Photo © F. Stop Fitzgerald

But the audience reacted with only mild amusement. We expected atheist subversives, but got a strange gang of friendly geeks instead.

The blossoming alternative cabaret scene was another story. Like the Pyramid Club in New York, we hit the mother lode at the 181 Club. Located in the Tenderloin on Eddy Street, the relic building had its original decor intact. The current owner had converted the dive into a trendy late-night membership club with DJs, dancing, and revue shows. A huge curved mahogany bar ran the length of one side of the room, dusty ornate red velvet lined the walls, and a classic 1920s-style cabaret stage jutted out into the audience. Perfect for a Nick show. Best of all, it was our kind of people—a boisterous artistic crowd that understood our offbeat style. And the club owners paid us a ton of cash.

The seedy Tenderloin neighborhood deterred us at first, but we would go on to play there as often as we could. "Once you were inside it was heaven," said Judy. "But getting in and out was horrible."

Our naïveté led to dicey situations. At one rehearsal, I had money stolen from my wallet. Another time, the police raided the place searching for a criminal while we were smoking pot in the dressing room. We hastily fanned the smoke out an open window, but it proved unnecessary. The police barely glanced at us as they rushed past.

Invitations to a 181 Club gig also proved risky. "My parents came to see us there," said Deb, "and after watching two lesbians in front of them making out, they concluded that I was a prostitute."

After that 181 Club performance, in a move that surprised no one, Monika bowed out. "I was less and less into it," she said. "It was getting old, the same songs over and over and over again. I wanted to be a professional actress, and the Nicks were getting to be like a feminist therapy group. I didn't feel as though I belonged any more. Everyone seemed to be getting uptight with me."

Monika *was* steering away from a feminist way of thinking. "She began to look at the Nicks' point of view as being an affront to God and decency," said Rose.

"I didn't want to cut off the friendships," said Monika. "I just didn't want to be a Nickelette anymore."

Monika's stint in Les Nickelettes epitomized her teenage rebellion, and now she was almost twenty and recently married. We veered in different directions but remained friends.

Meanwhile, my journey to parenthood launched in early July, when the doctor told Vince, "The reverse vasectomy surgery has healed, and your boys are swimming upstream again." *Whoopee*, I thought, *let's get this party started!* The green light had taken longer than anticipated, but only the quirky laws of nature could stop us now. This would be the fun part.

I had started charting my fertility cycle a few months earlier. On the Saturday marked on my calendar as the optimum day of the month to conceive, I woke up excited. Humming, I danced to the bedroom after my morning shower, thinking about what special outfit to wear. Vince walked into the room. My back was to him but I saw his reflection in the mirror of the highboy dresser. Without turning, I smiled at his image, "Guess what day it is?"

There was an uncomfortable pause. He cast his eyes downward. "There's no easy way to say this. I'm not happy. I'm leaving."

Stunned, my facial expression in the mirror slowly wilted, like a fragile lily deprived of water. "What? Is something wrong?"

"No," he answered.

"Is there someone else?"

"No. The relationship just hasn't been working for me."

Like witnessing a tornado strike with no warning on a calm, sunny day, I stood there in muted shock. A slow-motion movie reeled out in front of my eyes as he packed up a few belongings and walked out the door.

I couldn't breathe. I fled in my car to Ocean Beach. As I sat on the sand, I attempted to blot out reality by consuming the six-pack of beer I had picked up along the way. But even drunkenness mixed with the powerful crashing of the ocean waves failed to wash away my inability to comprehend what had just happened. The lyrics of a Nickelettes song kept playing over and over in my head. "How can he throw me away? / Dispose of me in this way?" What about our plans to have a child? Maybe he didn't want more kids? But then why had he reversed the vasectomy?

I couldn't bring myself to confide in anyone. For two days, I put a pillow over my head and slept. Monday evening, I got up and went to a previously scheduled Nickelettes rehearsal. I shielded my distress by plastering a phony, happy smile on my face. After a half hour, Judy turned to me and said, "You sure are quiet tonight."

"Vince dumped me," I blurted out.

Jarred by this bombshell, the Nicks asked, "Why? What happened?"

I had no credible answer. Like the others in the group, I had taken our rock-solid relationship for granted. Everybody in Les Nickelettes liked Vince, and no one questioned his position as silent benefactor. For me, the deeper link between him and the group existed with his role as originator of the troupe and his function as my trusted advisor. But I had no time to dwell on how this breakup would affect Les Nickelettes; we had a show to do that weekend. Concentrating on performing enabled me to hold it together through the rest of the week.

Following the weekend performances, I slipped into a sleepwalking twilight zone, and the Nicks took a break from rehearsing and performing. However, I couldn't defer my altered financial situation, so to pay the rent, I extended my cashier position to full time. But when I wasn't working I was a basket case, unable to do anything.

Vince avoided me. He didn't phone and wouldn't return my calls. One day, when I was at work, he came by the apartment and got the rest of his things (I had foolishly failed to change the locks). Coming home to empty shelves and a rifled closet dealt another blow. I longed for the nightmare to end. To stay sane, I daydreamed that it was all a mistake. I conjured up a vision of Vince sitting on the edge of the bed cooing, "It's okay, everything is peachy-keen. I want to come back."

Finally, after an impassioned plea on his answering machine at work, he agreed to meet with me. I needed answers. I deserved answers. As we sat side-by-side on the overstuffed sofa in the living room we shared for nine years, I grilled him.

"Did I do something wrong?"

"No, it wasn't you. I changed."

"Did you decide you didn't want to have another family?"

"No, it wasn't that."

"Is there another woman?"

"No."

"What then?"

"The relationship changed. I haven't been happy for quite a while. I don't want to hurt you, but I need to move on." Then he added breezily, "Let's stay friends." I didn't answer, and he let the statement hang in the air for a few moments before adding, "How are your folks?"

"You ruin my life and you want to know how my parents are doing? I don't think we can be friends."

From the front window, I watched as he walked away, his shoulders hunched in a familiar tan corduroy jacket, his hands shoved in pants pockets. Sadness evaporated in a rupture of kickass anger. Vince had stonewalled me. I paced around the apartment unleashing a torrent of furious frustration. Okay, so the relationship was really over, but the pieces of the puzzle didn't fit. "I've changed. It's time to move on," I mocked out loud. What kind of stupid bullshit is that? The encounter left me a beat-up, angry mess.

Anger sustained me for a couple of months. Getting a bit of revenge, I convinced Les Nickelettes, Inc. board of directors to default on the remaining loan amount due to Vince. I gloated; one has to pay.

But Les Nickelettes' thrust upstream slowed to the pace of a slug. August turned to September, and it was past time to put on the annual Salmon Awards event. But I dragged my feet. Tradition dictated that the 1983 Salmon Awards would serve to celebrate the New York production of *Anarchy in High Heels*. I had neither the motivation nor the energy to mount a full-scale fundraiser, so I suggested a scaled down, private version of the party.

Held at Mary's attic loft with only selected friends and nominees, the Tenth Annual Salmon Awards kept the familiar fish swimming upstream theme, but added Hawaiian Island decor and costumes—salmon disguised as mahi-mahi in muumuus. Tim Lewis, the *Spectator*'s Art Director, won the eighth annual Tanya Hearst Memorial Journalist award, an honor he had lusted after for two years. Not that he conceded it was a bribe, but on the eve of snagging his "devastatingly divine" bowling trophy, Tim reminded us that "three—count 'em *three*—rave reviews [of Les Nickelettes] had appeared in the sometimes smudgy print of the *Spectator*." The gala lifted a dark cloud from around my soul, and I allowed myself to laugh and have fun for the first time in months.

Thanks to Tim Lewis, we got a paying gig at the Fifth Birthday Celebration for the *Spectator* held at the Mitchell Brothers O'Farrell Theatre. Skepticism arose within the group about performing at the infamous porn palace.

"I think we should do it," I rallied. "It will be a triumphant return to the site of Les Nickelettes birthplace, and two hundred bucks for fifteen minutes is nothing to sneeze at."

I took this stand knowing full well that, as a Mitchell Brothers' employee, Vince would surely be there. This was the place where my relationship with him had blossomed, so perhaps I hoped for a confrontation (or a reconciliation?).

I had to muster every bit of bravado available in my being to perform that night. I stuck my stiff upper lip out as far as I dared and sang "You Don't Own Me" straight up to the projection booth where I knew Vince was hiding. But Vince never showed his face.

Naked girls gyrating in glass booths, and the hedonistic XXX-rated live sex show that included lascivious lap dancers personally entertaining patrons proved no nostalgic return to our virgin roots. The Nickelodeon and the 1972 porno films I recalled were quaint by comparison.

We continued to perform *Anarchy in High Heels* here and there, but the laughs turned stale, and it slowly ran out of steam. One day, sounding a death knell, Rose bellowed, "Fun is ruining my life!" I didn't have the strength to refute her. "I decided to leave Les Nickelettes," explained Rose, "because it didn't seem to me that staying with the group would lead to much exposure or recognition in the mainstream theatrical and film community. I wanted to do different types of plays and learn more about my craft."

I understood Rose's decision to drop out, and wondered if I should also pursue other acting opportunities. She scored a part in a Magic Theater play, and I went to see her. I tried to imagine myself taking on a similar straight role but couldn't.

Later, Rose moved to New York to try her luck, and she learned, like Judy, that her ethnic background hindered her chances. She told me this made her realize the rarity of her experience in Les Nickelettes, "Being a member in the Nicks, my ethnicity didn't matter in the least in terms of playing parts. There was a real spirit of democracy—everyone was equal to one another, no matter if you had an odd boyfriend or a different background."

Maybe that's why I stuck with Les Nickelettes. The core group shrank to five—Valerie, Deb, Judy, Mary, and me. But an extended gang of friends, significant others, and ex-Nicks hung out more than ever. We got together for kitschy slumber parties, staying up all night playing Trivial Pursuit and Pinochle. When you're struggling with loneliness, a supportive group of close, caring friends is a gift.

To untangle the confusing mixture of emotions swirling around in my brain, I began writing daily in a journal. One day, at the top of the page I underlined "L.A.V." (Life After Vince) followed by, "Time to get back to my creative core."

With that in mind, I discussed future plans for Les Nick-elettes with Deb, and she pressed for a European tour: "We need to think big." She and Annette were planning a vacation to Greece and Italy, and she proposed that they scout out possible venues. Perfect, I thought, if anyone could put together a tour of Europe it would be Deb and Annette.

To raise funds for this excursion, the two of them traveled two hundred miles north to rural Garberville (at the time the major illegal weed-growing hub in California) and took jobs cleaning, sorting, and packaging the autumn marijuana crop. Deb invited the Nicks to perform in Garberville for her twenty-third birthday celebration. The show took place at the rustic Garberville Community Center, followed by a birthday dinner for Deb. The audience was made up of locals, all involved in growing, harvesting, and selling the illicit weed. Our eyes widened at the sight of table centerpieces piled high with huge joints. But in this neck of the woods, this was just business as usual. When in the country, do as the country folk do—get stoned out of your fricking mind.

Cash in hand, Deb and Annette headed off for their European adventure stocked with promotional Nickelettes brochures and a video. "*Arrivederci*, girls," I bid them. "Let us know when we can start packing our bags."

Three weeks later, shocking news came from abroad. Deb and Annette had split up, Mediterranean style. Annette had taken up with an Italian girl, while Deb hooked up with a man in Florence. A man? "Debra Jean, Ms. Surprise Queen," I chanted when I heard the story. The guy led a heavy metal rock band, and Deb joined as lead singer. Later, they got married so she could stay in Italy. My vision of a European tour vanished quicker than a crunchy cannoli.

DENISE LARSON ★ 301

Determined to focus on the future and divert attention away from my present heartache, I packed my schedule from early morning to bedtime. There were eight-hour shifts working at Macy's followed by regular Nickelettes social get-togethers. I set up a regular exercise schedule and increased practice piano sessions in an effort to learn how to play the instrument. During other downtime, I pushed myself to research ideas for a new play.

But unresolved issues buried beneath the nonstop activities refused to be kept down. Dancing out from under the veil of sleep, the demons mocked my diversions. A nocturnal nervous breakdown came in the form of insufferable insomnia that jolted me awake night after night with loud palpitating heartbeats, an overheated body stinking with sweaty fear, and an overpowering sense that I was about to die. Daytime panic attacks have nothing on this.

Lack of rest forced me to seek therapy. A male therapist refused to give me drugs and suggested in scolding therapy-speak to "just man up." If I followed his advice I could move on with my life in no time flat. I requested a different therapist, and he thought I'd rejected him because he was Korean and blind, but the truth was simpler. I'd rejected him because he was a man.

A female therapist gave me Valium, which I didn't like to take because it made me drowsy the next day, but just knowing it was in the nightstand drawer calmed me when thoughts of dying seized me in the middle of the night. After hearing my story, she made the straightforward observation that to get on with my life, I needed to know the truth about why the relationship with Vince ended—asserting that I had a right to know.

The advice hit home. *I'm a damn wimp*, I thought. Finally, I screwed up my courage, and called Vince, demanding that he "tell me the whole truth."

"Not over the phone," he replied, casually brushing aside my query. "I'm very busy right now, but I promise we'll get together after the first of the year and talk about it."

Put on hold again.

A broken heart doesn't mesh well with Happy New Year. Add to that was another birthday to remind me of my ticking biological clock, and abject misery was bound to set in. I bid good-bye to 1983, the worst year of my life. 1984 couldn't possibly be as wretched as 1983, even if it was, well, *1984*. If the Orwellian Thought Police zeroed in on my state of mind, they'd be down in the dumps too.

After the holidays, I heard nothing from Vince—big surprise. I wanted to turn my attention to a new Nickelettes project but couldn't. Everything shut down except the resolve to know the whole story. Anger, and the thought that I had let him get away so long without accounting for his actions, bit me in the ass.

Refusing to be ignored, I called his office daily. All I got was a litany of brush-offs: "He's busy" or "In a meeting." It pissed me off but made me more determined. It took a couple of weeks, but I wore him down. Over the phone (so much for meeting face-to-face), he told me the truth.

Dropping his usual charming dodges, he gave me a straight-on confession: there *was* another woman, and she became pregnant. "That's why I couldn't talk to you a few weeks ago," he told me, "because the child was being born."

"Seriously?" I paused, did the math, and figured the child had to have been conceived only a few months after his reverse vasectomy surgery.

"I'm not even sure the baby is mine," he added.

"How pathetic. You're a bigger fool then I thought."

"Look, we had a good relationship, you always made me happy. I want the best for you. I hope you can forgive me."

"No fucking way!" I exploded in indignation. "How could you let me go on for months and months without telling me the truth? Now, I have to go back to point zero to deal with this."

Slamming down the phone I fumed at the cosmic irony that Vince started his new year with a newborn baby, and my prize was classic betrayal. Adding a kick in the butt was the stunning awareness that I had continued to harbor a pitiful hope for reconciliation. Now, I knew the truth. My new reality, I suspected, would involve massive amounts of self-medication and therapy.

My knee-jerk revenge plot involved a witch-like hex on Vince and his new family. But deep down I knew the best revenge was to reclaim my essential self, which meant a reboot of my witty artistic inclinations. Over the years, I had relied less and less on Vince's support, help, and advice. With my female collaborators, I'd gained the confidence to write, direct, and produce plays. Maybe that was part of the reason the relationship didn't work for him anymore.

"Let's immerse ourselves in writing an original full-length musical comedy from scratch," I proposed to Les Nickelettes. "We've been dancing around the idea of a new show, so let's get down to business."

"We do need new material," agreed Valerie.

"I've been researching ancient Goddess worship, and I think we should do a feminist satire on religion," I continued. "Here's the premise: Would religion and culture change if God were perceived as female instead of male?"

"That's sure to offend everyone," said Mary.

My experience with religion was limited to the Lutheran church. Vague childhood memories lingered of attending services until my father refused to go anymore, stating, "The minister only preaches about two things: how bad the Catholics are, and there's not enough money in the collection plate." Mom continued to take us kids to services on holidays, but my religious allegiance was weak at best.

I outlined my research on Goddess worship, which included witchcraft and reincarnation. Initially, my Catholic colleagues reacted viscerally: Blasphemy! Hell-bound! Damnation! Nevertheless, lapsed practitioners Valerie and Mary embraced the delicious heretical information. Judy, our only practicing churchgoer, struggled with the concept, but became engrossed with the modern tenets of Wicca.

"I was thinking black hats, cats on brooms, evil spells, and eye of newt, stuff like that," she said. "So it was an awakening to find out that Wicca actually celebrates nature. I thought that was kind of cool."

In the end, the theme didn't cause Judy to drop out of the writing team; instead, lack of patience for the process did. Plus, after marrying her longtime boyfriend, Gary, she took on a demanding retail management job.

The writing collective boiled down to Valerie, Mary, and me. We burrowed deeper into the subject matter. Valerie and I read *The Complete Art of Witchcraft* by present-day witch Sybil Leek.

"The word WITCHCRAFT was in bold pink letters on the front," recounted Valerie. "And as I read it on the bus going to work, people stared at me."

"Well, there was a time when women were burned at the stake for that kind of thing," I joked. But reading about the chilling murder of women accused of witchcraft offered nothing to laugh at.

Sybil Leek explained that in the old pagan religion, witches had been viewed as spiritual women with healing and psychic powers who revered nature. But reverence for the Goddess in medieval Europe led to vilification and a label of "evil." During the witch-hunts, it's been estimated that thousands of people (mostly women but also some men) were tortured, burned, or hanged for embodying Satan. These dubious witchcraft allegations lodged against women swept across Europe from 1450 to 1750. Why? Some scholars argued that the pagan belief of the female as the origin of life threatened the orthodox male monotheist Christianity. Whatever the reason, it's been surmised that these attacks on "witches" constituted a wholesale persecution against women.

Additionally, a general fear of the power of women led to laws in the church that required women to be chaste and subservient to men. It horrified and angered me that I had never heard this side of the story. It says something about who writes history.

But how could we take this serious stuff and shape it into a satirical play? At first, I envisioned a humorous mash-up of the 1950s TV show *Bewitched* with the iconic three witches in Shakespeare's *Macbeth*, but I couldn't get it to mesh.

And then I recalled a favorite childhood fable. At age eight, residing in the slim pickings of my family's bookshelf, I found the story of "The Ugly Princess" tucked inside an anthology of fairy tales. I read and reread it several times. I have searched for this tale to authenticate my memory without success. Who knows, maybe I made it up, but whatever the source, I remember it vividly.

The story revolved around a spoiled and pampered princess who was so disagreeable and ugly that no one wanted to marry her. The king offered a reward to anyone who could refashion his unlovely daughter. A humble peasant woman took on the task. The ugly princess, against her will, was whisked away to a modest cottage in the woods. For one year, the peasant woman and her three daughters patiently taught the princess the fundamentals of unselfishness, cooperation, and generosity. These lessons transformed the princess into a beauty. Her dull eyes sparkled, her downturned mouth was inverted into a graceful smile, and her stuck up snout straightened into a comely nose. Prince Charming married the princess, and, with a royal stipend, the peasants lived happily ever after in a spiffed-up forest cottage.

Recalling the fairy tale brought fond memories of lazy summer afternoons dreaming of living life in a royal castle. My eight-year-old mind imagined I was really a princess who had been placed in a lower middle-class American family to learn humility.

After relating this story to the writing group I said, "We could use the three peasant daughters like the three witches in *Macbeth.*"

"Yeah, and the ugly princess could be a Goddess in disguise," said Valerie.

"But to become a real Goddess, she will have to change, become transformed," said Mary.

"The Goddess can start out as a privileged, pampered rich girl from LA," I added. "Funny."

"She could appear as a contestant on *Queen Bitch for a Day*," suggested Valerie.

"But we'll have to give her some redeeming quality like being an avant-garde artist," I mused.

"And then she can be arrested by the Art Police," laughed Mary.

"Thrown in the slammer for bad art, which leads her to the witches," I said, giggling.

Valerie put the capper on it, "At the end, the witches reveal the return of the Goddess, like a female second coming."

We were on a roll.

In the midst of learning about the history of witches burned at the stake, we received shocking news about Ralph Eno, our guitar-playing comrade-in-arts. Ralph started out as Freaky Ralph at the Nickelodeon, followed us to the Intersection, performed "I'm on the Ward Again" at the Salmon Awards, and played guitar on our music tapes for *The DiDi Glitz Story*. In the late 1970s, Ralph changed his name to Ral Pheno, and launched himself into the emerging San Francisco punk music scene, later earning the moniker, "The Godfather of Punk Rock."

Now he was in the hospital after a suicide attempt. On the corner of Ninth and Irving, Ralph had doused himself with lighter fluid and lit a match. He lasted one day before succumbing to his burns. Ralph was a brilliant, sensitive genius who, like us, couldn't break through to get the attention of mainstream show biz.

Later, Fab Mab impresario Dirk Dirksen hosted a wake for Ralph at the On Broadway Theatre. The punk community and Ralph's friends showed up. Mary and I, representing Les Nickelettes, performed. I contributed my collection of photographs of Ralph from the Nickelodeon and Intersection days to the display in the lobby.

At the end of the event, as I retrieved the pix from the bulletin board, Robin Williams appeared and asked how I knew Ralph. Taken aback to be chatting with a world famous TV and movie star, I became tongue-tied. But Robin didn't comport himself at all like a star. He didn't try to steal the show—which he could have easily done. He didn't perform at all. He waited in the wings and only made a quiet appearance to express his regard and love for Ralph, a real pro.

Rest in peace, Ral Pheno, aka Ralph Eno.

I continued my Goddess/witch research, seeking inspiration. This led me to Marion Zimmer Bradley's witch coven. In her best-selling novel *The Mists of Avalon,* a feminist retelling of the Camelot story from the point of view of the women, Marion Zimmer Bradley lyrically conjures up the conflict between the Druidic old religion of the Goddess and the new patriarchal Christian religion.

I discovered that Marion Zimmer Bradley lived in Berkeley and ran The Center for Non-Traditional Religion. The center advertised an open invitation to attend the Mass of the Goddess. I talked Valerie into going with me.

"I was very brave," commented Valerie.

First to arrive on the night of the dark moon, we were directed to wait in the living room of Ms. Bradley's cottage. She wasn't there. The room was stacked with books everywhere: on dusty shelves reaching to the ceiling, on the floor in wobbly piles, and amassed haphazardly on the ratty furniture. The musty old-book smell added to the hidden thrill of being in this witch/writer's den.

"Look," whispered Valerie, pointing through an archway leading to a messy kitchen. "It's her word processor."

In a revered hush tone I added, "Where she invents her magical stories."

A young woman dressed in a flimsy white chiffon toga came in. "Follow me," she said, ushering us into a renovated garage behind the cottage. The witch sanctuary featured walls adorned with painted black female pagan symbols. Three women (also in white toga outfits) entered and acted out the three stages of womanhood: the Maiden, the Mother, and the Crone. We enjoyed their stories told in song and dance (like one of our shows without the jokes). Next, they invited us to join them in a circle and passed around a large oval hand mirror. Each participant was directed to stare at her image in the mirror and to repeat her name three times, followed by this self-affirming statement: "I am wonderful. I have power."

"I was shy, and it was awkward," said Valerie. "But it was pretty cool, too."

Later, reflecting on the experience, I concluded that Les Nickelettes had many of the characteristics of a coven.

~⌇~

The weight of my emotional burden began to lift with the first hints of spring. Renewal was in the air. One day, I came home and discovered I'd lost my watch. I backtracked and searched for it everywhere, but it was gone. The watch had been a gift from Vince. It was a gold circle around my wrist that I wore daily and looked at often, a constant unconscious reminder of our relationship. Had I lost it accidently, or on purpose? Either way, a message clearly screamed at me: "Time to move on, girl." I got a new watch.

I'd been taking piano lessons with ex-Nickelette Jill Rose for the past couple of years. This weekly focus on learning a new skill helped to distract from my melancholy. At this time in our lives, Jill and I shared a deep-rooted yearning—we both desperately wanted to have a baby. So, after I fumbled through an hour of botched chords and slaughtered melodies, we commiserated about the barriers preventing us from fulfilling our mutual burning desire.

"It's so hard getting back into the dating game after ten years," I moaned. "Not to mention trying to find a guy ready to start a family."

"My problem is different," Jill said. "I have a stable relationship with a woman, and we both want to have a kid, but I need a sperm donor. I don't want to go to a sperm bank; I want to know the father, but I also want no strings attached. I've thought about just going out to a club one night when I'm ovulating, and picking up a nice guy for a one-night stand."

"I've thought about doing something like that too, but it's not what I really want."

"Yeah, it's kind of risky. Hey, my ex-boyfriend isn't dating anyone; I should give you his phone number. I asked him to be my sperm donor, but he turned me down because he said if he became a father, he wanted to raise the kid."

I looked at the scrap of paper Jill gave me with the phone number of this ex-boyfriend—Vinny Mierjeski. "Seriously, Vinny, as in Vince?" I said. "I'm not sure about this." Was the universe playing a joke on me?

Nonetheless, on the first day of spring 1984, I found myself on a blind date set up by my piano teacher with a guy named

Vinny. We met for lunch at the Acme Café in trendy Noe Valley. Vincent hailed from New York and thus always went by the nickname Vinny. Whew, at least I didn't have to call him Vince. He stood six feet tall, had sandy blond hair, and his all-denim outfit included a well-worn shirt with the sleeves ripped out, revealing beefy biceps. The lunch conversation went along okay—at least, it wasn't awkward. Afterwards, he asked me for a ride to the taxi company where he worked as a cab driver.

As we drove to the taxi yard he spied an envelope propped up on my dashboard waiting to be mailed. Vinny glanced at the addressee: Fredericks of Hollywood (I was requesting a catalogue from the sexy lingerie retailer to pilfer language for a possible fashion show scene in the Nickelettes script). He raised his eyebrows and smiled at me lasciviously.

"No, no, you don't understand. It's just for research."

"Sure," he laughed as he got out of the car.

Embarrassing. I vowed never to see him again, but he called the next day and asked me to go the movies, and I said yes. We went to see *This Is Spinal Tap*, the hilarious mockumentary of a fictitious heavy metal band. As the parody jokes rolled out, Vinny's loud guffaws filled the theater. *Okay*, I thought, *there's potential here*—nothing like a shared sense of humor to break the ice. Afterwards we went out for a drink and talked for hours. We began to see each other regularly.

On one date, I invited Vinny to dinner at my apartment to meet my friends Diane and Bill (of *DiDi Glitz* and *Zippy* fame). Vinny discovered that, like him, Diane and Bill had grown up in New York. As they shared childhood memories, Bill mentioned that he had attended Division Avenue High School in Levittown, Long Island. Vinny said, "Oh, yeah? My dad was a teacher at that school."

"Wait," said Bill. "Your dad was my teacher for print shop, Mr. Mierjeski?

"Yep," replied Vinny.

"Sorry," said Bill shaking his head. In this small world, the fact that Vinny's dad had a reputation as a strict bastard, both as a father and a teacher, didn't need to be spelled out.

Meanwhile, the ambitious undertaking of creating an original script from scratch bogged down. The time-consuming, detail-oriented project proved too much for Mary. At meetings she would go off on unrelated tangents, and then fall asleep. "I was totally deluding myself," she confessed. "I was still living an underworld druggie kind of life, but kept telling myself that I was fine."

Finally, fed up with her mucking-up the process, I laid it on the line. "Mary, take a leave of absence, and when we're ready to perform again, you can come back."

"Okay," she replied. "I know that's the right thing to do."

I looked at Valerie, "It's down to you and me. Can we do this?"

"I don't know what I'm doing," answered Valerie. "The only writing I've ever done was *The DiDi Glitz Story,* and I didn't realize how easy that was when you already had the characters and plot ideas. We're just making up stuff that we hope is funny."

"This story line has so much potential, I don't want to quit."

Valerie and I soldiered on like neo-pagan worshipers at a full moon rite, even as we cycled back and forth between grumpiness and elation.

"Eventually we got a work-in-progress script," said Valerie. "It was unwieldy, but it felt very satisfying, too."

Valerie and I presented the rough draft of *Bitch Goddess* to the board of directors. We anticipated an encouraging boost from this group of supporters, but their comments sank in the mud like a rock thrown off a bridge.

"The play seems to have three different messages—it's all mixed up. What are you trying to say?"

"I don't know about the reincarnation part, it's a controversial and questionable theory."

"I'm never surprised by what Les Nickelettes do, but having witches save the world by promoting a Goddess as the second coming might be going too far."

Shaken, Valerie and I stumbled to defend our work. Then, Jane Dornacker, the talented six-foot comedienne who was visiting as a prospective board member, stood up, shook her mane of long shaggy brunette hair, and said, "You know, just believe in it. It's great. Of course it's a tricky subject matter, but that's what Les Nickelettes do. Go for it. Don't worry if people are going to accept it or not."

I could have kissed her. The wisdom of Jane's heartfelt words was the best advice we could have received. Sure, we could improve the script, but what we really needed was a vote of confidence.

⁓⌒〜

By the end of 1984, I counted up an all-time low of only four performances by Les Nickelettes all year. But this slowdown had an upside; with ongoing fundraising and no production costs, we managed to sock away $5,000 for the upcoming production.

But we feared our fans were fading away. To reassert a public presence, we sent out a holiday edition of *Nick News*: "Nicks Dead? Don't panic. It's just a vicious rumor without a shred of truth. You Nickel-maniacs will just have to wait for the exciting premiere of our all-new show: The Gospel according to Les Nickelettes. If someone walks up to you in a dark alley and whispers, 'The Nicks are dead,' tell them, 'Oh, yeah? Just wait for the second coming!'"

CHAPTER 13

OH GODDESS!

"Are you ready for the second coming?"

In the mid-'80s, the rich got richer and the working class waited bone-dry for the promised trickle down from the Reagan economics. This conservatism also led to a feminist backlash. Money, power, and righteous religion asserted a dominance that bit the head off the bold second-wave women's movement. The term "feminist" became akin to "slut." But this stiff-armed patriarchy only made progressive women hungrier for a paradigm shift. An exploration of Wicca, contemporary paganism, and Goddess worship exploded with hardy women libbers.

You can argue that God has no gender, but you can't overlook the fact that in Western religion, a male image prevails. Allegiance to a Father in Heaven implies a masculine Supreme Being meting out ethical conduct. In contrast, ancient pagan beliefs featured the Divine Being as Mother Earth. In Les Nickelettes' new play, renamed *Oh Goddess!*, we joined the sisterhood in an imagined return of Goddess spirituality. Our script combined the Goddess/witch resurgence with the spoiled ugly princess fairytale, added a splash of satire, and emerged as a futuristic fable. I anticipated this venture to be our gutsiest and most innovative achievement to date.

I embraced the challenge of directing the play, and with Valerie as co-producer, mapped out a production plan. It had been almost four years since our last full-scale play. Things had changed. Securing a small, affordable theater space used to take a few phone calls. Not anymore. Past venues were beyond our price range, already heavily booked, or had morphed into coffee shops. I searched for two months until I stumbled onto the Lab on Divisadero Street. The space was run by a group of students from the Interdisciplinary Experimental Arts Center at San Francisco State University (ah, memories of my alma mater). I pitched our female second-coming project to the manager, and he didn't flinch. "The commitment of the Lab is to present experimental works," he enthusiastically assured me.

Valerie and I sat down with this earnest young manager in early spring of 1985 to sign a contract for a mid-October opening. Although relieved we had secured a theater, motor memory kicked in about what the next whirlwind six months would be like. I hesitated. Signing on the dotted line meant putting into motion a sprint to the finish line. The script still needed to be revised, and hanging in the air was uncertainty about our dwindling support system. Deb, Rose, and Monika were gone. Judy announced that she couldn't commit to a performance schedule, but I coaxed her into doing the choreography. Liza was in a new-wave band with her brand new husband. Jan was freelancing as a costumer, and Diane was back to drawing comics. I was confident I could convince them to write the music, design the costumes, and do the graphics, but they hadn't been involved in developing the show, so there wasn't the same collective spirit. I swallowed hard, turned to Valerie so the manager couldn't see, and made a hand gesture of a salmon swimming upstream. Valerie nodded, and we signed. It was time to put up or shut up, but I felt as rusty as an old nail.

Amid this flurry of preproduction planning, circumstances in my personal life changed. My relationship with Vinny had deepened, and we made plans to move in together. This decision came during a couple's therapy session where each of us confessed a fear of commitment, followed by the revelation that we both desired to be parents. Couple's therapy was a wonderful way to cut through the crap and get to the heart of the matter. Not wanting to rush into this life-changing event, we decided to test our compatibility by first living together. So, a week before I revved up production on *Oh Goddess!*, I moved out of my apartment of eleven years and hauled my stuff across town to Vinny's place. Waiting for the moving truck, perched on the sidewalk with all my personal belongings stacked around me, caused an emotional floodgate to open. I broke down in tears. The heartbreak I'd endured in that apartment faced its final eviction. I took one last walk through the empty apartment and spotted a calendar still pinned to the bedroom wall. I noted it was July 31, the second full moon of the month, a blue moon. Once in a blue moon: some things end, some things begin, you have to take a chance.

Six days later, still consumed with unpacking, I threw myself into full-throttle director mode. The first duty was the scariest: auditions. The script called for twenty characters, and even with Valerie and Mary on board, plus double- and triple-casting, we still needed to recruit ten actresses. I reminded myself of other points in Nickelettes history when a new influx of soul mates resulted in a fresh new group. I was confident that the past would repeat itself. To bolster this notion, a cornucopia of great prospects to choose from showed up. But coming face-to-face with these new players caused my instinctive inner window to fog up. I thought moving into a new place with a new boyfriend would have no effect on my artistic activities, but it threw me off kilter. I shook the haze out of my brain and forced myself to focus on choosing the best cast.

One woman stood out immediately. Linda, with regal height and long limbs, was the physical epitome of our lead role, Gloria the Goddess. She read the character's lines flawlessly, sang well, and had a strong dance resume: The Goddess had been delivered to us in one neat package. But Valerie cautioned, "The Nickelettes cast against type, and it's always worked. Linda is almost too good to be true."

"Yes, but when the exact vision of the key character walks into audition, you have to believe in luck," I argued. "You can't just dismiss her because she seems too perfect."

During callbacks Linda continued to deliver, so she got the part. The other roles fell neatly into place, and I sensed a spark of clarity coming from adding these energetic women to our ranks. But, inexplicably, I also felt weighed down by duty.

Determined to shake off these unsettling emotions, I put my Capricorn nose to the grindstone. After all, this was the dawning of a new Les Nickelettes era. I gave a pep talk to the newly assembled cast. "Being cast in this play is more than just an acting role. As part of Les Nickelettes' theater collective, you share in the creative process that will shape the final version of this original play. But it also means you're part of the production team that puts the show on the boards. We can't promise any money, perhaps a stipend at the end, if all goes well, but we can promise an irreverent and fun adventure. So welcome to Les Nickelettes. Power to women in theater!"

Each newcomer nodded in agreement. Let the collective process begin.

⌒∾⌒

Liza agreed to do the music for *Oh Goddess!* but only if she could collaborate with her husband and fellow musician, Peter Marti. Their band, the Arms of Venus, was experimenting with a new style of electronic music. She also insisted on full autonomy in creating all the music and lyrics. This arrangement made me uncomfortable, as it was a break from our past partnership of shared contributions, but I trusted Liza's judgment.

But as I listened to the artificial electronic moog-synthesizer music recorded by Liza and Peter, I was at a loss for words. Liza characterized it as cutting-edge, but it didn't have the catchy, beat-heavy tunes we had come to expect.

"I was shocked by it," said Valerie.

"Maybe we just have to get used to it," I said hopefully. But the lyrics, mostly written by Peter, left me wanting. Like in the pivotal song "She's the One":

Hold onto your sister's hand
Take back the earth from the poisoned land
Hold onto your brother's hand
Rebuild the Garden—take a stand

It conveyed the intended message but didn't communicate the playful style of the play. Maybe it would grow on us?

Judy, coming on board to do choreography, struggled to design dances to what she described as, "that African oopi, chi-chi electronic music." Nevertheless, she created a couple of show-stopping routines. One was a Keystone Cops style shtick for the Art Police scene with bumbling officers arresting offending artists. Gloria, our heroine, gets busted for her painting *Premature Birth in a Taxi*.

The second was the energetic number "Premenstrual Syndrome Blues," sung by a nun and Catholic schoolgirl bonding over their monthly bloats.

As the performers learned the songs and dances, I concentrated on detailed scene work. Everyone worked hard to showcase their individual talent, and it pleased me to guide their progress. But try as I might, I couldn't conjure up a collective feeling among the different personalities. Still, the show took shape as expected.

After Judy and Liza wrapped up teaching the cast the musical numbers, Valerie took over leading vocal drills, and I put Mary in charge of physical warm-ups. Soon, Linda, a trained dancer, complained that Mary didn't know what she was doing. This opened a perfect opportunity to forge a Nick-elettes connection with my lead actress.

I set up a one-on-one meeting with Linda at her apartment. She lived in a modern style building located on the downhill side of Pacific Heights, which hinted at a desire for upward mobility. Sure enough, she greeted me at the door with apologies for the modest accommodation, explaining that it was just temporary until she and her husband hit the big time.

I placed the script on the coffee table, opened it to Act II, Scene 1, and launched into my spiel, "This is the most important scene in the play. Gloria's arrival at the Witch Headquarters has to project a character still self-absorbed, but also signal to the three witches that you are 'The One' they've been waiting for."

"Yeah, I get it," Linda nodded. "Excuse me." She got up, walked to the kitchen, and returned with a snack.

I reiterated the importance of this pivotal moment in the play. "If the audience is going to buy into Gloria fulfilling the witches' prophecy, you have to show a glimmer of transformation."

"I know, I know," Linda waved her hand dismissively. She took a bite of cookie and turned to stare at the TV tuned to the Phil Donahue show.

Searching for any kind of connection I commented, "Phil Donahue is pretty popular."

"I never miss him."

Clearly my presence didn't impede her daily fix. Shifting to the real mission of this get-together, I said, "Your dance resume is quite impressive. I could use your expertise in leading dance warm-ups."

She smiled. "Sorry, I'm an actress. I already have too much to do." She viewed my offer not as an opportunity but as an intrusion. It was as if she was saying, "Don't bother me, I'm watching Phil Donahue and eating cookies."

She had rebuffed me like an entitled upperclassman, and I left feeling like a dorky elementary school kid groveling to be liked. Why didn't I demand she turn off the TV? Damn! I was too nice. But I wasn't giving up. I just had to find a way to blast a hole through her smokescreen.

But soon, bigger problems loomed. Diane had completed a terrific design for the poster, but other commitments demanded her attention. She was forced to drop out. I'd been counting on her visual skills to help with the set design, not to mention pitching in on the grunt work. I asked cast members to lend a hand, but only got a litany of excuses. The task fell to the core production team: Valerie, Mary, and me.

Then, a week and a half before previews, Jan got a paying gig and left with only half the costumes finished. With way too much on my plate, I panicked. I begged the performers to help, but got only nonchalant shrugs. Finally, Nancy, cast as a bad poet arrested by the Art Police, stepped forward. "I know how to sew. I can finish the costumes." Nancy, a dead ringer for a young Carol Burnett, instantly became my new best friend.

The last two weeks of getting the production up to speed was like riding a rollercoaster. One rehearsal soared with the thrilling possibility of a great show, and the next plunged down to the pits with a glimpse of disaster. After a demoralizing tech rehearsal, I roused the troops with the old theater axiom, "You know what they say, 'Horrible tech, great show.'" And it worked. The preview performances turned out better than expected. The script was overwritten, but that could be fixed.

On Saturday October 19, 1985, Les Nickelettes premiered *Oh Goddess!* Friends from the audience joined us to celebrate after the show, and the positive feedback soothed my frayed nerves. There's nothing like a cast party to wash away stress.

The festivities provided another chance for me to form an alliance with Linda. She had taken on the responsibility of the party preparations including volunteering her Price Club membership to purchase discounted snacks and champagne.

"You're the munchies and bubbly queen," I complimented her.

"Like my character Gloria, I love to shop."

We both joined in a knowing laugh. Perhaps this was the beginning of a renewed Nickelettes collective.

The party wound down, and a woman draped in bangles and beads approached me. She swirled her long paisley gypsy skirt and introduced herself as the Cosmic Lady. Grasping my hand and gazing into my eyes, she said, as the tiny bells lining her headscarf jingled, "Your play is the most important thing happening on the planet."

"Yeah," I joked, "never mind Broadway."

"You mustn't make light of this; I'm deadly serious." She pivoted, walked away, and I was hit not only by her robust sincerity, but also by a whiff of her potent patchouli. Too bad she wasn't the *San Francisco Chronicle* theater critic.

Valerie and I hunkered down to fine-tune the overwritten script. Taking into consideration that the cast would have to quickly adapt to any changes, we concentrated only on cutting the fat. At the pick-up rehearsal before the next weekend of performances, we presented the changes. The cast looked at us as if we were out of our minds. As far as they were concerned, their job was done.

"We have to polish up the rough spots," I explained.

"If we keep working, we'll make the show better," added Valerie.

After some bickering, they agreed to the script cuts but refused to do any additional rehearsals. Stunned, I tried reasoning with

Poster for *Oh Goddess!*

Design by Diane Noomin

them. "Look, we may be limited by a shoestring budget of $5,000, but that doesn't mean the show can't be of the highest caliber."

"Five thousand dollars! Are you kidding me?" roared Linda. "I'm in a show that only spent $5,000 on production?"

That stung. Valerie, Mary, and I worked our butts off to accumulate that money. To add insult to injury, the actresses playing the three members of W.I.T.C.H. (Women In Touch Can Help) turned on us like ungrateful children. Libby, who played the nurturing mother figure of the trio chimed in, "It's kind of stupid to think you can do a production on only $5,000."

This was followed by Deidre (the play's prophetic Cassandra). "And it's not our fault the script has problems."

Mirroring the punk attitude of her Spike character, Hali jeered, "You can't even afford a backstage crew, so you make us move the sets."

Life had failed to imitate art. Who were these spoiled harpies? Certainly not the long awaited Goddess. Nancy came to our defense. "We were told when we started this was a grassroots operation."

"That's right," added Valerie. "Weren't you listening?"

This was a game changer. A line was drawn in the sand. The cast split into two distinct camps: Valerie, Mary, Nancy, and me on one side; Linda, Libby, Diedre, and Hali on the other; with the remaining five performers vacillating somewhere in between.

The negative energy caused my head to pound, leading to a major headache. In the past, no matter what obstacles Les Nickelettes encountered, there still remained a sense of community—that's what made the group unique. We experienced a diva here and there, but never a hardcore group of prima donnas. Like catty high school girls, they maneuvered to divide and conquer the uncommitted. Discouraged, Valerie and I dropped the idea of an extended run and plotted to just plow through the remaining three weeks hoping to avoid any skid marks on our backsides.

But then, there was more cheery news. A review by Barbara Shulgasser in the *San Francisco Examiner* critiqued the script as haphazard and uneven. And, after describing Valerie's performance as "good" and Mary as "perfect" she had this to say about our lead actress:

> Linda . . . as Gloria can be quite funny when she sets her mind to it, but on the whole [is] an undisciplined performer who tends to stand around on stage looking perplexed.

This didn't surprise me—the Nickelettes veterans were the best performers in the show. And Linda was rightly outed as not rising up to the potential of the role.

As the playwrights, Valerie and I acknowledged that the script was still rough around the edges. It needed more work to successfully weave the campy humor into the spiritual theme. Established Christian religion would have been an easy satirical target, but to parody an obscure Goddess theology was trickier. However, we also knew from experience that reviews from the mainstream press didn't necessarily define success for our shows.

After the write-up came out, Valerie, Nancy, and Mary reported to me that backstage grumblings from the prima donnas were becoming toxic.

"I can imagine Linda's miffed," I said.

"She's royally pissed about that review," warned Valerie. "She and Libby were huddled in a dressing room corner, giggling and making snotty remarks about you."

"They pretended to whisper," added Mary, "but everyone could hear."

"Screw them," Nancy said.

After the performance, I gathered the cast together. "We shouldn't let the review define the show," I argued. "We can use it to strengthen the play."

"The review would have been better if the script didn't suck," said Deidre.

"Not to mention the directing," added Hali.

"And *if* the director had any talent," Libby remarked.

Linda smirked, but said nothing. I ignored the bitchy remarks and went on, "The reviewer came to opening night. We've made changes and improved the play since then. Now, we can sharpen it even further with a rehearsal."

Out of the corner of my eye I caught Linda nudging Libby. Libby stood up and said, "No, we're not going to do it."

"Why not make the show better?" I asked.

"It's not going to happen," replied Libby. And with that Deidre, Hali, Libby, and Linda stomped out.

"They aren't walking out on the show, are they?" Mary asked.

"Don't worry—it'll be okay," soothed Nancy.

"It's just a bluff," I added.

"Linda is the instigator," noted Valerie. "She's clearly baiting Libby and getting her and the others to do the dirty work."

"I should never have cast to type," I lamented.

"Linda is a con artist," said Valerie. "She conned us. And then just sat back and basked in the glory."

My pride that Les Nickelettes were above these petty theater company dust-ups faded like an aging Hollywood ingenue. I had to confront this venomous animosity before the next performance, so I corralled the entire cast for a sit-down meeting to clear the air.

We settled into Mary's tiny living room, and, disguising my own misgivings, I tooted a confident trumpet of pleasant cooperation. But hostile vibes exuded out of every pore of Linda and Libby's body.

"If I'd known we were meeting in such a small place, I wouldn't have come," bristled Linda.

I paused for a beat to process her audacity, then plowed ahead with my prepared speech. "We all want to be in the best show possible. Original musical comedies need time to grow and develop, so if we all invest in the creative process, we can make it work."

"I don't think so," said Libby. "This show is a disaster, and I, for one, am ready to walk away."

"I second the motion," said Linda.

I took a deep breath, controlling an urge to scream. "You all made a commitment to a four-week run, and I expect you to honor that. Tickets have already been sold for this weekend. We have an obligation."

"I agree," said Nancy. "Besides, people in the audience last week told me they liked the show."

"My friends said it was poorly directed," countered Libby.

Linda glared at me. "The directing has been a big mess from the beginning."

Deidre and Hali nodded in agreement. I resolved to stay strong, but my backbone began to dissolve.

"My friends loved it!" enthused Mary. "They said, 'Wow, what a great show.'"

"My girlfriend Sandy thinks the concept is awesome and the jokes are hilarious," chimed in Valerie. "And believe me, she wouldn't say that just to be nice."

Linda and Libby sneered at the cheerleading, but in the end everyone agreed to complete the run. The meeting ended in an uneasy truce.

That didn't mean everything was hunky-dory. The following evening at the theater, Linda and Libby rubbed more salt in the wound by announcing that they weren't obligated to be stage crew and would no longer move the sets and props in between scenes. "As actresses, that's not our job," they smugly claimed.

The others in their camp also jumped aboard the anti-Nick-elettes mutiny ship. "I won't let them get to me, I won't let them get to me," I chanted under my breath as I figured out how to avoid backstage chaos.

To thwart the Bitchettes (my secret name for the mutinous cast members), I recruited a volunteer stage manager. But after doing only one show, she bailed, and I was forced to take over the duties. Linda plopped down on a backstage couch to watch me move the set into place. After I finished, I put on a cheery façade. "Have a good show."

"What's the point?" she replied as she sauntered back to the dressing room.

I toyed with the idea of taking on a more traditional director/dictator role and cracking the whip, but that seemed antithetical to the Nickelettes philosophy. I accepted the non-existence of a cohesive collective vibe, but refused to raise the white flag of surrender. Yet, this persistent black cloud threatened to erode my faith in a cooperative female esprit de corps.

Going into the final weekend of performances, the mood lightened—everyone looked forward to this being the last we would see of each other. For the sake of posterity, I videotaped the Friday performance, but messed up and skipped several scenes after pressing the pause button by mistake. So the next night's closing performance was my last chance to capture the show on home video. I set up the video equipment and was testing it, when Libby, who had just arrived appallingly late, ambled over to me.

"If you videotape the show tonight," she said calmly, "I won't go on."

"Wh-why?" I stuttered.

"I don't want my performance recorded. I have an Equity card, and you cannot videotape my performance without my written permission."

"This is home video for archival purposes only. It's not going to be used for profit or promotion."

"How do I know that? My husband will be in the audience to make sure that there is no record of me in this trashy play."

My blood pressure shot up so high I saw red. This plot had Linda's fingerprints all over it. "You can't blackmail me into not videotaping."

"Try me," she spun around and sashayed back to the dressing room. I shot invisible daggers into her back.

Valerie rushed from backstage. "What happened? Libby says she's not going on." I filled her in on the situation. "She can't do that," Valerie rolled her eyes. "You have to get in there and tell her she has to go on."

"I can't go into that she-wolves' den. They'll eat me alive."

"I'm going to talk some sense into her," Valerie said, heading back into the lair.

"Good luck," I said without conviction.

The box office was about to open, but I had to get out of there. I took a walk around the block to clear my head. When I returned to the theater, Sandy, who was working as our sound tech, confronted me.

"What the hell is going on? This must be really bad. You took off. Mary's bawling. Valerie's so upset, she's trembling."

"Libby threatened to walk out if we videotape."

"I'm going to kill her," seethed Sandy. "After the show tonight I'm going to beat the shit out of her."

I was as enraged as Sandy. I wanted to march into the dressing room and take out both Libby and Linda. But the audience was streaming in, and I didn't want them to witness a prototypical female catfight instead of *Oh Goddess!*

"Has it really come to this?" I said, more to myself than Sandy.

"You've got to do something," said Sandy.

"Go backstage, and tell Libby she can't leave now because the audience is already in the house." I held my breath until Sandy returned.

"Libby wants to be paid for the taping," she reported.

I shook my head.

"Look, let's take up a collection and pay her off," suggested Sandy.

"Over my dead body."

Sandy looked at her watch, "It's time to start the show."

I refused to back down. Likewise, Libby. It was a standoff.

Finally, Valerie appeared and whispered in my ear. "I'll tell Libby you've agreed not to tape, and then when the lights go down just turn on the camera."

"Okay." I could live with a little deception. I put a piece of tape over the green light on the camera, the show started, and I pressed record. I couldn't zoom in and out without risking Libby's husband/spy noticing our little trick, but at least we would have the show documented. If she found out about it later, she could sue.

Linda's performance was so sarcastic I wanted to slap her. And Libby's limited acting talents came into sharp focus. I chuckled to myself that if these two actresses lived in the reality of *Oh Goddess!*, the Art Police would have arrested them for bad acting.

At intermission, the minutes ticked by in slow motion. "I drank as much wine as possible," said Sandy, "and still be able to find the buttons on the sound board." But no drama queen craziness materialized. As soon as the second act started, I took up a position behind the camera and started zooming in and out. Fuck Libby and hubby. If they wanted to make a scene now—be my guest.

The applause faded after the final cast bow, and I hit stop on the video camera. As if on cue, the bottled up emotional pique in the pit of my stomach threatened to spew out in an unattractive public display. I fled to the only place nearby where I could be alone—the restroom. But both stalls were occupied. Waiting for my turn, pacing like a caged tiger, my focus slowly shifted to the two voices coming from the lavatory cubicles.

"I liked that song 'Shop Till You Drop,'" said the voice in cubicle number one.

"Yeah, and that part about the Goddess being revealed during White Flower Day at Macy's was so funny," said the voice in cubicle number two.

"I couldn't believe it when she got crucified on a sales rack," laughed the first young woman, who walked out of the stall and headed for the sink to wash her hands. She didn't give me a second glance as I darted into the stall and slammed the door. But why should she? I am the invisible director/playwright. "It made me realize that there really aren't any women in religion except a virgin mother, you know what I mean?"

"Yeah, why is that?" The second young lady joined the first at the sink. "I liked that it was serious and funny, at the same time."

"Are you a good witch or a bad witch?"

"Neither, I'm a *great* witch." The two girls exited laughing at one of the show's jokes.

Alone, sitting on a toilet in my locked refuge, I let the built-up sobs disgorge from a well deep down inside. I had done everything wrong. I'd failed. And I had no one to blame but myself for this dismal disaster. *Idiot! Idiot! Idiot!* my mind cried.

But, as I indulged in tears of self-pity, the words of those two young women reverberated in my head. They'd liked the show; they'd laughed at the jokes. And most importantly, they'd gained a new spiritual insight from the theme. I was hit with an epiphany, flashing back to something my college professor in Acting 101 told his class of beginners: "If you reach just *one* person in the audience you've successfully done your job." I had just heard evidence of *two* people being influenced by my play. They were the true critics.

My weeping stopped cold. I reflected on the significance of Les Nickelettes adopting the salmon mascot with its spawning metaphor. Those two young'uns were little salmon eggs beginning to hatch. With the pride of a new mother, I walked out of that bathroom with dry eyes and head held high.

The cast was collecting their things and clearing out. I bid them a buoyant, if not fond farewell. I grinned as Linda and Libby departed down the stairs. Just before they hit the exit door I crowed the words that had stuck in my craw for weeks, "You don't get it, Bitchettes!"

"I felt bad we weren't going to extend the show," said Mary, "because I could envision recasting and doing it again. I really liked the show; it deserved better." Despite my insight from the two women in the restroom regarding *Oh Goddess!* I had no inclination to take on the responsibility of another run. The fun of it all seemed to be fading like a fairy no one believes in anymore.

A simple summary of Les Nickelettes' tale could be of a brazen girl group trying to make it in show biz but never quite grabbing the star. But looking back, I see the importance of Les Nickelettes was not about getting our name in lights and making lots of money, but instead, it was about being part of a unique group of women laughing *with* each other, and not *at* each other. By fearlessly bonding together, we did outrageous things with an esprit of feminine camp. Infused with that sense of play, we'd stormed the stage at the topless Condor nightclub in our plastic tits and Girl Scout uniforms, appeared on the cover of *San Francisco Magazine* as rudimentary entertainers, scored a perfect thirty on the Gong Show, and written and produced five full-length musical satires. But through it all, what I treasured above everything else was the amazing friendships with over three dozen witty, astute, and audacious women—a shameless blast of zany escapades sheltered in the affinity of family.

"We did have a lot of fun. I was always hoping Les Nickelettes would make it," said Roberta Coleman (1973–1976).

We didn't catch the big break, but we "made" it in our own way, nonetheless.

One day, sometime after a gig at the 181 Club in 1984, I was walking in San Francisco's Mission District and spotted this graffiti anonymously scrawled on the side of a brick wall: "Anarchy in High Heels." Before Facebook and Twitter, this was akin to going viral.

The crux of the group's trajectory was that we refused to follow the paradigm of society-defined starlets of the time and resisted compromising our material to fit into an acceptable norm. No matter how much we sought to be taken seriously, we embraced an aesthetic of anti-seriousness and clung to our original, innocent female anarchy.

"The reviewers called us 'amateur' but I think the spirit really caught on with people and that's what came through," said Liza Kitchell (1979–1985). Definition of amateur: "a person who engages in activity for the pleasure rather than financial benefit or professional reasons." Punk rockers embraced the label of amateur, and maybe we should have, too. Still, there was no escaping the underlying message in the label "amateur"—it was code for, "These women aren't legitimate."

"People think, okay, it's just women being campy and silly and stupid, and it's easy to dismiss," said Diane Noomin (1981–1985). But despite the rocks and icebergs blocking our way, we never veered from our aspirations. We were in it for the freedom to theatricalize our feminine sense of humor; we were in it for the fun.

When I asked members of Les Nickelettes what being in the group meant to them, this is what they told me:

- "At the time, the kind of individual expression we did in Les Nickelettes was culturally taboo, but there was safety in numbers."
  —KATHY OPITZ (1973-1975)

- "I learned that humor is the most important tool. But satire is dangerous. I have to be careful; if I say what's on my mind, they want to put me away. But in Les Nickelettes, I always felt I could do anything."
  —DEBORAH MARINOFF (1972-1974)

- "Had I not met Les Nickelettes at that time in my life, I really don't know what would have happened to the girl in me. That girl was given room to be herself—to be her craziest, wildest, most expressive self. That was really important because it gave me courage, it acknowledged me."
  —BETSY NEWMAN (1975-1980)

- "It was really about being able to be me and be taken seriously, and at the same time not giving a shit who says what."
  —JUDY RAIN SCIFORD (1980-1985)

- "To me, it was about belonging."
  —MONIKA GURNEY ROTHENBUHLER (1979-1983)

- "[Before Les Nickelettes], I didn't know if I could trust other women. I was either a threat to them or they were a threat to me. With the Nicks, you could cut each other down and it was okay, it was fun, it was a joke; we could also praise each other and be each other's best friend."
  —MARY VALENTINO (1978-1985)

- "The emotional and spiritual connection that we had was real for me, and for us all. The best thing that ever happened to me was seeing that ad for the Nickelettes auditions."
  —VALERIE HELMOLD (1980-1985)

- "[After working in Les Nickelettes], I thought the whole world operated collectively, and when I went into other groups and situations, it didn't work out at all. It was like the Nicks were a special moment in time."
  —DEBRA JEAN POLLOCK (1980-1983)

- "The experience gave me a sense of assurance that I could accomplish things; being a woman was not an inherent handicap. There was a camaraderie that is usually depicted in movies and books as only existing among groups of men."
  —ROSE BIANCO (1981-1983)

- "I appreciated that the Nicks were brazen, like in your face, and going to say whatever it is you don't expect to hear. And it was just fun—fun in an unpretentious way."
  —JILL ROSE (1977-1978)

- "With all the research about the effects of laughter on health, I think how much good Les Nickelettes did themselves. Most people don't lead lives where they laugh themselves silly once a week."
  —ELLIN STEIN (1975-1980)

- "I still feel empowered from having done it. I have a lot more courage. That says a lot."
  —CAROL COLEMAN (1974-1977)

My youthful pipe dreams of a life in theater failed to foresee this accidental gathering of a bodacious sister-tribe. I came to San Francisco in search of the magical Land of Oz, and I found it. But it wasn't what I expected. As I danced and giggled like a hyena down the glitter-strewn Hot Pink Brick Road, my adventure in Les Nickelettes gave me permission to express my inner self and emboldened my spirit to do things I never would have dreamt of on my own.

❧

After *Oh Goddess!* closed, Vinny and I discovered we were domestically compatible and began talking marriage and babies. For thirteen years, my driving force had focused on keeping Les Nickelettes chugging along while putting off personal goals. Now, craving a more settled life, I took a break from Les Nickelettes. I didn't want the group to end; I just wanted to hit the pause button. In 1986, Vinny and I married. The following year, I gave birth to a baby girl. We named her Nicolette. She was an authentic joy and a wish come true, opening a different Nicolette chapter in my life.

Les Nickelettes never officially disbanded—just slowly faded away like Puff the Magic Dragon. But the desire to share in a community of heretical humor still remained. So Les Nickelettes morphed into a kind of club that met regularly for the private entertainment of the celebrants. Also, there was a Fifteenth Anniversary Bash, a Twentieth Anniversary Celebration, and a Fortieth year reunion. At one point, we even began to write a new show. But lives changed, priorities shifted, and members left San Francisco.

Social values in 1980s America took three steps backward. Competitiveness was favored over collective cooperation. Greed was good, and kindness weak. Women's Lib was out; feminist bashing was in. This cultural drought contributed to the drying up of Les Nickelettes' swim upstream. But now, over thirty years later, the waters are flowing again, and the salmon are jumping higher than ever—and spawning. Third- and fourth-wave feminist comediennes have ascended as bold, smart writers and performers. A bawdy style of women's comedy has come into the mainstream.

This is my sister Ruth and me doing our acrobat act. I could never had soared to fearless heights with outspread arms and a big smile on my face without my sister anchoring me on her shoulders. And metaphorically, I benefitted from being anchored on the shoulders of all of my Nickelettes sisters.

Second-wave feminists discovered and displayed power in alliances. They banded together with different callings: consciousness-raising groups, comic book and theater collectives, book and magazine publishers, record companies, music festivals, and political coalitions. These collaborations enabled women of the time to scale the barriers to emancipation. The movement pushed the evolution towards women's equality one step forward. Feminism ebbed in the mid-'80s, but it never went away. It was just gathering strength for the flow of a third and fourth wave. Like our cockroach character in 1980 said, "You can't get rid of us."

And so, one evening when I found myself listening to Psychic Horizons' students correctly tell me that my soul chose to be born into this lifetime because there was about to be a great advance in women's liberation, I wasn't surprised. But becoming a feminist wasn't the full story of my destiny. They missed that my most consequential fate belonged in the creation of Les Nickelettes.

SALMON AWARD HONOREES

Keeping the Spirit of Anarchy in High Heels Alive and Swimming Upstream Forever Awards: To all Les Nickelettes, past, present, and future.

Les Nickelettes All-Star Fan Awards: To—you know who you are.

Flashback Interviewee Contributor Awards: To Priscilla Alden, Rose Bianco, Jean Taggart Born, Stafford Buckley, Karl Cohen, Carol Coleman, Roberta Coleman, Jan Edwards, Valerie Helmold, Liza Kitchell, Deborah Marinoff, Sharon McNight, Betsy Newman, Diane Noomin, Kathy Opitz, Debra Pollock, Jill Rose, Monika Gurney Rothenbuhler, Amy Ryder, Rosalie Schmidt Galliher, Bermuda Schwartz, Judy Rain Sciford, Sandy Starkey, Ellin Stein, Goody Thompson, Ron Turner, Mary Valentino, and Rebecca Valentino.

Make It a Memoir Award: To Betsy Newman and Ellin Stein for their game-changing suggestion.

Perseverance Slog Through to the End of a Very Early Draft Award: To Betsy Newman and Vincent Mierjeski.

Tanya Hearst Journalist of the Year Award: To Ellin Stein. Her chronicles of Les Nickelettes events in newspaper articles helped jog my memory and fill in details.

Being There through Thick and Thin, Till the End Award: To Judy Rain Sciford, Valerie Helmold and Mary Valentino.

Thanks for the Memories (R.I.P.) Awards: To Priscilla Alden, Jean Taggart Born, Dirk Dirksen, Jane Dornacker, Ralph Eno, Clay Geerdes, Jane Huether, Yvonne O'Reilly, Larry Reppert, Elaine Schelb (Schelby), Bonnie Solliman, Vince Stanich, Mary Valentino, Bill Wolfe, and Martin Worman.

Hope We Meet Again Award: To all the people I've lost touch with over the years.

Saying Yes to Green Lighting My Book Award: To Brooke Warner and She Writes Press.

Project Manager of the Year Award: To Lauren Wise.

Book Cover of the Year Award: To Julie Metz.

Copy Editor of the Year Award: To Jennifer Caven.

Proofreader of the Year Award: To Laura Matthews.

Publicist of the Year Award: To Crystal Patriarche and BookSparks.

Unconditional Love Award: To all of my family.

Yeah, Go for It Award: To Vincent Mierjeski.

And finally, Love You to the Moon and Back Award: To Nicolette Mierjeski—just because.

ABOUT THE AUTHOR

Denise Larson is a native Californian; she went to elementary school in the Los Angeles suburb of Torrance and high school in the San Joaquin Valley city of Manteca, and finally, after college, she put down roots in San Francisco. With a BA in theater from San Francisco State University, she pinned her dreams on becoming an experimental theater artist in the 1970s counterculture milieu of the Bay Area. Along that path she founded Les Nickelettes. For thirteen years, she helmed the feminist theater company and assumed the role of actress, playwright, producer, stage director, and administrative/artistic director. Then she gave it all up to become a mother and teacher. After a twenty-year career in Early Childhood Education, she retired and took up writing. Denise still lives in San Francisco. She has also returned to her first love: theater. She is collaborating with other performers in a new theater venture: Cosmic Elders Theater Ensemble.

Author photo © Scott R. Kline

SELECTED TITLES FROM SHE WRITES PRESS

She Writes Press is an independent publishing company founded to serve women writers everywhere. Visit us at www.shewritespress.com.

Stutterer Interrupted: The Comedian Who Almost Didn't Happen by Nina G. $16.95, 978-1-63152-642-8. The funny, revealing, and unapologetic tale of how Nina G became, at the time she started, America's only female stuttering stand-up comedian.

Times They Were A-Changing: Women Remember the '60s & '70s edited by Kate Farrell, Amber Lea Starfire, and Linda Joy Myers. $16.95, 978-1-938314-04-9. Forty-eight powerful stories and poems detailing the breakthrough moments experienced by women during the '60s and '70s.

You Can't Buy Love Like That: Growing Up Gay in the Sixties by Carol E. Anderson. $16.95, 978-1631523144. A young lesbian girl grows beyond fear to fearlessness as she comes of age in the '60s amid religious, social, and legal barriers.

When a Toy Dog Became a Wolf and the Moon Broke Curfew: A Memoir by Hendrika de Vries. $16.95, 978-1631526589. Hendrika is "Daddy's little girl," but when Nazis occupy Amsterdam and her father is deported to a POW labor camp, she must bond with her mother—who joins the Resistance after her husband's deportation—and learn about female strength in order to discover the strong woman she can become.

Not a Poster Child: Living Well with a Disability—A Memoir by Francine Falk-Allen. $16.95, 978-1631523915. Francine Falk-Allen was only three years old when she contracted polio and temporarily lost the ability to stand and walk. Here, she tells the story of how a toddler learned grown-up lessons too soon; a schoolgirl tried her best to be a "normie," on into young adulthood; and a woman finally found her balance, physically and spiritually.

The Outskirts of Hope: A Memoir by Jo Ivester. $16.95, 978-1-63152-964-1. A moving, inspirational memoir about how living and working in an all-black town during the height of the civil rights movement profoundly affected the author's entire family—and how they in turn impacted the community.